T0319882

Pay and Employment in the New Europe

The research on which this book is based was funded by the Commission of the European Communities, DGV. The papers were specially prepared for a series of meetings at the Commission with the participation of other researchers, the social partners, members of the Commission, and other public bodies. The papers were also the subject of the special conference on pay and European integration held in Nice in June 1990.

The information contained in this publication does not necessarily reflect either the position or the views of the Commission of the European Communities.

PAY AND EMPLOYMENT IN THE NEW EUROPE

Edited by David Marsden

Reader in Industrial Relations
The London School of Economics and Political Science

Edward Elgar

© David W. Marsden 1992

All rights reserved. No part of this publication may be reproduced, stored in a retrieval system or transmitted in any form or by an means, electronic, mechanical or photocopying, recording, or otherwise without the prior permission of the publisher.

Published by
Edward Elgar Publishing Limited
Gower House
Croft Road
Aldershot
Hants GU11 3HR
England

Edward Elgar Publishing Company
Old Post Road
Brookfield
Vermont 05036
USA

A CIP catalogue record for this book
is available from the British Library

Library of Congress Cataloguing in Publication Data

Pay and employment in the new Europe/edited by David Marsden.
   p. cm.
  Includes bibliographical references and index.
  1. Wages - European Economic Community countries. 2. Compensation management - European Economic Community countries. 3. Labor market- European Economic Community countries. I. Marsden, David.
HD50 14.5.P39 1992   92-8920
331.12'5'094-dc20   CIP

ISBN 1 85278 564 0

Printed and bound in Great Britain by
Billing and Sons Ltd, Worcester

Contents

Notes on Contributors

Carlo Dell'Aringa: Professor of Economics and Director of the Centre for Labour Economics at the Catholic University of Milan, and currently President of the Italian Association of Labour Economists (AIEL). He has published several papers and books in the field of labour policies, including "Prezzi e Redditi", "The Duration of Unemployment in Italy", and "Rapporti sui Salari".

Luis Fina Sanglas: Director of Employment and Labour Market Affairs (DGV/B) of the European Commission since 1988. Previously, Professor of Applied Economics at the Autonomous University of Barcelona, and Visiting Fellow of the Institute of Employment Research at the University of Warwick (1981-82). He has also been "Executive Advisor" of the Cabinet of the Spanish Minister of Labour and Social Security (1983-85). Author of numerous publications and studies on Labour Economics.

Felix Fitzroy: Lecturer in Economics, University of St. Andrews, and previously Senior Research Fellow, Science Centre, Berlin, and Visiting Professor of Economics at the European University Institute, Florence.

Raymond Hara: Chargé de Mission with the Director of Personnel of the French railways (SNCF), in charge of the modernisation of its payment systems. Previously, he was head of the section on employment and wage policies at the Commissariat du Plan, Paris. There he was organiser and author of the reports for the Prime Minister on the evaluation and simplification of measures to help the unemployed; and rapporteur for the inter-ministerial study of employment subsidies. He also teaches at the University of Paris II.

Contributors

José Luis Malo de Molina: Head of Monetary and Financial Research at the Bank of Spain, and member of the European Commission's Economic Policy Committee and of the Monetary Policy Sub-Committee of the EC Central Bank Governors. Previously, he lectured in Applied Economics at the Complutense University. In 1987, he was appointed by the government as a member of the Experts' Committee to report on the problems of unemployment in Spain. His recent publications include "¿Rigidez o flexibilidad del mercado de trabajo? La experiencia española durante la crisis" (Madrid 1984); and "Estructura salarial y mercado de trabajo" (Madrid 1985).

David Marsden: Reader in Industrial Relations at the London School of Economics and Political Science. He has also been Visiting Professor at the Universities of Aix-Marseille, and Rome (La Sapienza), and Visiting Senior Research Fellow at the Laboratoire d'Economie et de Sociologie du Travail, Aix-en-Provence, and at the Institut für Arbeitsrecht und Arbeitsbeziehungen in der EWG, Trier. He has researched and published widely on questions of comparative industrial relations, wage structures and labour markets in Western Europe.

Jackie Morin: Administrator at the European Commission in the Structural Policies on Employment and the Labour Market Unit (DGV). He obtained his doctorate in the History of Economic Thought at the University of Paris I.

Pilar García Perea: is a Dr in Economics and Business Studies from the Universidad Complutense de Madrid. She is currently employed as an economist in the Bank of Spain's Research Department, principally in the field of economic forecasting and research. Her main publications address, inter alia, Spanish and EC labour market issues, and include the following: "Comparative analysis of labour costs in Spanish industry and the industrial sector of EC countries" (1985), "Potential risks of the developing single market: the Spanish economy's position" (1989) and "Changes in the Spanish wage structure since 1963" (1991).

David Shonfield: Senior Editor of Incomes Data Services, Britain's leading source of independent information and analysis on pay, employment and industrial relations. He writes IDS Focus, a quarterly magazine on personnel strategy. He has been an independent adviser to the European Commission for several years.

Jean-Jacques Silvestre: Director of Research at the Laboratoire d'Economie et de Sociologie du Travail (CNRS), Aix-en-Provence. His recent publications include "Les Inégalités de Salaire" (Paris 1978), and with Maurice and Sellier "The Social Foundations of Industrial Power" (MIT Press 1986). He is currently engaged on comparisons of engineers' work and pay in France and Japan, and of public sector pay in the European Community.

Daniel Vaughan-Whitehead: currently working at the Remuneration Section of the International Labour Office. Previously, he worked as expert for the European Commission, for the Cellule de Prospective (President's Prospective Unit), and then for the FAST Team (Forecasting and Assessment in Science and Technology). He obtained his doctorate in Labour Economics from the European University Institute, Florence. His recent publications have been on Social Europe and risks of social dumping; wage bargaining trends in the Community; relocation of industrial activities in the Single Market prospects; direct investment and technology in Southern countries.

Preface

Luis Fina Sanglas

In the services of the European Commission, we started work on the relationship between economic integration and wage determination more than a year ago, when we asked a group of prominent specialists in that area to reflect on, and to discuss, under the chairmanship of David Marsden, the whole range of issues concerning wage determination and the future of European integration.

At that moment, we felt, first of all, that concern with the priority problem of unemployment had fully occupied the minds of policy makers and specialists and that the 'wage question' had been somewhat neglected. With the economic recovery and the increases in employment already well established it seemed to us that this question would be soon back to the centre of public debate and that it was therefore important to detect in time which were the aspects that would be prominent during the 1990s.

We also felt, in the second place, that it was the right moment to assess what had really remained from previous debates, particularly, those of the 1970s and early 1980s. Before the first oil shock the main concern about wages was located at the macroeconomic level and centred on the still important question of how to ensure, at the same time, full employment, price stability and free collective bargaining. In the public policy field, this concern was paralleled in the debates about the effectiveness of 'income policies' as the instrument to ensure the compatibility between these three desirable goals.

The oil crisis shook all that. The old institutions were unable to accommodate its negative effects on the growth of incomes and were clearly leading to a wage-price spiral which was, in addition, also fueled in many countries by internal factors such as increased taxation. The question was then how to reform these old institutions in order to break the spiral and, in particular, how to dismantle indexation arrangements that had in the past contributed to the desirable stability in the growth of demand. The necessary changes were made successfully and there is little doubt that the current recovery of the economy and of employment levels owes much to that. In many countries, the contribution of the trade unions has been crucial as they have recognized that inflation was not good for anybody, and that it was indeed impairing the prospects for sustainable growth in the medium term.

Will the old institutions come back with the economic recovery? Will the old problems be posed again or, instead, is it the case that something important has changed for good? This is one set of questions that we deal with, but let me put forward my conviction that the answer to the first two questions should be negative. This conviction is based on two facts. First, the 'new consensus' as to the harmful effects of inflation represents a permanent change. It now seems well understood that there is compatibility, and even a 'virtuous circle' between 'wage moderation,' as defined at Community level by the 'cooperative growth strategy for employment,' and improvements in the standard of living. Second, greater economic integration and the establishment of a monetary union at Community level will profoundly affect wage determination, a question which I shall consider in more detail in a moment.

Before that, let me turn to the microeconomic aspects of the debates on the 'wage question' which should also be considered. During the 1960s and early 1970s, there was not much concern about the adequacy of existing arrangements for wage determination at the 'micro' level, understood as the level of the firm but also the level of a particular region or sector. 'Imitation' in wage bargaining ensured that the increases obtained in one part of the economy would rapidly spread to the rest. In some countries, through the fixing of minimum wages or through other arrangements, the public authorities ensured that these gains would also benefit those groups less well protected by trade union activity. In some countries, there was concern about 'leap-frogging' in wage bargaining and the harmful effects of a 'wage-wage' spiral, but this was seen as something that could be solved by greater synchronization of the leading wage negotiations.

Globally, however, and provided that ex post average wage growth was similar to average productivity growth, it was not seen as a problem that the wages for particular groups tended to increase at very similar rates and that, as a consequence, wage differentials were rather 'sticky' or rigid. On the one hand, the existence of new and better job openings was considered to be the main determinant of labour mobility, both geographically and occupationally, and on the other, the uniformity of wage increases among different groups was seen as an effective means for ensuring balanced structural change and, as a consequence, economic advancement. A common rate of wage growth would favour the more dynamic and technologically advanced activities, where wages would grow less than productivity, and, at the other end of the spectrum, it would cause the demise of traditional and technologically backward industries through increased unit labour costs and, at the same time, it would liberate the necessary labour for the more modern activities.

Particularly since the beginning of the 1980s, mostly in the context of the debates on the need to increase 'labour market flexibility,' all these ideas have been seriously called into question. The need for greater individualization of wage determination has been advocated in order to improve economic efficiency and the functioning of labour markets.

It is not clear what are the reasons for that important change of mood. One factor might have been the so-called crisis of the 'Fordist' mode of production which had been typified by a fixed grid of wages linked more closely to the job structure than to individual performance. The transition to a new system of production, where individual performance, flexibility to move from one task to another, and creativity and initiative have, arguably, become more dominant, would require a different system of wage incentives.

Another factor might be that the old model did not function in practice exactly as it was supposed to function in theory; in particular, the model led to compression rather than stability of wage differentials, and that, in turn, led either to different forms of 'wage drift' (a form of de facto or uncontrolled wage individualization), or to a decline in relative wages resented by those groups losing out. Finally, a third contributory factor might have been the increase in unemployment levels: in that situation, it is clear that the old argument that it is necessary to free labour from declining activities in order to ensure an adequate labour supply for the most modern industries loses much of its weight.

It was not clear either to what extent all the new proposals had effectively translated into the wage systems prevailing at the enterprise level, or whether they were really having any effect on wage negotiations in practice. For all those reasons, both of theoretical and of empirical nature, we felt that here there was an important area for new research and debate.

A third feeling and, without doubt, the most important reason we had to promote that line of work, was the need to make more explicit the relationships between the main Community policies and wage determination, and vice versa. We thought that these relationships were very important and that, although some very valuable work had already been done, there was a need to develop it further. In that context, I will briefly refer to some aspects of the relationships between wages and three of the main lines of Community economic policies: the strengthening of the internal market; the building of monetary union and the achievement of a true economic union; and, using the expression introduced by the Single Act, the reinforcement of the economic and social cohesion of the Community. Last but not least, I will finish with some considerations of the relationships between wage dynamics and issues of equity, which are central for the construction of a truly social Europe.

The strengthening of the internal market, with the elimination of remaining non-tariff barriers for the free movement of goods, services, capital and labour, and accompanying measures mostly in the fields of research and development and training, imply a clear option in favour of increasing Europe's competitiveness in the higher range of products to put it at a level comparable with the most advanced countries. This, on the one hand, raises the question of the relationship between wages and this type of competitiveness. More specifically, what kind of wage policy is most conducive to the production of high quality goods and to the encouragement of product and process innovations? On the other hand, it poses the question of what kind of wages policy will ensure the complementarity that should be sought with developing countries or, to put it another way, how much scope should be left for them to increase their production and trade in the more labour intensive and technologically more conventional types of goods?

As far as monetary union is concerned, the permanent and irreversible fixing of exchange rates will transform monetary policy at community level, providing a clearer and more stable monetary framework within which the social partners will have to conduct their pay negotiations. In addition, but also in consequence, the results of these negotiations will have a much more immediate effect on the determination of regional competitiveness and, in the last resort, on the employment levels of the different regions of the Community. In that context, we should be prepared to answer questions such as the following: Are existing institutional arrangements prepared for the new situation? What should be the necessary changes, if any? What will be the effects of the new situation on current practices of wage determination? Is it appropriate to devise special new arrangements at Community level?

The strengthening of Community economic union or, in other words, the reinforcing of its economic and social cohesion, poses a different set of questions in relation to wage determination. There is, first of all, the frequently debated question of the potential threat to living standards in the richer parts of the Community posed by the lower wages of peripheral regions, either through capital or labour mobility, or through straight product competition. There is also the fear among less developed areas of being caught for good in the 'low wage' trap, confined to production of labour intensive, traditional types of goods, without the possibility of joining the markets for higher quality, more sophisticated, and also more rewarding products. The relevant questions are then: what should be the minimum necessary measures to avoid potentially harmful effects of greater openness and competition; and what is the right mix of policies, relating to wages and also to other determinants of productivity, which can best promote the endogenous development of all areas in the Community?

As I have said, I wish to make some final remarks on some equity questions raised by the dynamics of wages and wage determination. This is perhaps one of the questions most frequently treated in public debate and it is also a question that concerns us at the Community level. Indeed, Article 2 of the EEC Treaty poses as one of the basic missions of the Community the acceleration in the improvement of living standards which should also be one of the basic goals of any system of wage determination.

We also think that it is essential to ensure that all individuals and groups of workers benefit from those improvements. To that end, the Community Charter of the Fundamental Social Rights for Workers proposed by the Commission and approved by eleven heads of government during the European Council of Strasbourg, in December 1989, establishes that 'all employment should be fairly remunerated' in the sense that 'workers shall be assured of an equitable wage, that is to say, a wage sufficient to provide a decent standard of living' and that 'workers subject to terms of employment other than an open-ended full-time contract shall benefit from an equitable reference wage.'

In that context, the questions to which we have to address ourselves, and of which the last extends beyond this book, are the following: to what extent are recent developments in wage growth at variance with these principles? If this is so, what can be done by the different parties concerned to reverse these trends? What are, in particular, the relationships between paid employment and poverty in our societies, and what are the conditions in terms of wages and social protection of the new forms of employment relations that have been spreading so rapidly during the last few years?

1. Pay and European Integration

David Marsden and Jean-Jacques Silvestre

1. Introduction

Progress towards the Single European Market, a stronger European Monetary System, and possibly, full monetary union will radically alter the macroeconomic environment of the labour markets of individual member countries. No longer will it be possible to use exchange rate depreciation to eliminate the consequences of a wages explosion in one country. Equally, free movement of capital, and further reductions in barriers to the movement of goods across national frontiers will reduce national autonomy in such areas as interest rate and fiscal policy.

All of these changes are likely to increase the pressures for economic adjustment on labour markets and on wage structures. This chapter, and this book, assess the nature of these new pressures, and the ability of Community labour markets to cope with them. It starts with an assessment of the likely impact of wage differences between countries on integration; it looks at wages as an adjustment factor in theory; and then looks in more detail at the scope for such adjustments in practice. It concludes with some thoughts on prospects and some tentative policy ideas for wider discussion.

2. The Extent of Wage Differences between Countries and Their Likely Impact on Integration

Because of wide differences in wage levels and wage structures between countries, increased European integration is likely to exert considerable pressure on labour markets. These pressures come from four main directions: the easing of intra-EEC trade; increased

1

possibilities for labour mobility; greater capital integration; and progress towards monetary union.

2.1 Inter-country Wage Differences and the Removal of Non-tariff Barriers (NTBs)

The removal of non-tariff barriers is expected to lead to a general increase in competition across the Community, especially in those sectors in which they remain extensive, and in which intra-EEC trade has remained low. Differences among countries in production costs will be one of the major influences on subsequent restructuring of European industry, and within this, labour costs are often a major component.

Variations in labour costs among member countries are considerable, ranging from about 75% below the EC mean for Portugal, to a little over 25% above the mean in the Netherlands (Table 1). Although the extent of such labour cost differences varies between sectors, their scale is greater across the Community than between sectors within countries (Table 2).

Table 1. Labour costs and unit labour costs in 1987, whole economy.

	Lab. cost/ employee (% of EC average)	Unit labour cost	Employees (000)	GDP (Bn Ecu)
Belgium	114.9	105.9	3,044	120.4
Denmark	114.7	109.6	2,302	87.9
FR Germany	122.1	104.0	22,643	969.5
Greece	44.0	75.4	1,932	41.1
Spain	73.7	88.8	8,303	251.3
France	118.5	102.8	18,166	764.1
Ireland	89.2	104.4	818	25.5
Italy	101.5	87.0	15,499	659.2
Luxembourg	115.7	122.5	151	5.2
Netherlands	127.6	104.0	4,130	184.9
Portugal	26.6	86.7	2,851	31.9
UK	77.0	107.3	22,174	580.1
EUR	100.0	100.0	102,013	3,721.2

Note: Labour cost (compensation) includes gross wages and salaries, employers' actual social contributions, and imputed social contributions; unit labour costs are calculated as labour costs per 1,000 Ecu GDP.
Source: Eurostat, National Accounts ESA Aggregates, 1970-87.

The inter-industry hierarchy of both labour costs and earnings displays a great deal of regularity both over time and between countries such that the low and high wage industries tend to be the same, whether they are located in a high or a low wage country (Table 2, and Zighera, 1989). Thus, the low paid industries in the high wage countries benefit from the high level of pay in the country in which they are located: textile hourly labour costs are about three quarters of the national average for all industry in both West Germany and Portugal, whereas West German hourly labour costs are roughly six times those of Portugal. Hourly labour costs in Electricity and Gas, the highest wage sector in Portugal shown in Table 2, were roughly four times higher in West Germany than in Portugal.

Table 2. Hourly labour costs in Ecu in five high and five low paid industries (1984).

NACE	FR Germany	France	Italy	NL	Belgium
14 Oil refining	23.4	21.0	13.0	19.8	21.5
33 Computers	20.8	21.1	12.7	15.9	-
16 Electricity & gas	19.0	18.5	15.1	16.9	24.8
25 Chemicals	17.8	15.4	11.9	17.2	16.4
36 Aerospace & ships	16.0	15.4	10.1	13.3	15.2
43 Textiles	10.5	9.2	8.9	11.8	9.9
44 Leather	9.4	8.8	8.7	10.7	9.3
46 Wood & furniture	11.8	9.2	8.7	10.8	10.7
45 Clothing & footwear	9.0	8.2	7.8	9.4	8.1
49 Misc.	10.7	11.6	9.1	11.1	9.2
1-5 All industries	14.2	12.4	10.7	13.7	13.4

	UK	Eire	Denmark	Greece	Portugal
14 Oil refining	16.2	-	14.2	5.8	-
33 Computers	13.4	9.9	13.7	-	-
16 Electricity & gas	13.7	12.7	13.9	6.0	4.9
25 Chemicals	11.1	11.1	13.2	4.8	3.7
36 Aerospace & ships	10.4	15.0	12.8	5.2	3.1
43 Textiles	6.1	6.8	10.5	3.4	1.8
44 Leather	6.3	6.7	9.4	3.6	2.2
46 Wood & furniture	7.5	6.9	10.1	3.3	1.8
45 Clothing & footwear	5.4	5.0	9.4	2.9	1.6
49 Misc.	7.4	7.6	11.0	3.0	1.7
1-5 All industries	9.0	8.9	12.0	4.1	2.4

Note: Manual and non-manual workers.
Source: Eurostat, Labour Cost Survey, 1984, Tab.17.

Differences in industrial structure among countries explain only a small part of the variation in national average labour costs, as the differences between average national labour costs are fairly closely reflected by those for individual sectors (Table 2). However, focusing on the extremes between the high and low labour cost countries may lead to an equally extreme view of the potential for employment adjustment in response to labour cost differences.

First, the contrast between the high wage countries on the one hand, and the very low wage ones on the other, obscures the broad similarity of labour cost levels between many of the economically most important Community economies. If we take the whole economy comparisons of Table 1 for Germany, France, Italy, Denmark and the Benelux countries, then the dispersion of average labour costs is much smaller: in 1987, the gap between Italy and West Germany was about 25%, instead of the 80% separating West Germany from Portugal (Table 1). The extremely low labour cost countries, notably Greece and Portugal, have only small labour forces, and it is unlikely that their wage costs would remain so low if there were a major relocation of production in those countries.

Secondly, the differences in labour costs are substantially reduced by productivity differences, and these may also diminish the pressures to relocate activities. The 80% differential between West Germany and Portugal in 1987 drops to only 20% if account is taken of productivity differences (taking the difference between labour costs in Portugal and Germany as a percent of those in Germany in Table 1). Economically more important is the gap between West Germany and Spain which is reduced from 40% to only 15%.

Even if the extreme variations in labour costs are greatly attenuated by concentrating on the main body of the European economy, and by focusing on unit labour costs, the differences among countries remain significant – especially in markets which are more competitive and in which consumers can switch easily between brands of different nationalities. Moreover, the increased competition, and the outlawing of discriminatory purchasing practices by national and local governments is likely to make sales more sensitive to such differences in costs. However, some caution is necessary in drawing out their possible effects.

First, there are considerable variations between sectors. The labour productivity comparisons in the car industry in the 1970s, for example, revealed somewhat greater inter-country differences, with West German productivity being more than 80% above that of the UK, which was one cause of the gradual shift of production away from the UK to other EC countries. This occurred partly through the decline of the national champion, British Leyland, and partly by gradual relocation of production within the two multinationals located in the UK, Ford and General Motors (Marsden et al. 1985).

Secondly, labour productivity, or more strictly, output per person, may vary for many reasons, including the effort, skill, and efficiency of workers, but also because of management efficiency, the newness of capital equipment, and the quality of the industrial infrastructure. Management efficiency and capital equipment are more easily exported than skill or infrastructure as the latter rely heavily upon national education and training systems and on public and private investment by others, and thus involve important externalities. Good examples of the former are provided in the car industry, by the good productivity record of the new production facilities in Spain, and by the transfer of management techniques and skills in the new Japanese plants in the UK.

There is a sense in which companies may see productivity as a variable controlled by management, at least to a certain degree, so that they would expect new facilities to have above average productivity in the host economy. Thus, although the multinationals' Spanish car plants might fall short of the productivity levels of their West German plants, they could still narrow the gap sufficiently vis-à-vis West Germany to operate with lower unit labour costs and take advantage of lower Spanish wages.

The problem is somewhat different when one is dealing with the renovation of existing plants and firms. Management and capital equipment are already given, and the experience of industrial adjustment in the 1970s and 1980s shows how difficult it is for firms to achieve major changes in the level of efficiency of such plants. This would suggest that the large-scale movement of jobs to existing plants in low wage countries is unlikely.

So far the discussion has been general, but it is worth looking in more detail at two types of adjustment problem: that of sectors which have been relatively protected by non-tariff barriers until now; and that of intra-sectoral specialization, which, in the past, has been as important, if not more so, than inter-sectoral specialization.

A clue as to the sectors which are most likely to be affected by the removal of NTBs can be found in the Commission's classification of economic sectors according to the level of remaining non-tariff barriers and the current degree of intra-EEC trade. The most affected sectors include a number in heavy engineering, food processing, but also in high technology, particularly when there have been favourable national public procurement policies. However, the influence of differences in relative labour costs is likely to be tempered by the degree of savings firms can make, which are clearly smaller, the smaller the share of labour costs in total costs, and in value added.

Equally, the more easily firms can find substitute labour, which is generally easier for less qualified labour, the more likely they are to move. A general view of the incidence of these characteristics on different industries enables the identification of a number of sectors which might prove particularly vulnerable to relocation pressures (v. chapter by Vaughan-Whitehead, Table 10). Among the sectors most likely to experience relocation pressures on these criteria were: glass, ceramic goods, foundries, structural metal products, footwear, timber and wooden furniture, and rubber products. But the majority of sectors of manufacturing looked set for some relocation on at least two of these criteria.

Because many industrial sectors are heavily concentrated in certain regions, these sectoral relocation pressures could affect employment in certain regions, as occurred with the restructuring of the steel industry in the late 1970s.

Less tangible, but possibly more important, are the potential effects upon intra-sectoral specialization. It has been argued that this is a more important effect of trade, and source of comparative advantage than countries simply specializing in discrete economic sectors. For example, within the engineering industry, Britain, France and West Germany have comparative specializations within different parts of the same sector [1] (Saunders 1978). Some such integration takes place within companies, as occurred with the restructuring of Ford's and General Motors' automobile European production during the late 1970s and early 1980s, which led to the creation of a number of fully integrated production systems spread across the Community. However, much intra-sectoral specialization also takes place through trade. In both cases, it is likely that the quality of the skills of national workforces and their cost are influential factors.

Relocation pressures as a result of the further removal of trade barriers will cause employment restructuring in both the sectors and regions gaining jobs and in those losing them. Initially new employees will more likely be attracted from other employment in the same region rather than from unemployment, as has commonly been the pattern in the past. Although large scale redundancies often attract a great deal of publicity, in fact, even in the darkest years of job losses in Britain in the early 1980s, they represented a comparatively modest component of the entries onto the unemployment register. Indeed, a major component of the steep rise in unemployment at that time was the increased duration of unemployment spells as compared with the rise in the number of entrants onto the unemployment register.

The quality of labour mobility is also an important question, notably whether it takes place among experienced skilled workers, which would seem to be the most economically desirable form as this would ensure that restructuring caused a minimum of loss to a nation's stock of skills, or whether it takes place primarily among young workers seeking stable positions in firms' internal labour markets,[2] and among displaced older workers. The available evidence does not permit a firm judgement as to the relative importance of these two aspects of labour mobility. There is some indication that the mix varies between countries (Marsden 1990a), with greater reliance on occupational structures favouring skill mobility in FR Germany and Britain, and on enterprise internal labour markets in France and Italy which tend to make workers' skills dependent on their current employer.[3]

One danger of integration for low wage and low productivity economies deserves mention: namely, that of attracting further low technology investment, and specializing in low productivity activities. For example, the low wages of the British economy, compared with those of West Germany, are reflected in the lower value added of many of Britain's exports to Germany even within the engineering sector. During the 1970s, the median unit value of engineering exports ('000$ per tonne, 1975) from Britain was 5.7, as against 7.4 from France, and 8.2 from West Germany, and Britain was exporting low unit value goods to, and importing high unit value goods from Germany (Saunders 1978 ch.5).

Although it is hard to draw firm conclusions for skill patterns and potential convergence, a recent study of the manufacture of kitchen furniture in Britain and West Germany (Steedman and Wagner 1987) highlighted the relationship between low skill, production methods, and unit values of goods produced. The lesser availability of suitably skilled labour left British firms with the need to substitute factory production methods using mainly semi-skilled labour to produce a basic, unsophisticated, low value added product. Once such a production system is set up, it is then difficult to integrate more skill intensive techniques. Similar conclusions concerning the relationship between choice of technology and choice of skills have been reached by Finegold and Soskice (1988).

2.2 Skill Mobility

Greater opportunities for the mobility of qualified labour between countries is a part of the broader Single Market agenda, so it might be thought that this would stimulate large scale migration of workers in response to the wage differentials noted above. In the past, labour mobility between member countries has been a major feature of the labour markets of countries such as France and Germany which experienced major inflows of Italian, Spanish, and more recently Portuguese workers. Within Italy, there has been a major migration from the south to the north, and wage differences, along with better employment prospects, were among the main causes. Currently, in France, there are about 1.5m people from Spain, Italy and Portugal, as compared with less than 100,000 from high wage Belgium and Germany (Marc 1987). The great majority of the immigrant workforce is concentrated in industry and construction, and in manual skilled and semi-skilled employment (Willard 1983).

There are several reasons to believe that such large scale migrations within the Community are now a thing of the past, most notable among these being the economic growth and higher incomes now available in Italy and Spain. Indeed, former cheap labour countries such as Italy and Spain are now experiencing their own immigration problems from North Africa (e.g. Venturini 1988).

Although the Treaty of Rome envisaged free mobility of EC citizens thoughout the Community, in practice this has been confined mainly to the unskilled and to certain professional groups. Mobility between Community countries among those with intermediate level skills, be they manual or non-manual, has generally been very limited. This is partly because such groups have not been very mobile geographically even within their own countries, and partly because of limitations on the recognition of their qualifications. In cases in which skill is based on long experience within the enterprise, such lack of mobility is to be expected; but among those with skills which are transferable across national labour markets, there is the problem that their skills are not recognized in other countries.

The task of breaking down such barriers to the free movement of labour has been undertaken by the CEDEFOP to promote mutual recognition of each country's vocational education diplomas, with the aim that vocational skills gained in one country should become more easily transferable to another. In pursuing this task, the CEDEFOP has sought agreement of governments and the social partners on 'mutual recognition' of vocational qualifications across the Community (Sellin 1989).

In practice, this operation faces two major difficulties, notably that of gaining acceptance of mutual recognition in the work place, and that arising from differences in labour market structure among countries, and notably, between those countries in which enterprise internal labour markets predominate and those in which inter-firm occupational markets prevail. Occupational markets may be more easily adapted to the requirements of mutual recognition because they are characterized by the transferability skills which are already recognized by many different employers and workers in a particular country. In contrast, skills based on internal labour markets lack even recognition by other employers and workers in the same country (Marsden and Ryan 1989).

In contrast, graduates of higher education have been more geographically mobile, and being better trained in languages, and sometimes partly educated in other member countries, are likely to display increased mobility. In part this is due to the greater transferability of diplomas resulting from mutual recognition, but it is also the result of the increased integration of European companies. There are already signs that European firms are recruiting heavily among graduates of neighbouring nationalities, so that graduate mobility would seem set to increase. To a lesser degree, mobility of those with scarce technician skills, for example in new technology, might also be expected to increase. This too may be facilitated by recent efforts to improve the teaching of other Community languages in schools.

How such workers will respond to inter-country wage differentials is hard to predict. At least two scenarios can be identified. In the first, highly skilled labour, especially in shortage areas, may be attracted by the earnings and good job opportunties of the high wage countries. There is, for example, a certain number of engineering graduates from Eire working in German firms in Stuttgart. Such moves are facilitated by the importance of the English language in computer related sciences.

In the second, young graduates may be attracted to work abroad by the possibility of learning another Community language, and thus enhancing their career prospects in their own country. Such moves could be towards higher or lower wage countries. A temporary drop in earnings might well be considered a worthwhile sacrifice in order to learn another language and to learn to work in another environment. Some British schools have been able to attract young German teachers who accept the lower salaries, for a time, because of the opportunity to perfect their English.

The likelihood that inter-country mobility should be primarily among younger workers who have not yet acquired family responsibilities should not conceal its economic importance as such people represent the newest vintage of technical skills arriving onto the labour market.

Thus, while the creation of a Community-wide labour market seems unlikely in the near future, moves in this direction are likely for certain categories of labour, especially the highly skilled and highly educated. This could cause new pressures on national pay structures and systems of pay determination, especially as entry rates of pay are the most sensitive part of the pay structure to labour supply and demand pressures. However, it seems unlikely that there will be a big movement of workers in response to inter-country wage differentials.

Finally, one danger arising from an increase in international skill mobility is that, because much skill training is employer financed, countries in which employers have not made adequate arrangements will be tempted to recruit skilled labour from those which have, and thus destabilize training arrangements in the latter group of countries. In addition, successful employer finance of transferable skills generally depends upon an understanding among employers of the importance of collective efforts in training, which commonly rest on moral pressures, as in West Germany. Foreign firms from countries lacking such traditions may prove less sensitive to this kind of pressure, and so be more likely to cut back on training.

2.3 The Integration of Capital and the Formation of European Labour Forces within Firms

The pace of capital integration between member countries has quickened in anticipation of 1992. Many national companies have sought partners in neighbouring EC countries in order to develop their activities in new regional markets, while other companies have sought new European partners for new technological and production ventures. Several elements of such integration affect labour markets.

The search for commercial partners with access to other countries' markets has been already mentioned in the context of graduate recruitment. The experience of coordinating activities between groups of employees raised each in their own national management styles is likely to shape the evolution of management techniques within the EEC, and in the future, make management skills more transferable between countries. One notable feature of recent links has been that smaller firms have been very active, whereas in the past, much of the international side of economic activity was left to large and very large firms.

Another source of pressure for greater management integration across the Community has been the move by many large companies to integrate their operations across the whole of the Community. The consortium of companies working on the Airbus project provides one illustration, and the articulation of automobile production facilities across several national borders, particularly within Ford and General Motors, provides another.

Apart from creating a European market in managerial skills, the integration of European firms influences management methods. In the past, multi-national companies have been major vehicles for the transmission of management and personnel practices from one country to another, particularly when the parent company took an active part in the management of its subsidiaries. These differences in management practice have often also been sources of greater efficiency. As a result, some multi-nationals have been able to take advantage of lower national wage levels in the host country, but achieving higher levels of productivity than had been customary in that country. In this respect, such companies might well choose to locate some of their activities in the low wage areas of the EEC because they believe that they know how to achieve higher levels of productivity there than do the existing national firms.

In a wider sense, management skills are not universal, as might be the case with technical aspects of engineering or information technology, but they are social skills developed within a particular national environment (or mix of national environments). Thus, a West German firm (used to working through the system of codetermination) taking over a British one (in which employee representation is more adversarial) has to adapt its managerial style, but it may also seek to change relations within the British firm. Equally, a French firm with a strong tradition of centralized management taking over a German firm would have to adapt to the more decentralized authority structure which is based on the high level of technical competence of those with intermediate level skills (v. Maurice, Sellier and Silvestre 1982).

Capital integration may often require more than just management integration if the kind of economies of scale indicated in the Cecchini report are to be realized (Cecchini 1988). There will need to be greater integration of the workforces engaged in different parts of the company's operations. At present, the workforce in one country is likely to be subject to one set of collective agreements and bargaining arrangements while that in another will be subject to a different one. In the past, much expatriate labour has been at the managerial and professional level, which has been only weakly unionized, and the somewhat exceptional nature of expatriates' status has insulated their conditions of employment from those of fellow workers in the same location.

If European collaboration is to be more regular and more routine, few firms will wish to pay the high premiums or be bound by the somewhat rigid system of conditions associated with expatriate employment. Moreover, as the level of contact spreads down the job hierarchy, it extends more into areas in which employment conditions and job classification systems are subject to collective bargaining. Hence, this degree of integration will place heavy pressure on existing systems of negotiation, and on existing systems of pay and work rules.

Companies developing their European links in this way will need, sooner or later, to develop policies to integrate key parts of their workforces in the different Community countries. For example, the creation of future management teams will require the development of suitable career development policies drawing on young managers across the firm's European operations - just as it is common now for large national firms to insist that their young managers should get experience of plant operations as a part of their career in the head office. The development of such career arrangements for technical staff may be even more critical, particularly in R&D intensive industries. Thus, a likely consequence of the increased integration of European firms is that firms' 'internal labour markets' (that is, the set of career flows within firms) will come increasingly to span national borders.

The impact of wage differentials across labour markets on career movements within enterprise internal labour markets is complex because the workers on such labour markets always have a choice between further career progression within the enterprise, and a move to a job in another firm. Entry rates are often important for recruitment, and external wage differentials appear to influence wastage among those with the most transferable skills, but otherwise, wage levels within internal labour markets are largely insulated from events in local labour markets, and internal differentials within the firm assume greater importance.

Until now, most firms have recruited from a single national labour market, or from neighbouring national labour markets with broadly similar wage levels, but tensions could emerge as a result of recruitment from labour markets with greatly differing wage levels.

Entry rates which would enable a company to pick the cream of graduates in a low wage country may be insufficient to attract enough graduates in a high wage country. Equally, internal wage structures could come under strain as the level of pay to keep down labour wastage in a low wage country could be wholly inadequate in a higher wage country.

2.4 Monetary Integration and Unit Labour Costs

The progress towards monetary union will also bring a new set of pressures on national labour markets and systems of pay determination (v. the chapter by de Molina and Perea). Although the working of the European Monetary System has, since its establishment in 1978, contributed to a reduction in exchange rate uncertainty, it has nevertheless allowed considerable flexibility: all of the fully participating currencies, except for the Danish Krone, have been either devalued or revalued at some point by more than 5%, and between 1981 and 1987, both the French Franc and the Italian Lira declined by more than 10% against the Ecu (Eurostat Money and Finance 2 1989). A stronger version of the EMS would reduce such scope for such variation (Richardson 1990). Full monetary union would remove possibility of exchange rate variation.

Since the early 1970s, exchange rate variations have enabled countries to cope with quite large differences in their underlying rates of inflation, the scale of which are illustrated in Table 3.

Although entry into the EMS may itself reduce inflationary expectations, as is illustrated by the recent Irish entry, inflation may also arise from tensions in 'real' economy, such as skill shortages, and unresolved pressures over wage differentials between different groups of workers, and between the recipients of different kinds of income. After a period as head of the British National Board for Prices and Incomes in the late 1960s, Aubrey Jones concluded that the 'wage-wage' spiral was as important a motor of inflation as the 'wage-price' spiral (Jones 1973). Clegg, who also had considerable experience of dealing with the wage claims of individual groups of workers during incomes policy, reached similar conclusions concerning the importance of pay comparisons between groups made by workers and their unions (Clegg 1970).

Although a tight national monetary policy could sustain a régime of semi-fixed exchange rates in the face of such pressures, its effect on labour demand and unemployment would be both severe and very uneven, biting most on weakly organized groups in the labour market. This is because many powerful groups of workers benefit from the investments that they and their employers have made in the development of skills which are often fairly specific to the enterprise in which they work. Such workers are costly to replace in the short run so that the burden of adjustment then falls predominantly on other less protected groups of workers. Even in periods of high unemployment, workers with more strategic skills can retain a high degree of bargaining power.

Table 3. Per cent change in labour costs, unit labour costs and exchange rates (1980-1987).

	Labour cost nat. currency %	Unit lab. cost nat. currency %	EcU exch. rate %	Unit lab. cost EcU %
Belgium	42.2	-3.5	-5.7	-9.0
Denmark	65.6	0.0	-0.7	-0.7
FR Germany	29.6	-22.8	21.8	-5.9
Greece	268.0	168.9	-61.8	2.6
Spain	109.2	27.5	-29.8	-10.6
France	78.9	11.3	-15.2	-5.6
Ireland	100.8	3.0	-12.7	-10.1
Italy	137.9	19.2	-20.2	-4.9
Luxembourg	50.5	5.3	-5.7	-0.7
Netherlands	18.5	-22.8	18.2	-8.8
Portugal	251.8	103.9	-57.1	-12.4
UK	73.3	9.3	-15.3	-7.4
EUR	-	-	-	-7.0

Source: Eurostat, National Accounts ESA Aggregates, 1970-87.

There are other circumstances too in which it may not be feasible to rely heavily on a tight monetary policy to restrain inflation. If there were a wage hike of the kind that followed the events of 1968-69 in France and Italy, it is unlikely that the government would risk letting it translate into unemployment. Equally, countries which already have very high unemployment rates may find it politically unacceptable to use a further rise in unemployment to cool wage inflation.

To control inflationary tendencies many countries in practice do not rely upon a single policy instrument, but use a range of policies because this enables them to spread the impact of the restrictionary measures. National governments may find their autonomy in taxes on savings and on capital reduced, and concentrated on taxes on items whose geographical mobility is restricted, such as employment incomes, consumption, and property. It will not be possible, in practice, to make up for all the reduced fiscal autonomy by taxing such items because of the likely economic distortions caused.

Although national governments will still retain some short-run autonomy – because markets are, in practice, highly imperfect and the degree of inertia in economic systems is considerable – it will prove more difficult to spread the burden of anti-inflationary policies. Consequently, a greater load will be placed upon labour market institutions to resolve inflationary pressures. Notable among these are the ability to coordinate the wage bargaining outcomes of a large number of bargaining groups, and to ensure that productivity grows in line with pay.

3. Wages as an Adjustment Factor in European Integration

Up until now, the main focus of this chapter has been upon the implications of wage differences between member countries for economic and monetary union. The emphasis now shifts to the potential role of wages and of wage fixing institutions in facilitating integration. The present section focuses mainly on the underlying theory, while the subsequent one takes a more practical view.

3.1 Allocation across Labour Markets

Although there is currently much controversy among economists, between those who believe that labour markets perform like competitive markets for other commodities and those who believe that non-competitive forces predominate, economic theory attributes a major role to wage adjustments in the general process of labour force adaptation. This section looks first at the role of wage differences across labour markets in reallocating labour, and then at the role of wage differentials within the enterprise as a means of promoting greater productivity and more flexible working, and finally at the role of collective bargaining and aggregate wage flexibility.

According to the standard competitive model of labour markets, movements in relative wages are one of the chief signals by which firms with expanding output can communicate their wish to hire additional labour. Except in periods of high unemployment, when there is excess supply, additional labour has to be attracted away from other firms whose output is stagnant or falling. Thus, in the short run, movements in relative wages between firms, and by extension, between industries, serve to reallocate labour in response to changes in demand.

A similar argument applies to labour mobility and wage changes between regions, except that interregional mobility involves usually considerably greater costs for the individuals involved, which is one reason why the great majority of job moves take place over very short distances.

Movement between occupations is more complex because of the longer term investments made by workers in acquiring skills which they expect to use over a large part of their working lives, thus short-run variations in relative wages between occupations have a correspondingly smaller role to play. Nevertheless, occupational choice does appear to be influenced to some extent by movements in occupational pay, particularly by the rates of pay applicable to new entrants (e.g. Freeman 1971: engineering graduates, Zabalza et al. 1979: school teachers). The same is probably true of workers seeking jobs in firms with well established internal labour markets (Doeringer and Piore 1971).

Flexibility of entry rates of pay has another, related, function. Inter-industry labour mobility often involves learning new skills, and may also involve learning new occupations, which implies the need for additional training and the acquisition of new kinds of work experience. During their initial months, and sometimes years, in a new industry, employees function as both productive workers and as trainees while they progress towards the output levels of experienced workers. For the most part, employers shoulder a considerable share of the costs of training and experience, and if this gives rise to transferable skills, then there is the risk that other employers will poach the trainees away once training is complete.

A common method by which the costs of training are shared is by the payment of special trainee (and apprentice) rates of pay which are below those of experienced workers. In periods of major restructuring the demands on employer-based training are increased, and one might expect the employment of workers from declining industries to be enhanced by the payment of temporarily lower rates in their new industry during their induction period. Special employment and training subsidies would have the same effect, and have been extensively used for young workers in recent years in Britain (Youth Training Scheme) and France (Travaux d'Utilité Collective).

3.2 Allocation of Labour Motivation within Internal Labour Markets

Apart from directing labour across labour markets, relative wages can also play a major role in determining incentives within the firm, within its internal labour market. This can take the form of incentives to accept promotion, or to move to more skilled or difficult jobs (Creedy and Whitfield 1988, Chabanne and Lollivier 1988, Sengenberger 1987). Indeed, in Italy and the UK, there has been much recent discussion of restoring differentials within the enterprise in order to increase management's ability to reward skill and responsibility (e.g. for Italy, Della Rocca 1989).

The role of wages in the motivation of individual workers within the enterprise is a controversial subject, and modern personnel management rarely relies on wage systems alone. Instead, it uses a battery of policies including, for example, those to build up organizational commitment. Nevertheless, it has often been suggested that the payment of a single rate of pay for all workers in the enterprise engaged in a particular occupation or classified in the same grade, harms motivation. This is because there is no reward for differences of ability and diligence between individual workers. For highly uniform work in which workers can exercise very little discretion, this may not be a problem. However, the search for improved product quality and reliability, and the introduction of new technology over the last decade, have increased the need for employees to exercise greater care and judgement in their work.

Under such circumstances as those outlined above, uniform rates of pay, irrespective of employee effort and quality, it has been argued, would tend to encourage individual performance to drop towards the lowest common denominator thus leading to under-utilization of the more able employees. Apart from these technical and market changes, there was also an increasing recognition by the early 1970s that older, Taylorist forms of payment and work organization had many serious disadvantages (e.g. Butera 1974).

One solution widely proposed is to introduce a system of individualized pay supplements, often called 'merit pay.' If these are to be effective, then employers have to monitor the performance of individual workers sufficiently accurately and fairly for workers to believe that their extra performance will be rewarded. Otherwise, such payments can be divisive as employees see the award of supplements as either arbitrary, or based on management favouritism. When done properly, employee appraisal takes up a good deal of management time, as it does, for example, in large Japanese firms (Best 1984). It also helps to reinforce the idea that pay is determined by factors within the enterprise, thus distancing pay determination within the firm from external, labour market pressures.

Close supervision can be very expensive and, where work involves the use of judgement and initiative, it may be counterproductive. This has led a number of economists to argue that many firms use another solution, namely wage and salary systems which offer increments based on age or length of service, or more generally, which offer the possibility of deferred income. These provide employers with a means of encouraging higher performance among their employees for two reasons: firstly, the employees stay far longer with the firm and so develop a longer term interest in the firm's performance, which should encourage them to be more conscientious; and secondly, the employees have more to lose if they are dismissed so that management's powers of discipline are enhanced. The effectiveness of such payment systems is also enhanced if the firm pays above the rate paid by its main competitors in the labour market. This also increases the power of the threat of dismissal.

The widespread use of this kind of payment rule has been recognized by many labour economists under the so-called 'efficiency wage,' 'contract,' and 'internal labour market' theories of wage behaviour.[4] The most important implication of such practices, and of the theories concerning them, is that a wedge is driven between the forces of labour supply and demand across labour markets and the wages paid to individual workers. Hence, the wages of incumbent workers are primarily determined by the personnel practices and collective agreements regulating work relations within the enterprise. To make their wages move in response to external supply and demand pressures would interfere with the motivational norms of the internal wage structures, and thus harm productivity.

Thus a conflict of function emerges for wages. On the one hand, the demands of inter-firm and inter-sectoral labour allocation require flexible wages, and on the other, motivation and flexibility of deployment of labour within the firm require stable wage rules, and a link between pay and quality of effort and cooperation. In practice, most EEC economies contain a mixture of such conditions, with some firms operating with predominantly stable pay relations, and others which are somewhat less protected.

The flexibility of aggregate real wage levels across the whole of an economy in response to changed circumstances, such as an external price shock, may also contribute to the maintenance of aggregate employment levels. For many small open economies dependent on international trade, the impact of such wage flexibility may often outweigh the employment effects of reduced incomes on domestic demand. Indeed, concern about the ability of countries to keep their unit labour costs in line with those of their EC partners discussed earlier is a variant on the same theme.

However, such aggregate real wage flexibility is something of a public good as it depends upon individual groups of workers (and recipients of other types of income) accepting reduced real incomes in the short term. Yet under many national wage bargaining arrangements, individual groups which forego wage increases that would compensate for the rise in prices may be left behind by other groups which do not show the same self-restraint.

The questions of aggregate, and of firm and sector-level wage flexibility are related. In an economy characterized by the competitive model of wage adjustment, micro-level wage flexibility would normally lead to aggregate wage flexibility. One major implication of the various internal labour market processes reviewed earlier is that large sections of the labour force lie beyond the reach of such micro-level competitive pressures, in the short-run at least, and this makes the attainment of aggregate wage flexibility more dependent on the achievement of voluntary restraint by one means or another. Moreover, these tend to be the more powerful groups, and those most likely to be able to press for wage increases even in periods of high unemployment.

This problem brings us back to the reduced scope for national governments to control inflationary pressures by means of the traditional instruments. It again highlights the likely need for greater reliance upon collective restraint by employer and union organizations in order to cope with the externalities associated with unrestrained pursuit of individual group interests. Although some of these may be contained by the expected general increase in competition, which should reduce the scope for sharing product market rents between employers and workers (v. the chapter by FitzRoy), many of the insider problems seem likely to remain.

4. Wage Structure and Wage Flexibility in Practice

It is often argued that certain kinds of flexibility in pay should help individual national economies to adapt to the pressures of economic and monetary union. This section reviews the principal ones and discusses the amount of flexibility they provide in practice.

On the whole, it will be argued that, on past experience, wage flexibility offers only limited scope for labour market adjustment, and its ability to provide flexibility in the level of labour costs is greatly diminished by the scale of non-wage labour costs. The relative inefficacy of pay in promoting external labour market adjustment serves to highlight the importance of pay and productivity within the enterprise, a point supported by the various studies of productivity growth in Europe in the 1960s and 1970s. These showed the relatively small contribution of inter-sectoral movements of labour to the productivity growth of the period [5] (e.g. ECE 1982).

Negotiation and employee participation and consultation play an important part in the search for improved productivity in the enterprise, but this should not obscure the importance of higher levels of negotiation for pay. As mentioned earlier, control of unit labour costs will depend on both productivity and pay.

The final theme of this section is devoted to coordinated pay bargaining and the problem of inflation. As with the tension between the role of relative wages as allocators of labour across labour markets and as motivators within the enterprise, so there is an equivalent tension between the reward for enterprise specific productivity increases and the wider concerns of the pay of other workers without such opportunities.

4.1 Inter-industry Relative Wage Adaptability

Empirical evidence - that changes in relative wage levels between industries play an active part in labour market adjustment – has, on the whole, been disappointing, despite attempts to test it systematically across several countries (OECD 1965 and OECD 1985 ch.5). The structure of relative wages between industries displays a great deal of stability both in the short-run and over longer periods, and this pattern appears to hold across not just the EEC countries for which there is suitable evidence, but also in the United States.

Moreover, within the industrial sector, for which the data series are most complete, the same industries recur among the high and low paid ones in each country (as illustrated in Table 2 above).

The slow pace of change of industry relative pay levels is not in itself at odds with the competitive interpretation of pay as an allocator of labour in so far as inter-industry wage differences are deemed to arise from differences in skill mix and in working conditions. Indeed, a sizeable fraction of the pay differences between industries can be explained in this way (CERC 1988 Tab. III-1): between one third and two thirds of the difference between high and low wage industries, depending on the country.[6]

Similar findings, using other sources, have been made for Italy by Dell'Aringa and Lucifora (1988), and for the US by Krueger and Summers (1987). However, what is harder to square with the competitive interpretation is the relative insensitivity of industry wage levels to changes in industry labour demand and supply conditions. The OECD (1965 and 1985) found little indication that wages grew faster in industries which were seeking to expand their employment. It appears that regional wage levels are also very slow to adjust to shifts in the economic fortunes of different regions, taking up to twenty years, according to recent evidence for the UK (Pissarides and McMaster, 1984).

In its earlier and more systematic study, the OECD (1965) pointed out that such evidence as could be found for wages increasing in industries with increasing demand was also consistent with a non-competitive interpretation. Namely, that firms with expanding sales simultaneously recruited extra labour and raised wages as a result of union pressures. More recent work by Krueger and Summers in the US (1987) and by Stewart (1990) in the UK provides additional support for the non-competitive interpretation (v. chapter by FitzRoy).

Occupational pay differentials appear to be just as insensitive to short-run variations in labour demand and supply as do industry differentials. Recent attempts to trace the responsiveness of differentials between skilled and unskilled, manual and non-manual, and managerial and clerical workers in a number of OECD countries, found no evidence of a general tendency for differentials between more and less skilled workers to increase as unemployment increased. This could have been expected because the demand for skilled labour generally falls less than that for unskilled labour in a recession (Oi 1961). This occurs as firms seek to retain their skilled labour, because of the subsequent difficulty of replacing it at the end of a recession, and because of their investment in its skills. Indeed, in

France, Germany, and Italy, even the steep rise of unemployment after the 1979 oil shock appears to have had no immediate impact on occupational pay differentials (OECD 1987, Marsden 1988).

The one significant area of sensititivity to short-run labour market changes appears to be that of entry rates of pay into certain occupations (Freeman 1971, Zabalza et al. 1979), and the pay of young entrants into labour markets (Marsden and Ryan 1990). In the latter case in particular, where evidence is available, rates of pay as a percentage of those of adults seem to have fallen, partly in response to public policy measures which have affected young workers' perceptions of alternative incomes, and partly as a consequence of the high levels of youth unemployment.

The failure of wage differentials to respond to labour demand and supply does not preclude possible adverse employment consequences for groups of workers whose pay is significantly out of line with the value of their output. Studies of the demand for skilled and unskilled labour in UK engineering (Nissim 1984) and German manufacturing (FitzRoy and Funke 1988a), and of that for young workers in the UK and the US indicate that the demand for these categories, and possible substitution between them and other categories, is sensitive to relative wages (e.g. Layard 1982).[7]

Although industrial and occupational wage structures appear insensitive to shifts in labour market conditions, and, consequently, to have made a relatively small contribution to the reallocation of labour in response to market pressures, they have, during the 1970s and 1980s, changed in response to government and trade union policies. In Italy, the equalizing pressures of the union policies for reducing wage differentials in the early 1970s (Santi 1981), followed by the equalizing influence of the system of flat-rate indexation of the 'scala mobile' in the late 1970s and early 1980s, have caused a considerable reduction in wage differentials between industries (Dell'Aringa 1988).

In Greece, the partial indexation provisions of the post 1981 incomes policy have also had a marked equalizing effect on industry differentials (Ioannou-Gianakis 1990). In Britain, various stages of the incomes policies of the early and middle 1970s had a marked compressive effect upon industry and occupational wage structures (Brown 1975, Saunders and Marsden 1981). In France, the operation of the minimum wage in the early 1970s, and again in the early and the middle 1980s, has caused a reduction in industry and skill differentials. The introduction of equal pay for women workers in both the Netherlands and the UK during the 1970s provides another example of such change.

The ability of government and union policies to alter wage structures is not without limit, as has been shown dramatically by the revolt of the skilled and supervisory workers at Fiat in October 1980 against the unions' egalitarian policies, and more recently, by the growth of the rank and file committees (the *Cobas*). In similar fashion, many skilled workers in Britain protested against the egalitarian policies of the 1970s by switching their vote from Labour to the Conservative party.

Nevertheless, the reaction against government and bargaining policies to change wage structures is not mechanical, and within certain limits, wage structures can be changed for the achievement of some higher goal. In the case of the incomes policies of Britain, Greece, and Italy, this goal was to reduce inflation, and to protect the incomes of the lower paid from inflation. In France, raising the minimum wage periodically has been justified by the need to improve the position of the weakest members of society.

What has proved more difficult is the bargaining in the opposite direction: instead of foregoing economic gain in the name of equality, making concessions on equality in the name of flexibility. The abortive national level flexibility negotiations in France in 1981-86, and in British engineering in 1984-89, and the limited success of bargaining over a partial reduction of the indexation system in Italy in 1983-84 illustrate some of the problems. However, they also show that such issues can be tackled by negotiation.

To conclude, the evidence of lack of flexibility of an industry's wages in response to its economic conditions has a number of important implications for European integration. First, one should not expect the industrial wage structure, in its present form, to provide a great deal of assistance in employment adjustment. Secondly, firms' personnel and remuneration policies have a major part to play. Thirdly, non-competitive factors are widespread, although some of them might be expected to diminish in the face of increased product market competition as a result of integration. Fourthly, in so far as the protection of incumbent employees' wages from labour market pressures stems from policies that contribute to better productivity, it seems unlikely that the flexibility of the industrial and occupational wage structures will greatly increase.

4.2 Pay Flexibility within the Enterprise

The increased concern of firms with competition over quality and technical sophistication, rather than competition over price for fairly standardized products, has made many of them take a greater interest in the motivation and training of their employees. This implies longer job tenures, at least for those receiving such training, and a concern by employers to select workers with potential for adapting to their personnel policies and evolving training needs instead of hiring those with standard qualifications for a standard job.[8] The introduction of new types of performance pay has also been stimulated by management's desire to 'restore' the pay differentials for skilled and managerial staff compressed during the 1970s and early 1980s, and to make existing pay scales and job classifications more adaptable to management's needs.

As concerns employee motivation, recent years have witnessed a revival among psychologists of the view that pay can be an effective motivater – as is evidenced by Lawler's exposition of 'expectancy theory,' and the large amount of experimental research he amassed in its support (Lawler 1971). According to that theory, pay can be effective as a motivator, but under certain conditions only: if employees see their effort as resulting in better performance; if that performance is adequately rewarded by the employer; and if employees value the rewards. However, it is not easy for management to meet these conditions, which no doubt helps to explain the mixed results obtained in practice. For example, individual effort may not produce the desired performance if management organize workflow badly, or staff are poorly trained.

Performance may not be adequately reflected in pay because performance measurement in many organizations is often inconsistent and unreliable. However, if suitable work and appraisal systems are designed, then, according to expectancy theory, pay can be an effective motivater. Lawler's framework is consistent with some recent research in economics that pay incentives can be effective (see Blinder 1990), although much work in sociology and industrial relations (e.g. Brown 1973) inclines to more sceptical conclusions because it has been focused on the breakdown of such incentives.

There are many reasons to expect that the impact of performance related pay will be modest because of difficulties in evaluating employee performance. For example, the most commonly used form of appraisal in European firms is by the employee's supervisor, yet the studies of such appraisal show that the mean correlation across several studies between raters' evaluations of the same employee is low (about 0.4), which implies a good deal of random variation in appraisals. This suggests a natural limit to which employees would accept the extension of individual merit pay schemes as they would not wish to see too substantial a part of their income dependent upon such inconsistent evaluation (Bishop 1987). It also suggests that there are limits to the capacity of merit pay systems to boost productivity by drawing forth greater, or different kinds of, employee effort.

New types of incentive pay have also gained popularity among managers as part of a wider shift of focus in personnel management inspired by developments in Japan and in the United States (Kochan et al. 1986) towards the enterprise and away from the labour market.[9] Under the 'human resource management' approach, firms seek to enhance their own training effort in order to improve quality in production; to encourage flexibility, especially in job assignments as distinct from remaining within the narrow specialist functions; to instill a sense of commitment to the firm's goals among its employees, rather than rely upon traditional incentive payment schemes; and to integrate human resources management into the general process of management decision-making rather than leaving personnel issues as problems to be dealt with downstream (Guest 1987).

The first three of these items represent a shift away from the treatment of labour as a resource to be hired when needed, and attribute to management a much more active role in shaping the skills it requires, and away from the idea that employees should be paid at the 'market rate' for their skills. Indeed, the more active management is in shaping the skills of its staff, the less readily these can be hired directly from outside. Equally, if management values a particular type of motivation, such as commitment, and adopts policies to develop this, its own behaviour must be consistent: hire and fire by management is inconsistent with the pursuit of policies to encourage employees to be committed to the goals of the organization.

As yet there has been little research in Europe on the spread of such management practices. Systematic adoption of all of the constitutive elements of human resource management, in Britain at least, where it has been much discussed in both academic and management circles, appears to have been fairly limited so far (Guest 1990), but there has been wide management interest in the adoption of individual components.

In Britain, a number of surveys have suggested that management in many sectors of the economy has been seeking to break away from long-standing skill demarcations and to adopt more flexible working patterns (e.g. Atkinson and Meager 1986), and in both France and Britain there have been many experiments with quality control circles (Eyraud and Tchobanian 1985, and Bradley and Hill 1983).

In West Germany, management and union concern with training within the enterprise has been long standing both as initial training under apprenticeships and as further supplementary training.

The third reason why many firms are seeking changes in their remuneration systems has been most in evidence in Italy and the UK where employers have sought to restore the differentials of reward and incentives for skill and management responsibility. In Italy, the system of wage indexation, in force from 1977, has caused an increasing share of employees' income to take the form of the flat rate increases to compensate for inflation, such that by the early 1980s, indexation increases accounted for up to 40% of their monthly earnings. This greatly reduced the percentage rewards for skill and for responsibility.

Since the Scotti agreements of 1983-84, which sought to reduce the coverage of indexation, employers have increased the share of employee remuneration which they control (Dell'Aringa and Lucifora 1988), and according to a Ministry of Labour survey, this freedom has been used in part to increase the rewards for skill and quality of work (Industria e Sindacato 14/1988). In the UK also, the restoration of differentials has been one of the concerns of management, and one of the causes of the big increase in pay inequalities since the early 1980s.

Fourthly, in France, but also in Italy and Britain, employers, in both the private and public sectors, have been concerned to reduce the influence of established systems of job and pay classification in order to facilitate technical and organizational change (Ministère du Travail,1988, Della Rocca 1989, Silvestre et al. 1991). Particularly in France, in a great many private and public sector firms, jobs are classified into a complex system of grades and of sub-grades into which workers are allocated. On top of this there are age or length of service increments, which means that individual employees' pay is largely determined by their position in the grading system. Ability and effort may still be rewarded by promotion, but most promotion systems run their course fairly quickly, leaving little additional reward for extra effort or care. The objective of 'individualization' in this context has been to introduce greater scope for employers to reward the behaviour they wish to encourage, but also to adapt to external pressures, such as retention difficulties.

Progress towards both merit pay and individualization has been limited in all three countries. The main obstacle seems to lie in the difficulty of assessing the effort, quality of work, or initiative of individual workers in large and complex organizations (v. chapter by Shonfield). Use of performance appraisal has increased in recent years in Britain (Long 1986), but in France, despite the spread of 'individualization,' it has proved very difficult to gain union agreement over the criteria for evaluation of performance (Reynaud 1989b), as it has also in Italy (Della Rocca 1989). The reason suggested for union suspicion in Italy, that the application of merit criteria is difficult for unions to monitor, hence the preference for easily observed criteria such as length of service, would seem to be of fairly general application in most countries.

Profit related pay and employee share ownership have also been much discussed initiatives in enterprise level pay determination aimed at fostering more flexible attitudes to change among employees. Evidence for both France and the UK shows some increase in such schemes in recent years, in both cases, encouraged by legislative incentives (CERC 1986, and Richardson and Nejad 1986). In most cases, such schemes brought additional benefits to normal earnings, and so were unlikely to encounter much union opposition, but the size of the benefits, outside executive compensation schemes, was small, and therefore unlikely to have a strong incentive effect. Nevertheless, a study of UK firms revealed some positive change of attitudes among participating employees (Dewe, Dunn and Richardson 1988).

Productivity bargaining may be considered another aspect of performance related pay, but in this case, employers generally negotiate productivity enhancing changes in working practices in exchange for increased basic pay. Such negotiations have been current in France, Italy and the UK in recent years, and more recently in Spain. Although the precise nature of the practices management has been seeking to change varies markedly between the three countries, there has been a common concern with bargaining over productivity enhancing concessions at the enterprise level. The emphasis in Britain has been on payment for specified changes in working practices, and in France and Italy, for general changes which result in the achievement of a specified output target (Eyraud et al. 1990: France and the UK, Zappi 1987, and Tommasi 1988: Italy).

The extent of such agreements is hard to ascertain: in Britain, Marsden and Thompson (1990) estimate that between 1980 and 1987 they covered about one tenth of manual workers in manufacturing, and Cahill and Ingram (1988) estimate that, over roughly the same period, 28% of pay settlements in the Confederation of British Industry's databank included productivity concessions. However, in none of the three countries have there been any detailed analyses of the direct impact of such agreements upon productivity.

27

If one is looking at these remuneration methods for signs of the emergence of systems which are more sensitive to the firm's product market conditions, then two additional factors need to be taken into account. The first is the widespread decline in the importance of traditional payment by results schemes which have lost ground in several countries in recent years (e.g. Reynaud 1989b: France, and Marsden 1990b: the UK) in favour of time-based payment systems. The second is the gradual growth in the share of non-wage elements in total labour costs (Hart 1989). In many EEC countries, non-wage elements represent a high proportion of total labour costs. If we include payment for days not worked (mainly holidays and sickness absence), then, in industry in 1984, such costs represented around two fifths of total labour costs in Belgium, France, FR Germany, Italy, and the Netherlands, and between one fifth and a third in the remaining countries (Table 4).

To conclude, given that many of the schemes for merit pay and profit sharing already represent only a small percentage of direct earnings, their impact on the flexibility of labour costs in relation to output changes is correspondingly smaller. Hence, such payment schemes have so far offered little in terms of labour cost flexibility, and their main benefits to date must therefore be sought in their effects upon employee motivation and the ability of management to buy change. Evidence of this is not easy to come by because of the difficulty of disentangling the effects of pay schemes from all the other influences on an enterprise's performance. However, the importance of productivity improvements as one of the means of keeping unit labour costs in line with those of competitors gives pay a central role as an instrument of management policy.

4.3 Collective Bargaining and Wage Adaptability

One of the notable features of wage determination in many EEC countries is the high proportion of the workforce whose pay is determined wholly or partly by collective agreement despite wide variations in union membership rates. In a number of countries, such coverage is supplemented by minimum wage legislation. For example, in France, Germany and Italy, industry-level collective agreements which fix minimum rates of pay for workers in the industry concerned may be extended by the authorities to cover firms which are not party to the agreement.[10] Although such powers may be rarely invoked, they strengthen the 'spill-over' effect which is commonly associated with collective agreements. Thus, collective agreements have a great deal of influence over movements in the level and structure of nominal earnings, and not surprisingly, past efforts to control inflation in many European countries have involved either formal or informal discussions between the state and the social partners.

As mentioned earlier, a low rate of inflation without a high rate of unemployment[11] has many characteristics of a 'public good,' in other words, something from which all groups in society benefit. At the same time, it is often difficult to achieve in a decentralized and competitive economy, as individual groups may be tempted to exploit the self-restraint of others in order to gain an exceptionally large increase for themselves.

Success in resolving this problem, plus the relatively low rates of inflation experienced by a number of small countries with highly centralized wage bargaining systems, have caused attention to focus on the organization of wage bargaining in different countries. Does the negotiation of a central wage agreement between the peak organizations of the unions and the employers, as used to occur in Sweden or is still the case in Austria, for example, provide a mechanism by which the wayward behaviour of some individual bargaining groups can be contained in the interest of the majority?

As the scientific debate evolved, it became clear that centralization was only part of the answer, because of the good inflation performance of a number of decentralized economies, such as the United States, and the number of exceptions to the centralization rule, such as Switzerland, which have coordinated, but decentralized bargaining and low inflation. Thus, Crouch (1985) has argued that the structure of bargaining is only important where unions are strong, or where the coverage of collective bargaining is great. In the United States, weak unions and low coverage leave competitive market pressures to keep down wage inflation. However, as collective bargaining has a wide coverage in nearly all EEC member countries, the US solution is not an option.

Centralization alone is not sufficient. The degree of horizontal integration between the constituent parts of union and employer organizations has also proved critical. Thus, an interest organization which is able to represent a large fraction of the workforce in a particular economy, or in other words, which 'encompasses' a large part of the workforce, is better able to take a long view on issues of collective concern than one which represents only a narrow interest (Olson 1982). The encompassive group must be able to formulate acceptable compromises between the diverse interests of constituent

Table 4. Structure of monthly labour costs in industry (1984).

Percentage of monthly labour costs (a)				
	FR Germany	France	Italy	NL	Belgium
Direct pay	56.5	52.5	53.4	56.1	54.9
Periodic bonuses (b)	8.6	5.0	8.0	7.1	10.9
Pay for days not worked	11.4	9.4	10.9	9.6	9.1
Pay in kind	0.2	1.2	0.3	0.1	0.1
Total direct costs	76.7	68.1	72.6	72.9	74.9
Social security payments					
Statutory (c)	16.4	19.4	24.1	16.3	22.5
Voluntary/agreed	4.6	8.7	1.3	8.1	1.4
Other	2.3	3.9	1.2	2.7	1.2
Total	100.0	100.0	100.0	100.0	100.0
Ecu	2008.4	1733.6	1544.7	1891.1	1718.6
	UK	Eire	Denmark	Greece	Portugal
Direct pay	71.3	69.7	83.6	62.0	58.7
Periodic bonuses (b)	1.1	1.0	0.7	12.0	10.3
Pay for days not worked	10.4	11.7	8.0	7.0	5.3
Pay in kind	0.2	0.2	0.1	1.0	0.2
Total direct costs	83.0	82.6	92.4	81.0	74.5
Social security payments					
Statutory	7.6	8.6	4.6	18.0	16.3
Voluntary/agreed	7.0	6.1	1.1	-	2.1
Other	2.6	2.7	1.9	1.0	
Total	100.0	100.0	100.0	100.0	100.0
Ecu	1417.1	1423.0	1732.4	623.4	385.5

Notes:
(a) Establishments with 10 or more employees. Coverage: NACE 1-5, Industry and construction.
(b) Eurostat defines these as 'bonuses and gratuities not paid regularly at each pay period.' They include employee share ownership schemes.
(c) Italy: reduced by the effect of subsidies, notably the effect of the Cassa Integrazione Guadagni, equivalent to about 8% of labour costs in 1984.
Source: Eurostat, Labour Cost Survey (Tab. 201A).

groups, which calls for a high degree of internal integration (Visser 1988). Such encompassiveness can be found in the union and employer organizations of many of the Scandinavian countries, and in West Germany, but is much weaker in countries such as France, Italy, and the UK.

The detailed evidence concerning the effect of various measures of centralization and encompassiveness on the achievement of both low rates of inflation and low rates of unemployment (a low score on the Okun index of economic misery) is reviewed by Dell'Aringa (in this volume). It confirms the earlier results of Paloheimo (1990) that both decentralized and encompassive countries scored well on inflation and unemployment, and that those placed in between, which includes many of the major EEC economies, fared worst.

Achieving greater coverage and integration among wage bargaining organizations (of both workers and employers) offers a key to a lower 'misery index' and control of a critical component of unit labour costs, namely wages. It would be utopian to suggest that countries such as Britain or Italy could imitate the detailed institutional arrangements of countries such as Sweden or Austria. Nevertheless, both Britain and Italy experienced collective restraint of inflation at various times during the 1970s, although their success was of limited duration.[12] Also, there is currently debate on the reform of pay bargaining arrangements in both countries with a view to achieving greater coordination.

5. Prospects and Policy Implications

The brief review of the potential impact of wage differences and wage flexibility on economic and monetary integration in this chapter points to a number of conclusions. We shall deal first with the overall influence of wage differences between countries on integration; secondly, with the potential for wage adjustments to facilitate integration; and thirdly with some policy questions.

5.1 The Impact of Economic and Monetary Union

The broad conclusion concerning the impact of current wage differences between countries on integration is that nominal wage differences give a highly misleading picture, and that they are offset to a great extent, but not wholly, by differences in productivity. Lest this should create too sanguine a view, it should be noted that when firms set up new facilities in another country, they often achieve productivity levels above the average for the host country, so that they reap the advantage of lower average wage levels and achieve higher productivity. Of course, not all aspects of productivity are under management's control, notably those of the economic infrastructure, and the quality of skills available locally.

The balance between these different factors is likely to weigh heavily in any decisions to shift production to lower wage countries, as is the possibility that the country will not remain for ever a low wage area. It was also noted that most of the major EEC economies lie within a much smaller range of unit labour costs, and there has also been some convergence in recent years (Economie Européenne, 11. 1989, Sup. A). Moreover, the degree of exposure of sectors to the removal of NTBs varies greatly as some already compete on a Community-wide market, and so will be little affected by the advent of the Single Market.

Intra-Community labour mobility seems unlikely to increase much in the immediate future, except among some of the more highly qualified groups. Over the longer term, the wider recognition of vocational diplomas may facilitate greater inter-country mobility, but it seems unlikely that, in the short-run, the wage differences between Community countries will provoke major shifts of population.

More important, but also less easy to observe, will be the impact of the integration of European firms upon their internal labour markets, particularly for managerial and technical staff. For many years, much inter-regional labour mobility has occurred within firms in Britain, and there seems little reason to believe this is atypical of other countries. While such moves are generally the result of management decisions, and are not made in response to wage differentials, it is easy to see that a big increase in their frequency will pose severe problems to company remuneration policies as staff move between high and low wage areas of the Community.

Finally, moves towards monetary union will progressively deprive individual countries of the possibility of using exchange rate depreciation as a means of correcting undesired movements in unit labour costs. Exchange rate flexibility is not an unmitigated benefit as depreciation itself can boost domestic inflation, and the knowledge that the currency can be allowed to slide may encourage firms and employers' organizations to concede higher wage increases than they might otherwise do. Nevertheless, depreciation can be a useful way out when other policies have failed, or seem politically too expensive. Perhaps the most important conclusion from that section is that stable exchange rates will place a premium on wage bargaining arrangements which have a less inflationary bias, notably, ones in which a large number of claims of different groups can be coordinated in the interest of achieving lower inflation.

5.2 The Contribution of Wage Flexibility to Adjustment

Turning to the contribution of wage flexibility to adjustment, the general conclusion is that wage flexibility across labour markets has, at best, only a limited role and that the pursuit of productivity within the enterprise – facilitated by suitable payment systems – offers greater potential. As concerns external wage changes, perhaps one of the most promising areas is that of entry wages into occupations and into enterprise internal labour markets, both because these have displayed more sensitivity to labour market conditions, and because they influence employment opportunities for the categories most affected. However, the danger that flexible relative pay for entry positions could become a source of cheap labour, and thus a threat to established workers, could prove a major obstacle to its acceptability. Joint regulation of such flexibility through collective bargaining or works councils could greatly reduce this problem.[13]

Productivity based pay increases offer short-term advantages, enabling employers to buy changes which enhance the efficiency of working practices, but they also have certain major disadvantages. First, workers engaged in activities which cannot produce large productivity increases, such as personal services, may well feel that the resulting increase in inequality is unfair. Such groups are likely, sooner or later, to seek larger pay increases in order to 'catch up.'

Secondly, localized productivity bargaining also raises a serious problem in relation to more encompassing approaches to national pay bargaining. Pursuit of productivity is best undertaken at the enterprise level, yet enterprise and plant level bargaining may undermine restraint at higher levels of wage determination. In Germany, the tendencies of plant level negotiations to generate such increased inequality have been controlled by setting them within the framework established by industry-regional level bargaining. Greater competition would also temper firms' willingness to pay too much for productivity increases.

Turning to performance of internal labour markets, it is useful to distinguish between linking pay to productivity increases, and performance related pay and remuneration policies which reward more productive employees of the kind implied by 'individualization' and 'merit pay.' Whereas the former are based on sharing the gains of an increase in productivity related to a particular change in working practices, the latter seek to promote more cooperative and more efficient behaviour generally.

The latter kind of payment, merit pay, remains a potential threat to coordination of bargaining. Unions are often suspicious of such payment schemes because their application is hard to monitor, and they fear that they may weaken employee support for the collective action, on which higher levels of bargaining ultimately rest. However, the dangers should not be exaggerated because there is nothing inherent in such remuneration policies to exclude joint regulation by management and employee representatives, for example, over appeal procedures. Indeed, lack of support from the latter group has been one of the causes limiting the progress of merit pay schemes.

5.3 Wage Flexibility and Social Dialogue

The potential role of social dialogue and collective bargaining as a framework for discussion of greater flexibility in wage structures should not be overlooked. In several countries, by far the greatest force for change in wage structures, in recent years, has been union and government policy on pay inequalities. This suggests that there is scope, temporarily at least, to alter wage structures in line with some other social or economic objective, and that such change can be legitimized by either union policy or government policy. If such changes can be brought about to combat inflation or to reflect changed norms of equality among the workforce, then it should be possible to seek to negotiate limited changes in wage structures to facilitate adaptation to the Single Market. This could be achieved, for example, by increasing the rewards of skilled workers if it is necessary to encourage training,[14] to vary entry rates, or to alter the focus of existing payment systems.

Wage flexibility would still have a limited role in assisting the adjustments of economic and monetary union, and would need the help of public active manpower policies in retraining and in job placement. These, too, could be under overall tripartite administration as is the case in Sweden.

Finally, a substantial role for the social partners in introducing greater flexibility into certain aspects of wage structures, such as those discussed here, would help to ensure that this was used for adjustment to the Single Market, and not for the pursuit of competitive cheap labour policies.[15]

Appendix: Major Changes in Labour Costs and Wage Differentials 1970-1990: France, FR Germany, Italy, Spain and the UK[16]

1. Inflation and Wage Differentials in the 1970s

Across Western Europe, the 1970s were a period of high inflation, with inflation slowing, but by no means disappearing during the 1980s. Annual labour costs increased by more than 200% across the twelve Community countries during the 1970s, and by over 50% during the 1980s. Of the five largest countries, four experienced faster increases than the average for the twelve in both decades, with Italy and Spain suffering the fastest inflation (Table 5).

Of the five, all except West Germany resorted to some kind of incomes policy during the 1970s. The most notable of these were the Plan Barre of 1976 in France, the national solidarity measures of 1975-77 in Italy, which included the revision of the indexation system, the Moncloa Pact of 1977 in Spain, and the incomes policies of the British Conservative government of 1971-74, and the Social Contract between the unions and the Labour government between 1975 and 1979.

The Italian and UK policies of the middle to late 1970s relied upon heavy involvement and support by the main trade union organizations. In Spain, the Moncloa Pact was initially drawn up by the government and other political parties, owing to the weakness of the unions and employers' associations, but by 1980, the latter were strong enough to conclude their own agreements in-keeping with the main tenets of the Moncloa Pact.

Part of the price of support for the last three countries' anti-inflation policies was that the incomes of lower paid workers should be specially protected. In Italy this was achieved by flat-rate increases, and in Britain, by a mixture of flat-rate and percentage increases. In Spain, the agreement maintained the reduced level of wage differentials brought about during the transition period. These policies either had, or sustained, a compressive effect upon wage differentials between both occupations and different industries. With the relaxation in Italy and Spain, and the ending in the UK of these policies, there has been an increase in both kinds of wage differential in the 1980s (see Tables 6 and 7).

Table 6. Summary of the main changes in wage structure (1970-1988).

Country	Dispersions		Occupational differentials		Industry differentials	
	1970s	1980s	1970s	1980s	1970s	1980s
France	-	+ >84	-	+ >86	-	+ >84
FR Germany	-	n.a	=	- <84	+	+
Italy	--	n.a	--	+ >84	--	+
Spain	n.a	n.a	-- <77	+ >77	+<77	+

Notes:+ indicates increase; - decrease; = not much change; +/- changes in different directions depending on categories; double sign major changes; n.a not available. Where the turning points in trends are known to deviate markedly from the turn of the decade, they are indicated: < indicates before, and > after.

Table 7. Differentials of hourly earnings between industries (1972-1988).

Coefficient of variation (%) of earnings between two-digit industries.

	1972	1975	1978	1980	1984	1988
France	18.31	17.85	15.55	14.61	13.89	15.44 (a)
FR Germany	11.64	13.29	13.19	13.35	13.84	13.61
Italy (all ind.)	25.95	22.25	15.61	13.42	14.11	14.04 (b)
Italy (mfg.)	14.89	14.00	10.67	9.43	9.91	10.06 (b)
UK	15.95	13.44	12.96	13.02	16.13	16.67
Spain (e)	29.91	31.56	23.11	23.80	24.45	25.74 (f)

Notes: (a) April; b) 1985; c) males only; d) 1970; e) difference series from other countries; f) 1987.
Based on average gross hourly earnings of manual workers in two-digit industries, October of each year. Unweighted coefficient of variation (the standard deviation expressed as a percentage of the corresponding mean).
Sources: Eurostat, Harmonised Earnings Statistics; Spain: de Molina (1989).

Although a government austerity package (and not based on union support) in France, the Plan Barre, introduced in 1976, allowed pay increases for workers below a certain level of earnings. However, the threshold was set very high, and did not affect the great majority of wage and salary earners. More recently, the socialist government's austerity package introduced at the end of 1982 included action by the state, as employer, to 'de-index' public sector pay, and issue guidelines to the private sector employers. Again, it did not rely on union support, although the CFDT argued for tacit support. In France, one of the main sources of pressure on wage differentials has arisen from government decisions periodically to boost the national minimum wage, but this has not been directly linked to the control of inflation, or the desire to create a wider consensus on which such control could be based.

In West Germany, through the 1970s, there was no official incomes policy, although in the early 1970s, there were formal discussions between the unions and employers as to the scope for improving real wages under the auspices of the 'Concerted Action.' However, after the employers challenged the 1976 codetermination legislation in the constitutional court, the unions withdrew from concerted action in protest, and it has not been formally resumed since then. Nevertheless, the ability of the West German industrial relations system to produce low inflation outcomes owes much to its structure, notably its combination of both horizontal integration, through the existence of broad units covering large sections of industry, and vertical integration, through the relationship between the unions in their collective bargaining, and the works councils (Streeck 1981). This is not to deny the importance of monetary and other economic policies for controlling inflation, but concentrated action in pay determination can make them both more effective and less painful than otherwise would be the case.

2. Increased Wage Differentials in the 1980s

Just as wage differentials declined in many countries during the 1970s, so they increased during the 1980s, although not all from the same date. The increase started first in Britain in 1979-80 with the break-up of the Social Contract and the election of Mrs Thatcher's Conservative government. The break-up of the Social Contract signalled the end of the consensus among wage bargainers which had supported it, and under which more skilled groups had accepted a reduction in their pay relative to the less skilled. At the same time, among employers faced with the economic crisis of 1979-81, there was a recognition of the need to restructure and to raise productivity. This signalled a shift of emphasis towards linking pay rises to increased productivity and concessions on working practices, and towards increasing the rewards for skill and management responsibility.

The steep rise in unemployment may also have been influential, although the evidence of the 1970s and 1980s does not reveal any consistent relationship between wage differentials and aggregate unemployment (Marsden 1988).

In Italy also, the start of the 1980s signalled the end of the consensus on which the egalitarian union wage policies of the 1970s had been based, the most symbolic event being the strike by skilled and supervisory workers against their unions' policy at Fiat in 1980. Similar concerns to those of their British counterparts led many Italian employers to seek increased wage differentials, but it was not until the partial de-indexation agreed in 1983-84 that they began to find the leeway to accord non-negotiated wage increases to certain groups of employees.

In Spain, the social accord held more or less between 1977 and 1986, but broke down in the subsequent years, releasing pressures for greater pay inequalities. The parallel between Spain and Italy and the UK has two major limitations. First, the equalizing pressure on differentials was in fact greatest during the transition period leading up to 1977, whereas the Moncloa Pact and subsequent agreements sought to maintain the more egalitarian status quo which had been reached by that year. Second, during the period after the Moncloa Pact, one of the chief problems was that of moving from a system of authoritarian wage fixing, in which indexation had played a major part, to one based on collective bargaining. Moreover, the very high stability of employment during the Franco period greatly reduced any impact which labour market pressures might have had.

In France, Italy, Spain and the UK, a common force for greater wage differentials has been the search by employers for increased productivity, and for methods of payment which enable them to differentiate between workers according to their performance. With the exception of managerial pay, performance related pay has spread in coverage but still does not represent a major component of workers' pay. Moreover, as noted in the main body of this paper, merit pay has frequently been used to restore skill differentials, and thus to reward whole categories of workers.

Compared with most of the other countries, in West Germany, industry and occupational wage differentials were fairly stable, although skill differentials showed some tendency to decline in the early 1980s.[17] One factor would seem to the absence of incomes policies and solidaristic social pacts to restrain inflation. The greater long-term stability of West German industrial relations, and its ability to provide low inflation wage settlements when its neighbours were experiencing sharply rising inflation may have obviated the need for emergency policies. In doing so, it also avoided the need to build a new consensus based on concessions on relative wages of higher paid workers, and the subsequent problems posed for worker motivation.

It is also striking that the debates about 'merit pay,' individualized pay and performance related pay have attracted less interest among German employers and unions, as has the debate about productivity agreements. One of the reasons for this would seem to be the high degree of flexibility of deployment of labour in German firms, and the ability of German employers, in conjunction with their works councils, to achieve good levels of productivity growth outside the arena of wage bargaining.

Notes

1. Within the engineering sector, for example, at the three digit level, in Britain, France and West Germany, the branches which have the highest export ratios also tend to have the highest import ratios (Saunders 1978 Ch.3). Employment adjustment within such broad sectors as engineering may well be less difficult than between more diverse sectors on account of the broad similarity of the skills involved.
2. An internal labour market may be said to exist for certain jobs in an enterprise when the employer regularly seeks to fill vacancies occurring in them from among the firm's current employees.
3. Although long term employment is an established feature for many employees, for example, with between a third and a half of males in Britain and France in 1986 having job tenures of over ten years (OECD 1989 p. 187), job mobility among mature workers remains an important component of inter-sectoral employment changes. There is little difference in the employment shares of those aged under 25 between sectors and industries with growing or declining employment (OECD 1989 Tab. 5.5): if anything the share is higher in the declining industries. A similar picture can be found for the employment shares of workers aged over 55.
4. Many of the efficiency wage theories are well summed up in Akerlof and Yellen (1986).
5. The importance of workers' motivation and cooperativeness within the enterprise as compared with the movements of labour between sectors as a source of economic and productivity growth is illustrated by the small proportion of the growth in labour productivity, during the 1960s and 1970s, which could be attributed to shifts of labour from low to high productivity sectors as compared with intra-sectoral factors (ECE 1982 Ch.1.).
6. This calculation included also establishment size which does not have a ready competitive interpretation.
7. A recent paper by FitzRoy and Funke (1989) seeks to test for a similar relation for skill differentials in West German manufacturing. However, a significant negative relationship between relative pay and employment was found only for unskilled women.
8. Estimates for Britain show that the average completed job tenure of full-time adult males was about 20 years in 1968, and that three fifths of the workers in this group were in jobs which would last at least 10 years (Main 1982). Evidence of a similar nature has been assembled for other major European countries showing a similarly high proportion of long term jobs in these economies (OECD 1984). In the United States, among males over the age of 30, about 40% will have remained in their current job for 20 years or more (Hall 1982).
9. In Britain, a recent survey of large firms revealed that many of them were concerned to move away from the traditional skills available on their local labour markets toward skills which bridged the existing divisions between skills, notably between manual and technician skills (Atkinson and Meager 1986) Evidence of similar moves can be found in France (Maurice et al. 1988) Research on the spread of 'Human Resources Management' techniques suggests a shift

of emphasis in personnel management towards policies designed to focus employees' activities on the enterprise and away from their occupational labour markets.

10. In Italy, (Scardillo 1977 Ch.4), France, (Lyon-Caen and Pélissier 1988), and West Germany, the labour market authorities have the power to extend industry agreements to cover firms which are not members of the signatory employers' organizations. According to Reynaud (1989b), in France, in 1986, about 85% of industrial establishments with more than 10 employees were covered by an industry-wide collective agreement.

11. The so-called 'Okun index' of economic misery was obtained by adding a country's inflation and unemployment rates.

12. In Britain, the position of employers' associations has been weakened by the power of large firms which have less to gain from pooling their resources. By the middle 1980s, in British manufacturing for example, the 50 largest employers accounted for about one quarter of the workforce in that sector. The emergence of such large scale employers has been one of the causes of the demise of industry-wide bargaining as they had little to gain from pooling their strength with other employers. The emergence of major multinationals may affect the ability of employers to organize at the European level as they also have little need to pool resources with other employers for negotiating and consulting with unions.

13. Marsden and Ryan (1990).

14. To date, most such changes have been in the direction of greater equality. There seems to have been no negotiation of greater inequality, except possibly in the domain of concession bargaining. This has mostly focused on productivity enhancing changes in conditions rather than changes towards greater pay inequalities. Nevertheless, in both Italy and the UK, unions sought to negotiate increased relative pay for skilled workers in the late 1970s, and some of the action organized by the *Cobas* in Italy has been in order to restore the differentials of more highly paid workers. However, such issues have generally been pursued as sectional interests rather than as the objectives of encompassing unions, indeed, in Italy, the *Cobas* have acted for sectional interests against the encompassing unions.

15. The pursuit of such policies via labour market channels would probably have less effect on national wage levels than on the lower tail of the earnings dispersion within a particular country. Substantial reduction of the average wage level would depend on currency depreciation, ruled out by monetary union. However, there would remain the possibility of reducing the protection of less organized, lower paid, groups of workers which would increase the dispersion of earnings around the national mean.

16 The material in this appendix is based upon short reports on recent wage developments in France, FR Germany, Italy, Spain and the UK by J.J. Silvestre, F. FitzRoy, C. Dell'Aringa, and D. Shonfield, and also draws on Marsden (1990b).

17. In the same period managerial differences increased.

2. The Internal Market and Relocation Strategies[1]

Daniel Vaughan-Whitehead

Introduction

As the completion of the single European market grows ever closer, firms' locational strategies are once again in the limelight. On the one hand the liberalization of movements of capital is perceived as a generally positive step that will help firms channel resources towards the most productive jobs and, through rationalization, to take full advantage of economies of scale. On the other hand, since wage costs and standards of social protection are lower in the southern regions of Europe, this expansion in trade may lead to further strengthening of specialization based on comparative advantage.

Trade unions - particularly in the industrialized countries - have shown themselves to be worried about the adjustments that will be required as a result of this process. Does the internal market threaten to affect employment in the more highly developed regions?

The less highly developed countries are also concerned about relocation although, conversely, their main fear is that development will be concentrated in the already established industrial sectors.

This paper is a contribution to the emerging debate on the social dimensions of the internal market. Its aim is to identify those relocation strategies likely to exert an influence in this area and to assess their possible social consequences. The first part consists of a theoretical investigation of the determinants of locational strategies which will help to describe the transfers of activities or investment that can be expected within the European Community, from firms in both member and non-member states.

In the second part of the paper, we shall return to the dynamic of relocation within the Community in order to identify, by means of multi-criteria analysis, those sectors where this process is likely to be experienced on a large scale. Taking this preliminary reconnaissance work as a basis, the third part will investigate the possible impact of firms' movements on the equilibrium of the various regions within the Community as well as the measures that will be required for coherent development of their industrial fabric.

2. The Effect of the Internal Market on Locational Behaviour

2.1 The Determinants of Decisions on Location: A Survey of the Theoretical and Empirical Studies

On the basis of a review of the economic literature on the subject, we have drawn up a complete list of the factors affecting locational decisions (Table 1). Two types of motives seem to lie behind this process:

- A firm may decide to establish itself in another country or region in order to exploit comparative advantages in production costs. In this first case, relocation is generally the consequence of the divergent evolution of the production factors endowment in the countries of origin and destination.[1]
- The establishment of activity in another country may also form an integral part of a clearly defined commercial strategy designed to position a firm in a particular market. This might be called strategic relocation.

These two separate sets of motives may lead to very different forms of locational strategy when risk factors are taken into account. Firms seeking to reduce their production costs will minimize the risk inherent in the project by providing their own assets in the form of management, technology and capital. Conversely, firms seeking new outlets for their products will begin by granting licences in order to minimize the financial consequences of a possible failure.[2]

Factors listed in Table 1 play differing roles, depending on the type of locational strategy adopted. For example, import restrictions imposed by the country of destination are one of the main determinants of strategic locations but are virtually ignored by firms seeking comparative advantages. The latter are attracted above all by cost advantages (low wages, tax incentives, etc.) - factors which are of secondary importance in a positioning strategy.

Table 1. Factors Influencing Locational Strategies.

Market potential
- demand in the local market; prospects for development.
- opportunity to exploit economies of scale.

Macro-economic/economic policy context
- economic growth rate; capacity of economy to react to shocks;
- exchange rate; cost of credit; income/company tax;
- industrial policy: R & D, subsidies, energy policy;
- trade policy: import controls, non-tariff barriers;
- environmental and health and safety standards.

Labour market
- labour costs;
- labour force skills;
- labour market: work time regulation, redundancy legislation, etc.;
- social climate: industrial relations, flexibility; trade union activity.

Geographical situation
- proximity to customers and suppliers;
- transport and communications costs.

Infrastructure
- energy costs (electricity, gas, water);
- industrial sites (costs and opportunities for expansion);
- services market (banking, insurance, etc.).

Type of activity
- product life cycle;
- labour intensiveness.

Other factors
- social, cultural and language factors.

2.1. In Search of New Markets: Location as a Commercial Strategy.

From a theoretical point of view, the size of the local market is the first strategic motive for firms in their search for new locations. In order to ensure high profits, firms set up in regions where the market is large enough to justify a production unit. Table 2 summarizes the results of several studies conducted in the Federal

Republic of Germany on transfers of establishments from one region to another. Sales are one of the most important factors.

Table 3 also summarizes the results of 21 studies designed to determine the competitiveness of the state of New York in terms of locational factors. The 'size of market' factor was the largest single consideration, closely followed by labour and raw materials.

The locational process in the Italian food industry between 1971 and 1981 also seems to have been determined in part by the potential markets in the various regions.[3]

Relocation is also a means of circumventing non-tariff barriers which impose high transaction costs on exports. Even in cases where direct investment is a more costly option than exporting, these additional costs enable multinationals rapidly to obtain increased control of the local market, making it more difficult for new firms to enter the market and offering the likelihood of net profits in the longer term.

Thus it was in response to restrictions on imported cars imposed by the Spanish government in 1950 that Renault, which had had a commercial presence in Spain since the beginning of the century, decided to have its cars built by a local manufacturer, FASA (Fabricacion de Automobiles Sociedad Anonima). It was the Valladolid assembly plant, built for this purpose and employing 450 workers that, in 1953, was to turn out the first four cv models assembled in Spain.[4]

During the same period and for the same reasons, another manufacturer, Fiat, joined forces with a local company, SEAT (Sociedad Espanola de Automobiles de Turismo).

In the case of Renault, the venture was a success and led to the creation in 1964 of FASA Renault. In 1972, despite customs restrictions, Renault's rate of penetration in the Spanish market was 24.9%, rising to over 33% in 1981.

It should be pointed out that, although 'strategic relocation' accords priority to the above-mentioned criteria, in no case is it possible to disregard the possibility of obtaining comparative advantages. In any event, firms must take account of all the various factors that determine their competitiveness.

2.1.2 Exploitation of Comparative Advantages.

The second type of motive behind locational strategies arises out of the pressure exerted on firms by certain factors[5] which leads them to maximize the differences in costs (wages, raw materials, etc.) that exist between different countries or regions. These factors may be technical in origin (transport costs, economies of scale) or institutional (preference for nation states).

This strategy takes account of the evolution of the major macro-economic variables: the rate of inflation and the exchange rate are some of the factors that determine the competitiveness of an industry, both at home and abroad. By way of illustration, attempts to reduce inflation through the use of monetary instruments (notably a high exchange rate as in the FRG) affect competitiveness abroad in the short term. On the other hand, incomes policies, which undoubtedly enhance the competitiveness of products in foreign markets, have proved to be less effective in bringing about improvements in productivity. A firm seeking to relocate will allocate differential weightings to these elements depending on whether their products are destined for export or for local markets.

Government decisions relating to industrial policy may have an even more direct effect on location. The 1972 decree in Spain that changed the regulation of the motor industry is a good example. The lowering of the compulsory rate of inclusion of locally manufactured parts, coupled with a demand that new French manufacturers should export 80% of their production, meant that the Spanish government could achieve two objectives. First, new manufacturers were attracted to Spain (Ford was the first beneficiary of these measures, followed later by General Motors) and second, the volume of cars exported by the Spanish motor industry was increased.

The relative burden of taxation on incomes, the regulations governing tax allowances and the way in which tax is collected may also encourage firms to move (see Table 2). In recent years, many foreign firms have set up in Belgium, attracted by the tax concessions they were granted for ten years from the date they first established themselves in the country. Some of them left at the end of this period to seek more advantageous tax conditions elsewhere (examples of firms in section 3.1). Ireland has also used attractive tax arrangements to tempt a significant number of firms in the micro-electronics industry (investment costs reduced from 40% to 60%).

Table 2.Ranking of the factors determining decisions to relocate within Germany (FRG) (a).

Authors of the studies	Period of investigation	Relocation
Jochimsen and Treuner	1955-1965	Labour supply (2), industrial sites and buidings (1-3), transport (4), sales (5), raw materials and energy (6), state subsidies (7)
Brode (IFO)	1965-1967	Industrial sites (1), labour supply (2), taxes and other state subsidies (3), sales (4), staff preferences (5), transport (7)
Ballestrem Förtsch	1966-1971	Industrial sites and buildings (1), transport (2), labour supply (3), local contacts (4)
Fürst and Zimmermann	1966-1970	Industrial sites (1), financial aid (2), transport (3), labour supply (4), politicaL climate (5), sales (6)
Ruppert	1974-1981	Industrial sites (1), labour supply (2), local taxes (3), sales (4), transport (5)
Schliebe	1976-1979	Industrial sites (1), sales (2), labour supply (3), state subsidies (4), raw materials (5)

Note: (a): Ranking in brackets.
Source: IFO - Institute for Economic Research, An Empirical Assessment of Factors Shaping Regional Competitiveness in Problem Regions, first interim report, Munich, November 1988.

Various standards and regulations, fixed at national or regional level, exert considerable influence on location decisions. Environmental protection standards affect production processes and also the industrial structure of a region. Transport restrictions - such as those on lorry routes, night flights and movements of hazardous substances - increase operating costs in certain sectors. The regulations governing competition are also taken into account by firms to the extent that they control monopolies and determine consumer rights.

As Tables 2 and 3 show, firms are very sensitive to regulations governing labour markets, for example: regulations for health and safety, as well as national legislation of working time, redundancies and forms of flexibility, sometimes encourage firms to look abroad for more flexible employment conditions.

For some regions, the state of the infrastructure is a barrier to the setting up of new firms. All the empirical studies on the Italian regions have shown that even if all the expected conditions (i.e. potential markets, lower wage costs, availability of raw materials) were met, the process of relocation from the developed to the less favoured regions could not take place unless the regions had crossed a critical development threshold, below which firms would not relocate.

The importance of the regional infrastructure has also been observed in the FRG. The various studies carried out in Germany between 1955 and 1981 (and presented in Table 2) are unanimous on this last point: whatever the period under investigation, the availability of adequate industrial sites appears to be the most important factor considered by German firms when deciding on the regional distribution of their activities. The existence of banks, insurance companies and consultancy firms are also factors that influence the final choice of location, particularly for large companies.[6]

Production costs are directly dependent on the price of raw materials - including energy, water, or even telecommunications - the supply of which is generally controlled by the public sector. To judge from Tables 2 and 3, the supply of natural resources also seems to be important.

Transport costs are of particular importance for some sectors. Plant Location International (PLI), a company which helps firms to find the ideal location to meet the criteria they specify, has developed a computer program for calculating transport costs on the basis of four variables: distance, load quantity, weight and frequency.

Other national characteristics, such as culture and language, sometimes help to sway the decision in favour of one region or another. Thus the education system makes an essential contribution to competitiveness, to the extent that it feeds the stock of human capital and produces the various skills of the labour supply. Germany, for example, is known to have a highly developed training system which gives it an undeniable comparative advantage. The nature of the links between industry, research institutes and colleges of technology is also significant.

High union membership may also be an obstacle to relocation. According to PLI, several pharmaceutical firms requiring continuous production for fermentation have refused to relocate in Italy and Ireland for fear of frequent strikes. Finally, studies of multinationals have shown that their perception of a country's political stability is an element taken into account[7] before deciding on new locations.

The results of studies of relocation between regions carried out in Germany and the USA show that firms that relocate are seeking above all to profit from comparative advantages in labour costs.[8] Thus the labour supply is ranked either in second or third position in Table 2, while it climbs to second place in Table 3, just behind size of market.

E. Hoover has demonstrated the dynamic of location with respect to the labour supply:

> The differences and the variations in the qualities required for a given kind of work...have profound effects on industries' locational choices. An industry requiring a specialized, highly trained labour force will have a concentrated and relatively stable configuration. However, since the production processes in all industries can become routine, it may be possible in the future to use an ordinary work force with no specific training. The result is that this industry will spread or move to other regions, with its dispersion from its original centres being motivated principally by the relatively high wages and inflexible conditions established there by a skilled elite.[9]

Depending on the position of the product in its life cycle, capital is substituted for labour and the production process is deskilled. Thus, firms belonging to the so-called 'mature' sectors, and which also require a large supply of unskilled labour, will have a strong tendency to relocate because of wage costs.

On the basis of these theoretical observations, we can now identify the locational trends that should come into play within the European Community with the introduction of the single market.

Table 3. Summary of literature on the ranking of locational factors (a).

	Markets (b)	Natural resources	Climate (c)	Labour	Threshold (d)	Agglomeration (e)	Urban atractivity (f)	Quality of life	Taxes	Industrial mixes
Mclauglin and Robcock (1949)	1	2	N	3	-	4	-	-	N	-
Floyd (1952)	-	-	-	-	-	-	-	-	N	-
Cohn (1954)	1	N	-	-	I	-	-	-	-	-
Ullman (1954)	1	-	I	-	-	-	-	I	-	-
Thompson and Mattila (1959)	1	-	-	2	-	-	-	-	N	-
Chinitz and Vernon (1960)	1	-	-	3	-	2	2	-	-	-
Lichtenberg (1960)	1	-	-	3	-	2	2	-	N	-
Fuchs (1962)	N	2	I	1	-	-	-	-	N	-
McCarthy (1963)	1	2	-	-	I	2	-	I	N	-
Perloff (1963)	1	I	I	I	I	2	-	I	-	-
Jorta and Stein (1964)	1	-	-	I	-	I	-	-	-	N
Fantus (1966)	1	N	-	2	-	3	3	-	-	-
Advisory Commision (1967)	I	I	-	I	-	-	-	-	N	-
Williams (1967)	-	-	-	-	-	-	-	-	N	-
Bretzfelder (1970)	-	-	-	-	-	-	-	-	-	N

Continued...

Table 3 (cont.) Summary of literature on the ranking of locational factors (a).

	Markets (b)	Natural resources	Climate (c)	Labour	Thresh-hold (d)	Agglom-eration (e)	Urban attrac-tivity (f)	Quality of life	Taxes	Industrial mixes
Wheat (1973)	1	5	2	3	4	7	6	-	-	-
Chalmers and Beckhelm (1976)	1	-	-	3	-	2	-	-	-	-
Joint Economic Committee (1978)	-	-	-	-	-	-	-	-	I	-
Lund (1979)	2	3	-	1	-	-	-	4	5	-
Schmenner (1980)	2	4	-	1	-	4	-	3	N	-
Kieschanick (1981)	-	-	-	1	-	-	2	-	-	-

Notes: I means important; N means not important.
a) Ranking in descending order with 1 being the most important.
b) Includes transportation costs and services, proximity to customers.
c) Includes energy and raw materials, and their costs, but is separated from climate.
d) Includes labour supply, costs unioniZation, state manpower training assistance, and labour climate.
e) Or foundation of development.
f) Includes supply of intermediate goods, supplier availability, and external economies.
Source: Tran, D.T., 'Declining Industrial Competitive Advantage in New York', *Regional Science*, Vol. 26 (February 1986), S. 124.

2.2 1992 and Expected Locational Trends within the Economic Community

2.2.1 Non-member States and Strategic Locations: The Desire for a Presence in the European Market

The main reaction of firms in non-member states to the prospect of the internal market seems to be an increase in strategic locations. Several factors of a strategic nature explain this renewal of interest in the 'old continent.' The most important of these is size of market. 'Getting a foothold' in the European market in order to operate in a trading bloc with 320 million consumers, and no borders, seems to be the prime motive behind these moves. A survey conducted in 1988 by EGIS shows that almost a third of direct Japanese investment in Europe is intended to increase their sales in the European market.[10]

Similarly, a survey carried out at the beginning of 1989 by the Bank of Boston among 1,200 heads of American manufacturing companies reveals that 84% of them see 1992 as an opportunity to increase their sales and operations; 53% intend changing their marketing or production strategies in order to exploit this opportunity. The removal of barriers between member states and the reduction of transport costs will facilitate this search for economies of scale.

The anticipated potential of this vast market is in itself sufficient justification for the conclusion that it will be necessary to have a production capability within the Community in order not to lose market shares. For example, the UK, where Nissan, Toyota and Honda have all set up factories, has become the European bridgehead for the Japanese motor industry.

In February 1984 Nissan became the first Japanese manufacturer to go down this road when it opened its factories in the North of England. At the beginning of 1989 it was Toyota's turn to announce its intention of building an assembly plant in Derbyshire at a cost of some £850 million. Finally, on 13 July 1989, Honda took a 20% stake in Rover and decided to build a factory in Swindon capable of turning out 100,000 cars a year from 1994 (both Honda and Rover models). At the same time, the Honda chairman, Mr. Kume, announced that 60% of this output would be destined for the European market.[11] Thus the three major Japanese manufacturers should be producing almost half a million cars a year, an ambition in keeping with the scale of the European market.

There is a second factor reinforcing this desire to exploit the potential of the European market from within, namely the fear that 1992 will see the development of 'fortress Europe,' with community-wide barriers replacing national restrictions.

According to the Jetro survey, 15% of Japanese firms cite the existence of trade barriers (quotas, standards, protectionist practices by both private and public purchasers) as the main reason for establishing themselves in Europe. There is no shortage of examples: in 1989 the electronics company Fujitsu set up a factory in the UK in order to get around community quotas.[12] Similarly, Nissan UK succeeded in exporting its cars to France without them being included in the 3% quota of Japanese cars authorized for import.

The results of the EGIS survey show that the objective behind the proliferation of Japanese factories in the high-consumption sectors - such as cars, video recorders, microwave ovens and television sets - is the mass production of bottom-of-the-range models for the European market. More up-market models, requiring increasingly advanced technology and aimed at a very specific market niche, will be exported to Japan.

The motives of the American firms are exactly the same: fear of failing to profit from all the advantages offered by the single market dominates their decision to come to Europe.[13] The rush by the Japanese to get into Europe seems to have occasioned this decision. Thus industrial groups from non-member states are now engaged in a race against time in order to be well positioned in the market before 1993.

Other advantages of the single market might well be encouraging this rush to set up in the European Community. The liberalization of financial services should reduce financial costs and make it more beneficial to use local finance, which is particularly appreciated by medium-sized firms. According to the EGIS survey, 50% of Japanese SMEs setting up in Europe call upon the services of local banks, whereas subsidiaries of multinationals usually benefit from finance from the parent company.

Japanese and American companies should also benefit from a strengthening of their major banks' positions in the European market, since the 'single assent' contained in the new directive on banking will enable them to extend their activities to the whole of the EC.

The link between banks and foreign companies is obvious. For example, Fuji Bank decided in 1988 to open offices outside London in order to follow the Japanese manufacturing companies that are investing in the Midlands and the North of England.[14]

In the eyes of foreign investors, the exchange rate stability arising out of monetary union is an additional advantage of the single market. The desire to avoid exchange rate fluctuations is cited by 20% of the Japanese firms surveyed (JETRO survey) and the Japanese finance minister cites the appreciation of the yen as one of the main factors in direct Japanese investment in Europe.

The current increase in foreign investment is also taking place through subsidiaries of multinationals already established in Europe. This capital is generally being used to finance rationalization programmes, the ultimate purpose of which, clearly, is to increase market domination. Thus Ford, for example, a company already very well established in numerous European countries, will be investing almost US$17 billion in the next five years in order to exploit the advantages offered by the single market.

Other examples include IBM, Digital Equipment Corp., Heinz, Westinghouse and other major American companies that already have a presence in Europe - all are planning to increase their operations in this market.[15] Whirlpool and Philips merged two years ago, thus giving Whirlpool a foothold in the European market and, through a French subsidiary, K-Way, acquired a 75% stake in the French company, Eider, which specialises in ski and mountaineering clothing. This acquisition has strengthened K-Way's position in the European skiing market.

The final example is a significant one: the American Sara Lee farm produce and textiles group, has just established its new headquarters in Utrecht (NL) and is trying to build up a dominant position in the European coffee, tea and tobacco markets.

Recent statistics on foreign investment reveal the new attraction of the European market for investors from non-member states. The diagram below shows the evolution of direct American investment in the EC since 1981.

At the beginning of the 1980s, it seemed that the Americans were about to withdraw from Europe, considering it to be in economic decline. In 1985, however, this trend began to be reversed. Since then, American investment has continued to increase, with a very sharp rise being recorded in 1987. A sharp increase was also noticed in 1985, and seems to have been confirmed in 1990.[16]

The prospect of the single market in 1992 has increased the presence in Europe of small and medium-sized enterprises: 42% of the 200 medium-sized American firms surveyed by International Media Inc. had already started to look for acquisitions in Europe and 41% were prepared to embark on a joint venture in order to penetrate the European market. As shown in Table 4, the countries favoured by American companies are the UK, Germany and France, with Spain also attracting substantial inward investment.

Figure 1. Direct American investment in the EEC.(In billions of dollars)

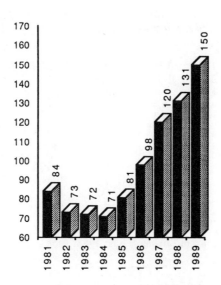

Source: Survey of Current Business, June 1989 and June 1990.

Direct investment in Europe by Japanese firms is proceeding at a very rapid pace. There was a very sharp increase in 1987, with a growth rate of 14.7%, and this appears to have been repeated in 1988. Indeed, the last available figures, at the time of writing (until September), show a large increase over the same period of 1987. Most of this investment is in the electrical and electronics and transport sectors. Northern European countries, principally the UK and Germany, are the favoured locations. The internal market will undoubtedly encourage this investment to be more evenly distributed between regions.

Spain is already in the lead in this respect. In 1987, Japanese investment there reached a record 33 million pesetas, and it continued to increase in 1988. It is useful to note that Spain has not been chosen simply for its cheap supply of labour - for example, in the motor industry - but also and more particularly because of the potential market that exists there. Spain lies in third place for

55

investment in the electrical and electronics sector (Table 5) and an increase has been recorded in the chemicals sector.[17]

Table 4. Direct American investment in Europe.(In billions of dollars)

	1987		1988		1989	
	All industry	Mfg. sectors	All industry	Mfg. sectors	All industry	Mfg. sectors
UK	42.0	17.7	49.3	19.8	60.8	22.1
FRG	24.8	16.2	21.8	14.1	23.1	14.4
F	11.8	8.0	13.2	8.7	14.7	9.5
I	9.0	6.4	9.5	6.9	10.7	6.8
NL	14.4	6.1	16.0	6.2	17.2	7.5
IRL	5.1	3.8	6.2	4.5	6.2	5.1
B	6.8	3.3	7.4	3.9	8.3	4.4
E	3.8	2.3	4.9	3.0	6.0	3.9
L	0.8	0.2	0.8	0.5	0.9	0.6
DK	1.1	0.3	1.2	0.3	1.2	0.3
P	0.4	0.2	0.5	0.2	0.6	0.2
G	0.1	0.1	0.2	0.1	0.2	0.1
EUR	120.1	64.7	131.0	68.2	149.9	74.9

Source: Survey of Current Business, June 1988- June 1989.

Japanese firms have recently begun to establish a presence in Portugal.[18] Their investment there has been upstream of the production process, in the form of technological assistance. For example, Mitsubishi has a 25% stake in the synthetic fibre company, Fisipe, while the Fitor company will produce and export artificial silk under Japanese licence.

Other non-member states have established a tactical presence in Southern Europe, particularly the Arab interests grouped together under the umbrella of the Kuwait Investment Office (KIO), which has been calling the tune. In 1988, having taken a controlling interest in EBRO (Spain's leading sugar refinery company), the KIO purchased the TORRAS paper mills and the two chemical companies, CROS and ERT, whose merger provided the basis for the establishment of the first Spanish chemicals group. The KIO is currently trying to extend its interests to Portugal and has acquired, through its Spanish interests, a 45% stake in Vasco da Gama, the largest canning company in Portugal.

Finally, Swedish and Norwegian companies have made a number of strategic investments in Portugal and Spain, in the wood, paper and shipping sectors.

2.2.2 Relocation within the Community: Optimization of the European Space

If location as a commercial strategy is very much in fashion among companies from non-member states, the imminent introduction of the single market has led companies already established in Europe to consider relocation as a means of exploiting comparative advantages. After 1992, the factors described as having led to strategic relocations should, for these companies, become irrelevant.

Figure 2. Direct Japanese investment in the EEC.(Cumulative totals: in millions of dollars)

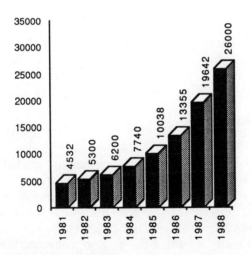

Notes:
(1) The Japanese tax year begins on April 1.
(2) The 1988 total is an estimate based on the figure for the first half of the year (23,520 millions).
Source: Japanese Ministry of Foreign Trade.

Table 5. Cumulative direct Japanese investment in the Community (Distribution by country and industry)

	EUR	UK	FRG	F	NL	B	L	I	IRL	G	E	P
Electricity/ electronics	21.8	36.2	24.5	11.8	1.1	1.5	1.5	1.5	9.0	0.1	12.5	0.0
Transport equipment and motor vehicles	20.6	3.9	0.1	0.8	0.0	5.6	0.0	16.7	0.0	0.0	70	2.4
Machinery	10.5	26.9	28.5	13.8	15.4	9.2	0.0	0.7	0.0	0.0	3.8	1.7
Chemicals	10.5	1.5	15.7	7.7	32.6	12.4	0.0	9.3	0.0	6.2	13.9	0.7
Metallurgical industry	8.7	0.0	0.0	0.9	15.7	22.6	0.0	0.9	0.9	41.6	17.9	0.0
Textiles	8.5	1.9	0.0	18.4	0.0	0.0	0.0	0.9	52.8	0.0	19.3	6.7
Food	3.9	18.7	4.2	58.3	0.0	0.0	0.0	14.6	0.0	0.0	4.1	0.1
Other manufacturing	15.5	11.8	14.5	7.5	11.8	40.9	0.0	4.8	3.8	0.0	2.7	2.2
TOTAL manufacturing sectors	100%	14.5	12.4	10.1	8.5	11.9	0.3	6.2	7.2	4.3	23	1.6

Note: DK not included.
Source: Japanese Ministry of Finance, 1986.

The tactic of choosing a location in order to circumvent barriers to trade will become obsolete when national boundaries are opened up. Similarly, the size of a local market will no longer seem sufficient justification for a transfer of activities: all firms within the Community will benefit from a single market and will be free to sell their products to any of the 320 million consumers throughout Europe. As a result, exports will become the main route to success for European companies. According to a survey of 696 firms,[19] by KPMG, access to a much expanded market and a reduction in operating costs are seen by actors within the community as the two principal advantages of the single market.

The scale of the new European market and the intensification of competition are going to encourage producers within the Community to try to exploit economies of scale in order to reduce their costs.

This drive for competitiveness could be assisted by concentrating production units in those regions of the Community where production costs are lowest. The expected reduction in transport costs should make this strategy more viable.

Thus the single market may lead to a system based on the principle of one factory per country being replaced by one based on specialized production units supplying the whole of the European market. This new dimension has already begun to influence locational decisions taken by manufacturing companies: almost 19% of the companies surveyed by KPMG intend to relocate part of their production within the Community. This strategy is particularly favoured by German producers, who are making it their first priority in the fight against their competitors. A survey by HSD-Arthur Young would appear to show that French companies are also considering adopting a similar relocation strategy.[20]

There is no doubt that regions with the lowest wage costs, such as Spain, Portugal, Greece or even Ireland, will be among the most popular for relocation. Statistics confirm this: in the past three years there has been a veritable tidal wave of foreign investment in Portugal and Spain, most of it from within the Community.

The figures for Portugal speak for themselves: with a total of $960 million, foreign investment in 1988 showed an increase of 120% over the figure for 1987 and a more than five-fold increase over that for 1986 (192 million). Foreign investment in Portugal also doubled during 1989. The majority of this investment, 64% of the total, is from within the EC. The UK and Spain account for 37% and 38% respectively of this flow from within the Community, followed by France and Germany.

Spain has also seen a spectacular rise in foreign investment: 280 billion pesetas in 1985, 400 billion in 1986, 730 billion in 1987, 849 billion in 1988, 1,247 billion in 1989 and more than 1,800 billion in 1990. Investment in manufacturing industry in particular seems to be breaking all records.[21]

Again, more than half of this investment has come from within the Community. Holland heads the list with 24.7%, followed by the UK with 11.2% and France with 8.8%. Within the space of a few months in 1988, companies as prestigious as Fiat, Siemens, Michelin, Carnaud, Montedison, SIV, Bayer and Hoechst announced they would be setting up in Spain (see Part II). According to T. Casilas of Cegos-Spain, many investors within the Community are currently setting up in Spain in order to take advantage of lower costs to supply markets in other economic zones, both in Europe and other parts of the world (e.g. Latin America and Africa).

Foreign investment in Ireland has also reached very high levels: almost 75% of firms in the Irish textiles sector are controlled by foreign capital, most of it from within the Community.

Part of this investment in southern Europe could replace some of the investments made recently by companies from member-states in countries outside the Community. Indeed, foreign investors are becoming increasingly interested in Southern Europe as a platform for their export businesses, not only to the European market but to other areas outside the Community. In 1988, the management of Grundig explained its decision to locate production units in Portugal by saying there was no point locating certain activities in South-East Asia when Portugal offered equally competitive wage levels and good levels of productivity.

A number of firms in the textiles sector are now relocating in southern European countries, reversing the recent trend in this sector towards moving production to South-East Asia (PLI). This substitution phenomenon seems to apply to some of the foreign firms that have set up in Spain[22] and, although it does not seem to be a consideration for large multinationals that already operate transnationally and are able to manoeuvre simultaneously in several different markets, it seems more likely to be a factor in the decisions taken by medium-sized international firms, whose greater involvement in Europe requires a renewed concentration of investment within the Community. This is all the more true since, according to the KPMG survey, a shift of focus back to the European market requires enormous expenditure on R & D.

In the following section these intra-Community relocations will be analyzed in greater detail. First, the factors which might be taken into account in this search for comparative advantages will be outlined, and then an attempt will be made to identify those sectors in which this dynamic of relocation from north to south will be strongest.

3. Relocation within the Community: Identification of the Sectors Likely to be Affected

3.1 Emergence of the Wage Factor

3.1.1 The Declining Influence of Non-wage Determinants: the Belgian Example

Trade unions, particularly in the northern European countries such as Germany, have expressed the fear that this process of redistribution of activities and investment will be accompanied by plant closures and job losses in the more developed countries.

For José Verdin, of the Fondation André Renard of the FGTB (Fédération Générale des Travailleurs Belges), the threat of relocation is exaggerated. He does not think that the internal market will bring about a massive exodus of firms and investment from Belgium to, say, Portugal or Spain. This opinion is based on analysis of two phenomena: the factors behind recent locational trends in Belgium and a typology of firms that have transferred their activities.

For multinationals in the light manufacturing sector, the tax factor seems to have been the main reason for relocation. A number of firms left Belgium at the end of the 10 years during which they were granted tax concessions by Belgian law. One important example is Memorex, a manufacturer of tapes and computer diskettes, which left Belgium in 1986, having come to the end of its period of fiscal grace. The company transferred all its stocks and equipment in one weekend to Maastricht in Holland, just 35 km away from Liäge, the site of its factory in Belgium. The tax situation was the only reason the company gave for this move. It did not change its suppliers and even kept on some of its Belgian work force. There is reason to believe that the harmonization of tax regimes should reduce the number of firms relocating to countries with more favourable regimes.

Several producers of basic products, such as non-ferrous metals and those whose activity is based on mineral processing, have also left Belgium in recent years. These departures were caused by high energy costs, the highly concentrated primary resources sectors being dominated by monopoly pricing. Again according to J. Verdin, if companies such as EDF (Electricity of France) and ENI

(Italian National Electricity) could supply companies in Belgium at more competitive prices, this would encourage them to stay in the country.

A third factor seems to have played a decisive role in decisions to transfer production activities abroad, namely the cost of credit. This is particularly high in Belgium, where substantial risk premiums have the effect of increasing the interest rate by almost 1%. The burden of interest payments has been felt particularly keenly by small and medium-sized firms which, unlike large groups, do not generally have any opportunities for internal financing. The opening of frontiers and the free circulation of capital ought to reduce the cost of borrowing and thus increase the competitiveness of firms established in Belgium.

These few examples show that, paradoxically, the single market should reduce the importance of the factors - mostly unconnected with wage levels - that have caused a number of firms to leave Belgium in recent years. These observations based on the Belgian experience highlight the possible effects of the single market on firms' locational strategies; in particular, they show that the influence of certain factors, mainly non-wage ones, will be lost.

Gradual harmonization of health and safety and environmental protection standards and, in the longer term, of regulations governing labour markets, should eliminate the advantages gained from transferring activities in order to benefit from the existing differences between countries.

Total freedom of movement for capital, and increased competition in the banking and insurance sectors will help to equalize the real cost of credit. Differences in energy and raw material costs should also become less significant due to both the injection of competition into hitherto protected public sector markets, and a reduction in transport costs. Both of these will make it easier to supply firms abroad.

The prospect of a move towards the harmonization of direct taxation will help to solve the problem of 'fiscal dumping' as a factor in firms' locational strategies. Moreover, the harmonization of indirect taxation will help to discourage companies from flitting from one country to another in search of comparative financial advantage. At the same time, the internal market - by encouraging high-volume production - will make it more attractive for firms to relocate to areas with lower wage costs.

3.1.2 The Wage Differentials between Member States: An Invitation to Relocate

In order to assess the importance of wages as a factor it is essential, first of all, to have a general idea of the relative extent of wage inequalities between one country and another. To determine this we carried out a statistical analysis based on the harmonized half-yearly earnings statistics compiled by the Statistical Office of the European Communities. Only figures for manufacturing industry are included here, since relocations for reasons of wage costs are rare in the service sector. As for the year selected, we opted for the most recent one for which figures were available, 1985. Only Spain and Luxembourg are missing, because of a lack of data. The calculations were carried out in a common currency, the ECU. In consequence, the results reflect both the internal structure of each country and the influence of exchange rate fluctuations.

This study covers only money wages paid directly by employers. It could therefore be extended in order to calculate unit production costs, which would make it possible to ascertain whether the wage differentials observed are in some cases offset by differences in productivity. However, as far as relocation strategies are concerned, it was essential to begin obtaining an adequate assessment of wage differentials: while firms that relocate certainly take account of wages when doing so, they do not always place the same emphasis on productivity levels.

In particular, large multinationals often depend on their own resources (advanced technology, skilled management, own remuneration system - including profit-sharing and fringe benefits) in order to develop their levels of productivity. It should be added that a number of studies of locational strategies take account only of wage levels.[23] The two histograms below clearly show the gap that exists between countries in northern Europe and those in the south. The main distinction to be made is between countries like Greece and Portugal with a low average wage and those such as Belgium, Holland and, in particular, Germany, where the average wage is high.

The differences in wages between countries are considerable, particularly for manual workers. The hourly wages of manual workers in Denmark are more than six times higher than their Portuguese counterparts. There is also a considerable gap in the case of white-collar workers, who earn almost four times more in Germany than in Portugal, and two times more than in Greece.

Figure 3. Gross hourly wage for manual workers. (in ecus)

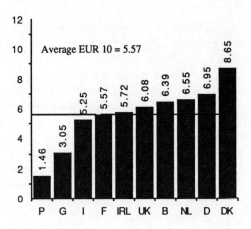

Source: Derived from Eurostat, Harmonised Earnings Statistics, 1985.

Figure 4. Gross monthly salaries for white-collar workers.
(in ecus)

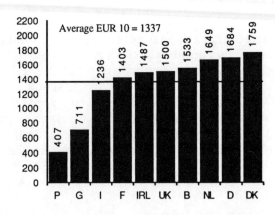

Source: Derived from Eurostat, Harmonised Earnings Statistics, 1985.

The largest gap between blue-collar and white-collar workers is in France. The hourly wage for French manual workers is just equivalent to the average for the Community as a whole (and thus lower than the average for northern European countries), while monthly earnings for white-collar workers are considerably higher than the Community average. In consequence, France has a different ranking in the two histograms. This result confirms those obtained by the CERC,[24] which highlighted the much wider gap that exists between manual and non-manual workers in France and, to a lesser extent, in Belgium and Luxembourg. Manual workers seem to be more highly valued in Germany, Denmark and Italy. Indeed, it is in these first two countries that wages for manual workers are highest.

The gap between North and South widens still further if employers' social security contributions are taken into account. These contributions are particularly high in Italy, France, Holland and Belgium, increasing the risk of companies moving out of those countries. Conversely, they are low in the less developed regions such as Portugal, Greece and Ireland, as well as in the UK and Luxembourg.

Statutory and contractual social security contributions.

(As % of total labour costs for manual and non-manual workers)

P	G	I	IRL	UK	F	B	NL	DK	D	L	E
18.4	18.0	33.5	14.7	14.6	28.1	24.0	24.4	5.7	21.0	14.9	NA

Source: Eurostat, Labour Cost Survey.

Denmark is clearly the record-holder, with social security contributions accounting for only 5% of labour costs; however, this only partially compensates for the high wage levels in that country. Taking into account employers' social security contributions seems to put the UK into the group of countries with moderate wage costs. On the other hand, it puts Italy into the high-cost group and shows that this southern European country is no longer a cheap labour region. Furthermore, high social security contributions are one of the reasons for the massive expansion of the black economy in that country.

3.2 Identification of the Sectors with a High Risk of Relocation

3.2.1 The Method Adopted: Multi-criteria Analysis

In the first part we concluded that the introduction of the single market might encourage firms established in the European Community to transfer part of their activities in order to exploit the comparative advantages offered by the less developed countries. As we have seen, differences in wage levels between member states should play a leading role in this process. Our task here is to assess the likely extent of these transfers.

We have subjected the various sectors of the European industrial fabric to a range of filtering processes with the aim of identifying those activities likely to be relocated when the internal market is introduced. These successive filtering processes are based upon three sets of relocation criteria:

1. The wage costs criterion, illustrated by:
- the dispersion of wages between member-states (filter 1);
- the share of wages in turnover (filter 2);
- the share of wages in value added (filter 3).

2. The industrial structure criterion, illustrated by:
- the skill structure of the labour force (filter 4);
- the evolution of visible consumption since 1981 (filter 5);

3. The criterion of openness, illustrated by:
- the level of non-tariff barriers (filter 6);
- the level of intra-community penetration (filter 7).

The sectors that pass through the greatest number of filters are those in which, on the basis of the above three sets of criteria, there is the greatest risk of relocation. The final results are shown in Table 5.

3.2.2 The Wage Cost Criterion

A company will only contemplate transferring all or part of its activities if wage levels in the country of destination are lower. Table 6 lists the industries with the greatest wage differentials between member states. A distinction is made between manual and white-collar workers. It shows that, in some sectors, firms which relocate could benefit from high dispersion in both categories of wage-earners. This double advantage may prove to be of fundamental importance where these two categories are equally represented as, for example, in shipbuilding and mechanical engineering (see Table 8).

In the traditional sectors, the only significant wage differential is for manual workers. The advanced technology sectors, on the other hand, benefit from this advantage only for white-collar workers. The risk of relocation is thus greater within the first group, to the extent that the main advantage of the southern European countries lies above all in the availability of a supply of cheap, unskilled labour. The predominance of white-collar employees in the second group could, however, encourage some firms to transfer at least part of their production, provided the local labour force was sufficiently skilled.

Of the industries identified in Table 6, only firms in those sectors in which wage costs constitute the most important variable will be encouraged to exploit the wage differentials that exist between member states. Table 7 lists the sectors concerned. The two indicators selected for this purpose are complementary: the use of value added - which does not include intermediate consumption - makes it possible to relativize performance in terms of sales. This intermediate consumption is important in, for example, the motor vehicle industry. In consequence, the share of wages is high relative to value added, but low in proportion to turnover.

In general, however, these two filters highlight the same sectors (Table 7). A total of twelve industries pass through the first three filters. The shipbuilding industry, for example, has a high level of wage dispersion and the highest share of wage costs in both turnover and value added. Thus, the wage criterion and its three filters immediately make this industry one of the candidates for relocation. The wage criterion is also a decisive factor in the industries of: structural metal products, mechanical engineering, timber and rubber.

Table 6. Dispersion of wages by sectors between Community members.

Filter 1: Dispersion of gross hourly wages for manual workers
(and gross monthly salaries for white-collar workers)

CRONOS code	Sectors	Differentials code	
		Manual	White-collar
20	Manufacture of glass	33.7	31.4**
21	Manufacture of ceramic goods	34.4*	29.9
22	Chemical industry	33.3	30.4
23	Man-made fibres industry	31.4	30.2
26	Foundries	34.2	31.6**
27	Manufacture of structural metal products	35.7*	32.3**
28	Tools, finished metal goods	33.8	30.9
29	Mechanical engineering	34.7*	31.7**
30	Office machinery, data processing	33.1	35.8**
31	Electrical engineering	32.7	31.8**
33	Motor vehicles	36.9*	35.2**
35	Shipbuilding	36.1*	33.2**
36	Aerospace equipment	34.3	32.9**
37	Instrument engineering	33.4	32.1**
39	Food industry	36.7*	30.9
40	Drink industry	39.1*	32.0**
41	Tobacco industry	35.3*	34.4**
43	Wool industry	37.6*	30.2
44	Cotton industry	35.5*	30.8
45	Knitting industry	33.8	30.9
46	Leather and leather goods	35.5*	31.2
48	Manufacture of footwear	34.4*	30.8
49	Manufacture of clothing	32.1	30.7
50	Timber, wooden furniture	37.1*	34.9**
52	Manufacture of pulp, paper and board	36.7*	33.7**
53	Processing of paper and board	37.2*	30.8
54	Printing and publishing	39.2*	31.4**
56	Manufacture of rubber products	34.5*	31.3**
57	Processing of plastic	34.6*	30.9
58	Other manufacturing industries	38.4*	35.3**
	Average for all industries	34.4	31.3

Notes: Risk of relocation higher in:
* Sectors in which the dispersion for manual earnings is equal to or higher than the average for all industries (34.4).
** Sectors in which the dispersion for white-collar earnings is equal to or higher than the average for all industries (31.3).
Source: Derived from Eurostat, Harmonised Earnings Statistics, 1985.

Table 7. Share of earnings in costs.
Filter 2: Share of earnings in turnover
Filter 3: Share of earnings in value added

CRONOS code	Sectors	Share of earnings in Turnover	Value added
20	Manufacture of glass	22.1*	74**
21	Manufacture of ceramic goods	28.4*	79**
22	Chemical industry	13.1	59
23	Man-made fibres industry	16.8	65
26	Foundries	27.1*	83**
27	Manufacture of structural metal products	22.4*	82**
28	Tools, finished metal goods	22.8*	74**
29	Mechanical engineering	24.2*	78**
30	Office machinery, data processing	14.7	52
31	Electrical engineering	23.7*	75**
33	Motor vehicles	18.0	81**
35	Shipbuilding	33.8*	93**
36	Aerospace equipment	23.8*	72**
37	Instrument engineering	27.3*	74**
39	Food industry	8.8	63
40	Drink industry	8.4	62
41	Tobacco industry	4.4	68
43	Wool industry	16.2	66
44	Cotton industry	18.3	73**
45	Knitting industry	21.6*	75**
46	Leather and leather goods	13.5	67
48	Manufacture of footwear	22.2*	76**
49	Manufacture of clothing	23.2*	78**
50	Timber, wooden furniture	22.4*	77**
52	Manufacture of pulp, paper and board	13.9	62
53	Processing of paper and board	18.4	71
54	Printing and publishing	26.9*	63
56	Manufacture of rubber products	24.3*	78**
57	Processing of plastic	20.1*	69
58	Other manufacturing industries	21.2*	70
	Average for all industries	20.1	72

Notes: Higher risk of relocation in:
* Sectors in which the share of earnings in turnover is equal to or greater than the average share for all industries (20.1).
** Sectors in which the share of earnings in value added is equal to or greater than the average share for all industries (72).
Source: Eurostat Luxembourg, CRONOS data bank.

3.2.3 The Industrial Structure Criterion

Through filters four and five, Table 8 highlights those industries characterized by an intensive production process with a relatively unskilled work force and saturation of product markets. These mature sectors will also be increasingly dominated by a drive to reduce production costs through economies of scale. With the opening up of national frontiers, the risk of relocation will be increased in these sectors.

In the first instance, Table 8 shows the distribution of the labour force in each industry among four categories of wage earners (manual workers, supervisory staff, white-collar workers and managerial staff) as well as the proportion of white-collar to manual workers - a simple and precise measure of the skill level of the work force. This latter ratio is particularly low in the traditional sectors of footwear, clothing, and timber (between 0.16 and 0.19), where the work force is composed mainly of manual workers (up to 80%) and which have only a small proportion of white-collar (14%) and managerial staff (1%). Conversely, the ratio is high (between 0.5 and 1.5) in industries based on advanced technology - chemicals, office machinery, electrical and electronic engineering - in which white-collar workers sometimes account for half the work force, and there is also a high proportion of managerial staff.

Most of the low-skill sectors also have to face a situation in which demand is falling. The only exceptions are the motor vehicle and food industries, where demand is still rising.

3.2.4 Openness as a Criterion.

Two filters can be used to assess the degree to which each of the industries studied is open to community imports. The first of these is an assessment of the significance of the various existing non-tariff barriers in a given sector (standards, fiscal or administrative barriers, open markets, etc.). The second is the rate of penetration by firms from member states, which indicates the share of domestic demand satisfied by imports from EC countries. Taken together these two indicators make it easier to identify those sectors where the introduction of the single market is most likely to lead to significant transfers of activity or investment. Grid 1 presents this typology.

Table 8. The structural characteristics of sectors.

Filter 4: Skill level of work force
Filter 5: Evolution of consumption (index 100 for 1981) as an indication of mature industries

CRONOS code	Sectors	Skill levels					
		Manual workers	Supervisory staff	White-collar staff	Managerial staff	Ratio w.c./ manual	Evolution of consumption
20	Manufacture of glass	76.9	5.0	17.1	1.0	0.22*	124**
21	Manufacture of ceramic goods	76.9	5.0	17.1	1.0	0.22*	115**
22	Chemical industry	52.7	7.5	37.0	2.8	0.50	153
23	Man-made fibres industry	73.6	5.9	19.0	1.5	0.26*	125**
26	Foundries	73.6	5.9	19.0	1.5	0.26*	120**
27	Manufacture of structural metal products	73.6	5.9	19.0	1.5	0.26*	128**
28	Tools, finished metal goods	62.6	4.9	31.4	1.1	0.50	130**
29	Mechanical engineering	63.8	6.1	28.6	1.5	0.45	127**
30	Office machinery, data processing	35.9	8.3	53.7	2.1	1.49	226
31	Electrical and electronic engineering	62.6	4.9	31.4	1.1	0.50	147
33	Motor vehicles	76.5	4.3	18.4	0.8	0.24*	154
35	Shipbuilding	65.2	6.3	28.0	0.5	0.43	148
36	Aerospace equipment	65.2	6.3	28.0	0.5	0.43	132**
37	Instrument engineering	62.9	6.5	29.8	0.8	0.47	120**
39	Food industry	70.9	5.8	22.1	1.3	0.31*	143
40	Drink industry	70.9	5.8	22.0	1.3	0.31*	135**
41	Tobacco industry	70.9	5.8	22.0	1.3	0.31*	168
43	Wool industry	77.2	7.1	14.4	1.3	0.19*	133**
44	Cotton industry	77.2	7.1	14.4	1.3	0.19*	121**
45	Knitting industry	77.2	7.1	14.4	1.3	0.19*	131**
46	Leather and leather goods	82.2	3.9	13.1	0.8	0.16*	127**
48	Manufacture of footwear	80.1	5.7	13.3	0.9	0.17*	119**
49	Manufacture of clothing	77.2	7.1	14.4	1.3	0.19*	127**
50	Timber, wooden furniture	77.5	6.2	15.0	1.3	0.19*	108**
52	Manufacture of pulp, paper and board	65.6	5.1	27.8	1.5	0.42	144

Continued ...

CRONOS code	Sectors	Skill levels					
		Manual work-ers	Super-visory staff	White collar staff	Manag-erial staff	Ratio w.c./ manual	Evolu-tion of consum-ption
53	Processing of paper and board	65.6	5.1	27.8	1.5	0.42	140
54	Printing and publishing	65.6	5.1	27.8	1.5	0.42	136**
56	Manufacture of rubber products	73.6	5.6	19.6	1.2	0.27*	124**
57	Processing of plastic	73.6	5.6	19.6	1.2	0.27*	143
58	Other manufacturing industries	71.9	5.7	21.3	1.0	0.30*	120**

Notes: Higher risk of relocation in:
* Low-skill sectors with a ratio of manual to white-collar workers equal to or less than 30%.
** Sectors experiencing low growth in consumption since 1981 (less than average for all industries = 137).

Where frontiers are already open, transfer of activity to the south will be limited. The highly internationalized sectors have, for the most part, already benefited considerably from the wage differentials that exist between member states. The drive to relocate began just after the entry of Spain and Portugal into the EC. Since then, there has been a levelling off of wage levels within the Community, with the result that the wage factor alone no longer seems sufficient justification for a fresh wave of relocations within the sectors that are already internationalized.

In the nationally oriented sectors the low level of trade with the community can be explained not by trade barriers but by structural factors such as high transport costs, limited economies of scale and the small size of efficient production units. The single market is not likely to change this situation, unless the reduction in transport costs and the dynamic created by the drive towards '1992' suddenly propel these sectors (e.g. the timber industry) towards concentration and the exploitation of economies of scale (following the example of the Swedish company, IKEA).

Table 9. Industrial sectors and degree of openness.
Filter 6: Scale of non-tariff barriers
Filter 7: Rate of EC penetration

CRONOS code	Sectors	Non-tariff protection	Rate of EC penetration
20	Manufacture of glass	average*	23.0
21	Manufacture of ceramic goods	average*	25.5
22	Chemical industry	average*	N.A.
23	Man-made fibres industry	low	60.4
26	Foundries	low	6.5**
27	Manufacture of structural metal products	average*	9.0**
28	Tools, finished metal goods	low	14.9**
29	Mechanical engineering	average*	30.1
30	Office machinery, data processing	high*	42.3
31	Electrical engineering	high*	low**
33	Motor vehicles	average*	33.4
35	Shipbuilding	high*	3.5**
36	Aerospace equipment	average*	36.4
37	Instrument engineering	low	high
39	Food industry	low	low**
40	Drink industry	high*	low**
41	Tobacco industry	low	6.4**
43	Wool industry	average*	31.7
44	Cotton industry	average*	42.5
45	Knitting industry	average*	37.8
46	Leather and leather goods	low	27.9
48	Manufacture of footwear	average*	37.8
49	Manufacture of clothing	average*	19.7
50	Timber, wooden furniture	low	15.8**
52	Manufacture of pulp, paper and board	low	18.0
53	Processing of paper and board	low	17.4**
54	Printing and publishing	low	7.1**
56	Manufacture of rubber products	average*	22.2
57	Processing of plastic	average*	25.1
58	Other manufacturing industries	average*	high
	Average for all industries		17.6

Notes: High risk of relocation in:
* Sectors with high or average non-tariff protection,
** and those that also have a rate of EC penetration lower than the EC average of 17.6%.

The risk of relocation will be higher where non-tariff barriers existed. The lifting of barriers to trade in those industries which already have a high rate of penetration will not, it is true, modify competition between producers, but it will lead to a reduction in costs. In turn, this will encourage large-scale production for the

European market. From this point of view, firms will seek to relocate towards the south, particularly those producing for mass markets (see Table 9).

Those sectors in which significant barriers to trade coincide with a low rate of penetration will be the sectors with the highest potential for relocation.

Table 9 shows that only four industries pass through these last two filters. Firms in these industries are operating in protected markets, either as suppliers of state companies (as in the metal industry) or as national standard-bearers receiving government subsidies (as in the shipbuilding or drinks industries).

Grid 1. Indicator of openness and relocation.

NON-TARIFF PROTECTION

		low	high
		Nationally oriented sectors	Protected markets
R A T E O F E C	l o w	**Little benefit in relocating** unless Single Market encourages concentration and exploitation of economies of scale	**The sectors most likely to experience** relocation, because of blocking of competition and high level of wage dispersion
		e.g.: printing and publishing, foundries, timber	e.g.: metal industry, shipbuilding, drinks
P E T R A T I O N	h i g h	Already internationalized sectors	Sectors already open to competition but technical standards still a burden on production costs
		Little benefit in relocating if not already moved	**Considerable risk of relocating** particularly if wage dispersion is still high and not yet exploited
		e.g.: man-made fibres, instrument engineering, leather goods, paper-box	e.g.: textiles, glass, footwear, rubber products

3.2.5. Sectors with a High Risk of Relocation: A Summary of the Successive Filtering Processes

Table 10 enables us to identify, on the basis of the criteria adopted, those sectors where there is a high risk of relocation. These are the sectors that pass through the highest number of filters. One sector stands out very clearly, having accumulated all seven indicators of the risk of relocation; this is the manufacture of structural metal products.

Six of the seven indicators are satisfied by six of the other sectors: glass, ceramics, foundries, footwear, timber and rubber. Next in line, with five indicators, are the industries linked to the textiles sector (knitting, cotton, clothing) and those of mechanical engineering, shipbuilding and aerospace and drinks.

Using Table 10 as a basis, the various sectors can be grouped into several categories according to the degree of risk of relocation. These are: mature, protected markets; consumer goods; mature industries with limited wage advantage; and sectors with a high technology content.

Mature, protected markets. The sectors most affected by relocation will be the 'national standard-bearers' that are still relatively protected from intra-Community trade and that also display the characteristics of industries at an advanced stage in their 'life cycle' (low-skill work force, low growth in demand). The example of the structural metal products industry, which passes through all the filters (and thus fulfils all the criteria) is significant. This is a sector which has reached maturity and in which obstacles to trade have clearly blocked the development of intra-Community trade. As a result, there is still a high level of wage dispersion between member states.

The importance of wage costs in this industry might encourage firms to relocate some of their production units in order to revive their competitive position in a saturated market. Thus, in 1988, the Belgian company Bosal invested 4.35 million pesetas in a new exhaust pipe factory in Valencia in Spain. In the same year, the French company Carnaud decided to set up a new metal box factory in the Rioja region of Spain. Prior to this the company's metal box production had been located exclusively in France.

The protected drinks market (characterized by the highest levels of wage dispersion for all manufacturing industry) could well be undergoing a similar process. In 1989, for example, International

Distillers and Vitners (IDV), a subsidiary of the British Grand Metropolitan group, acquired the entire capital of Sileno, the main distributor of wines and spirits in Portugal.

The shipbuilding industry is also a sector with a number of indicators which point to a high risk of relocation (Table 10). It is not impossible that, at some stage, some European shipbuilding companies will consider transferring part of their production to southern Europe. This will occur in order to acquire a cost advantage in the face of particularly fierce competition from the newly industrialized countries and Japan, which may well sharpen still further with the removal of non-tariff barriers. However, the shipbuilding industry is currently trying to cope with the problems of restructuring, as illustrated by the recent unrest at the French shipyards in La Ciotat. Government influence (e.g. in France) and the large number of people employed in this sector make it difficult now to envisage a transfer of activity of this type.

Consumer goods. As can be seen from Table 10, those sectors specializing in products accounting for a significant proportion of ordinary household expenditure (shoes, sports goods, cotton, wool, cars) or in intermediate goods (glass, ceramics, rubber) would also have good reason to relocate to southern Europe. Wages which were much lower would enable these traditional industries, already open to trade despite barriers, to benefit from the economies of scale that remain to be exploited. This need to exploit wage advantages is all the more pressing with the introduction of the single market, since the distribution networks will systematically turn to the least costly suppliers within the Community.

Several examples show that this strategy is already being put into practice. In the sports goods industry (classified under 'other industries'), Donnay and Snauwaert have already closed their factories in Belgium and moved to Portugal. In the household electrical industry Electrolux took a controlling interest in 1988 in Carbero-Domar and United Hermetica of Barcelona. Ford of the US and Volkswagen of Germany have decided to launch an ambitious joint vehicle programme in Europe, which will include building a new assembly plant in Portugal.

Relocation strategies are also noticeable for intermediate products. In the glass industry in 1988, the Italian company SIV set up a factory in both Valencia and El Ferral in Spain. These produce parts for the motor vehicle industry. Through Cristaleria Española, the French Saint Gobain company is also planning to invest in the construction of a new glass fibre production unit in Madrid. In the rubber industry, Michelin launched a plan to invest 95 million pesetas over the four year period between 1988 and 1992.

Mature industries with limited wage advantage. Already, other traditional industries - open to trade from within and outside the Community - have at least partially exploited the wage differentials that currently exist between member states, and relocated to southern Europe. This would seem to be the case in the clothing, knitting and finished metal goods industries, which are characterized by a lower level of wage dispersion. This reduction in wage advantage could, however, be compensated for by increased specialization and greater know-how in the countries where these sectors are less developed (see section 4.2).

Sectors with a high technology content. High-tech industries in which consumption is evolving favourably should seldom be tempted to relocate. This is the case in the office machinery, electrical and electronic engineering, and precision instrument industries.

These sectors are already open to trade with member states as well as with non-Community countries (Japan and America provide particularly strong competition). Only for white-collar workers is wage dispersion above the average for manufacturing industry (see Table 6). Moreover, the trade war in these sectors is reflected more in R & D expenditures, licences and new technologies than in competitive salaries. Other factors which make relocation more likely, such as an adequate infrastructure in the country of destination, a relatively unexploited local market and tax incentives, may play a fundamental role.

Firms in these sectors may of course decide to transfer to southern Europe only those parts of their activities that are intensive in low-skill labour and require less sophisticated technologies. That might well be the case in electrical engineering (31), which is still relatively protected. Thus, in 1988, there were two significant investment projects in the electrical and electronics industry in Portugal. Legrand purchased the Sipe company (turnover $12 million), which has 35% of the Portuguese market for low-voltage electrical equipment. The French company intends to invest $8 million over two years in order to expand Sipe's production capacity - with the eventual aim of supplying other European markets. In

1988, the German firm Siemens acquired a controlling interest in the telephone equipment manufacturer Emptel.

To conclude this multi-criteria analysis, it can be said that this identification process is worthwhile, but that any conclusions must be qualified. Alarmist talk about the social consequences of the single market, associated with the risk of relocation, should not be taken too seriously. In the great majority of cases (highly internationalized sectors, nationally oriented sectors, high-tech sectors, those in which wage costs are relatively unimportant), the specific impact of the single market on transfers of manufacturing activities will be limited.

On the other hand, this analysis makes possible early identification of those sectors in which there is a high risk of social disruption because of transfers of activity that may occur after the opening of national frontiers. Once these sectors have been identified, it becomes possible to analyze the possible consequences of these transfers for the industrial equilibrium of the various EC countries.

4. The Impact of Relocation on the Various Regions of the Community: Threats and Potential

4.1 Job Losses and Comparative Advantages in Northern Europe

Our study confirms that some regions of the Community will be able to exploit lower wage costs and standards of social protection and attract investment and transfers of activity. However, the debate surrounding this topic conceals the equally great, if not greater, advantages enjoyed by the more developed regions, including better trained work forces, more advanced financial, administrative and educational infrastructures and more rapid marketing methods. Under these circumstances, the fear of a widespread trend towards relocation would seem to be exaggerated.

Table 10. Identification of the sectors with a high risk of relocation, in the light of successive filters.

CRONOS code	Sectors		Wage criteria			Structural criteria		Openness criteria	
			High wage dispersion	High share of earnings in turnover	High share earnings in v.a.	Low skill work force	Low demand	High non-tariff barriers	Under-developed trade with EC
			Filter 1	Filter 2	Filter 3	Filter 4	Filter 5	Filter 6	Filter 7
20	*Manufacture of glass*	!!	*	*	*	*	*	*	-
21	*Manufacture of ceramic goods*	!!	*	*	*	*	*	*	-
22	Chemical industry		-	-	-	-	-	*	-
23	Man-made fibres industry		-	-	-	*	*	-	-
26	*Foundries*	!!	*	*	*	*	*	-	*
27	*Manufacture of structural metal products*	!!	*	*	*	*	*	*	*
28	Tools, finished metal goods		-	*	*	-	*	-	*
29	Mechanical engineering	!	*	*	*	-	*	*	-
30	Office machinery, data processing		*	-	-	-	-	*	-
31	Electrical engineering	!	*	*	*	-	-	*	*
33	Motor vehicles		*	-	*	*	-	*	-
35	Shipbuilding	!	*	*	*	-	-	*	*
36	Aerospace equipment	!	*	*	*	-	*	*	-
37	Instrument engineering		*	*	*	-	*	-	-
39	Food industry		*	-	-	*	-	-	*
40	Drinks industry	!	*	-	-	*	*	*	*
41	Tobacco industry		*	-	-	*	-	-	*
43	Wool industry		*	-	-	*	*	*	-
44	Cotton industry	!	*	-	*	*	*	*	-
45	Knitting industry	!	-	*	*	*	*	*	-
46	Leather and leather goods		*	-	-	*	*	-	-
48	*Manufacture of footwear*	!!	*	*	*	*	*	*	-
49	Manufacture of clothing	!	-	*	*	*	*	*	-

Continued ...

CRONOS code	Sectors	Wage criteria			Structural criteria		Openness criteria	
		High wage dispersion	High share of earnings in turnover	High share earnings in v.a.	Low skill work force	Low demand	High non-tariff barriers	Under-developed trade with EC
		Filter 1	Filter 2	Filter 3	Filter 4	Filter 5	Filter 6	Filter 7
50	*Timber, wooden furniture* !!	*	*	*	*	*	-	*
52	Manufacture of pulp, paper and board	*	-	-	-	-	-	-
53	Processing of paper and board	*	-	-	-	-	-	*
54	Printing and publishing	*	*	-	-	*	-	*
56	*Manufacture of rubber products* !!	*	*	*	*	*	*	-
57	Processing of plastic	*	*	-	*	-	*	-
58	Other manufacturing industries !	*	*	-	*	*	*	-

Notes:
!! Very high risk of relocation (6 or 7 filters)   * = yes
! High risk of relocation (5 filters)   - = no

In order to confront greater competitiveness, many firms in northern Europe are considering various other moves, such as increased rationalization, the development of new, higher quality products and improvements in marketing and distribution. Evidence for this is provided by the KPMG[25] survey, which indicated that only 19% of the firms questioned seem to want to relocate, compared with the 27% that are planning improvements in productivity and the 21% that are seeking to rationalize existing sites.

On the other hand, transfers to southern Europe will take place in labour-intensive firms suffering from declining demand. Those regions of orthern Europe with relatively advanced technologies and large capital stocks enjoy their own comparative advantage in the high-tech and capital-intensive industries which are characterized by high demand. Thus northern Europe will benefit a great deal from the economies of scale made possible by the introduction of the single market.

Finally, the size factor should stimulate further expansion in the developed regions. In the run-up to the single market, it may be seen that a number of firms from outside the Community, particularly from Japan, South-East Asia and the United States, are currently setting up in these regions. This trend, which is particularly marked in the high-demand sectors, should benefit industries in northern Europe - not only in terms of transfers of technology but also in terms of employment. Certain stipulations are necessary, however, along the line of the agreements on the compulsory inclusion of a locally produced component in order to sustain the link between the goods produced by these multinationals and the local supply.

Thus by virtue of their infrastructure and technology, northern European regions will not be disadvantaged by the opening up of national frontiers; however, it is now necessary to face up to the job losses which are likely to occur in the traditional sectors. Large-scale national training programmes are required in order to 'recycle' the redundant workers and to ensure that they adapt to the new market requirements without the occurrence of major social problems.

4.2 Moving to the South: A Chance to Enhance Traditional Specialization

The theoretical and sectoral analyses presented in Parts I and II cast doubt on the viability of any catching-up process that may be taking place in southern Europe. According to the life cycle theory, growth in a region is stimulated by the presence of industries in a rapid growth phase and hindered by the presence of industries in a slow growth phase. There is empirical evidence to show that mature industries are not only declining but also preventing the development of new industries.[26]

If, as has been shown, relocation to southern Europe is likely to occur only in the mature sectors, this may in fact prove to be an obstacle to the development, in these regions, of new industries characterized by strong demand, thus undermining the catching-up process.

4.2.1 The Candidates for Relocation: Key Sectors in the Economies of Southern Europe

The argument that relocation to the South by the mature sectors will thereby create obstacles to the development of new industries and

81

consequently undermine the catching-up process, does not take sufficient account of the central role played by the traditional sectors in southern European countries and their evolution in recent years. Analysis of their performance will enable us to see the place of relocation in the development of these economies in a different light.

The contribution of each of these sectors to the balance of trade (figures which are available for both Spain and Portugal) is an indicator that will highlight those activities with surplus capacity and those with a shortage. As Table 11 shows, the traditional manufacturing sectors, using old technologies, are the major assets of these economies. Thus the group of sectors contributing most to the trade balance (with a BCI > 2) include most of the industries with a high risk of relocation. Portugal is highly competitive in the drinks, food, timber, paper, clothing and footwear industries. The leading sectors in Spain are food, footwear, clothing and motor vehicles.

Table 11 also highlights the weaknesses of the Spanish and Portuguese economies in the advanced technology sectors (precision instruments, for example). However, from the mid-1970s onwards, the traditional sectors have been sufficiently strong to launch both economies into a phase of rapid growth. Their performance led the OECD to classify them in successive years (Spain in 1979 and Portugal in 1980) as newly industrialized countries (NICs). Between 1981 and 1985, Spanish exports grew annually by 3%, while the corresponding growth for Portugal was 5.5%.[27] As a result, the share of imports covered by exports rose from 42% in Portugal in 1981 to 74% in 1985, and from 63% to 81% in Spain.

Since 1985, however, there has been a definite reversal of this growth trend. The trade surplus recorded by Spain in that year ($852 million) gave way to a deficit of $4 million in 1987. Furthermore, Greece, having eliminated its deficit between 1981 and 1984, went into the red in 1987, to the tune of $6,942 billion.[28]

Manufacturing industry in southern European countries must tackle two crucial problems arising out of membership in the EC. These are:

- a considerable increase in imports from other member states;

- the potential erosion of their export markets (particularly within the EC) by imports from non-member states. This form of competition is emerging in sectors with low value added, which is precisely where southern European countries are strongest.

Table 11. Foreign trade of Portugal and Spain: contribution to trade balance (BCI) by sector.

Sectors with high relocation risk as identified in Section 3:		BCI Spain	BCI Portugal
20	Manufacture of glass	+ 0.12	+ 0.37
21	Manufacture of ceramic goods	+ 0.98	+ 1.21*
26	Foundries	+ 1.51*	- 0.16
27	Manufacture of structural metal products	+ 1.91*	+ 1.26*
28	Tools, finished metal goods	- 0.23	- 1.21-
35	Shipbuilding	+ 0.93	+ 1.11*
36	Aerospace equipment	- 0.04	+ 0.15
40	Drink industry	+ 1.23*	+ 3.17**
44	Cotton industry	+ 0.07	- 1.63-
45	Knitting industry	+ 0.58	+ 9.53**
48	Manufacture of footwear	+ 3.38**	+ 5.43**
49	Manufacture of clothing	+ 1.97*	+17.21**
50	Timber, wooden furniture	+ 0.73	+ 2.27**
56	Manufacture of rubber products	+ 0.56	- 0.91
58	Other manufacturing industries	+ 1.63*	+ 0.32

Other industries:		BCI Spain	BCI Portugal
22	Chemical industry	- 2.61--	- 2.55--
23	Man-made fibres industry	- 0.48	- 1.57-
28	Foundries	+0.49	- 0.38
30	Office machinery, data processing	- 2.06--	- 0.49
31	Electrical engineering	+0.21	+0.30
33	Motor vehicles	+8.04**	- 4.54--
37	Instrument engineering	- 2.29--	- 0.95
39	Food industry	+1.53*	+4.82**
41	Tobacco industry	- 0.85	- 0.20
43	Wool industry	0.02	- 0.39
46	Leather and leather goods	+0.44	- 1.37-
52	Manufacture of pulp, paper and board	- 0.04	+ 4.75**
53	Processing of paper and board	- 0.04	+0.56
54	Printing and publishing	+0.57	- 0.06
57	Processing of plastic	+0.32	- 0.88

Notes:
** Strong sectors (BCI > 2)
 * Relatively strong sectors (1 < BCI < 2)
 - Relatively weak sectors (-2 < BCI < -1)
-- Weak sectors (BCI < -2)
Source: Société Internationale pour le Développement, November 1987.

This sudden change for the worse can be explained by the gradual removal of two types of protection from which these countries benefited: a tariff system designed to increase the price of imports above those of domestic products, and large export subsidies that reduced the price of goods exported to markets abroad.

Southern European countries have adopted a dual strategy in a bid to overcome this erosion of their trade advantages. They are seeking first, to stimulate large-scale production and second, to concentrate that production on segments of the market where consumption is highest. As we shall see, foreign investment may play a central role in this process.

4.2.2 Foreign Firms and the Exploitation of Economies of Scale

According to the new theories of international trade, the size and international base of multinationals make them prime movers in the exploitation of economies of scale.[29] Fishwick, for example, in an econometric study of four countries (UK, F, It, FRG), highlighted the positive and statistically significant relationship that exists in manufacturing sectors between the level of foreign investment and performance as measured by sales.[30] This process is currently under way in southern Europe.

Dokopoulou and Hamilton's studies on Spain show that foreign investment shapes the strategies of the four leading firms in each of the following traditional sectors: footwear, textiles and clothing and plastics. Consequently, foreign capital is making a significant contribution to Spanish export performance.[31] Similarly, Dokopoulou and Hamilton have shown that more than a third of the manufactured goods exported by the 200 largest Greek companies in 1987 were produced by subsidiaries of multinationals.[32]

Finally, the S.I.D. report attributes the increase in exports from both Spain and Portugal to the opening up of these two economies to foreign investment.[33]

It should be pointed out that the increase in economies of scale encouraged by direct foreign investment does not always come solely from the parent companies of multinationals. A number of medium-sized Spanish companies are currently forging links with similarly sized firms within the Community which do not have the investment capacity of multinationals, but which can help them to win market share. These agreements are important for the Spanish market, in which 80.1% of manufacturing firms employ fewer than 10 people, and only 0.2% of firms are classed as large.[34] Of Spanish firms surveyed by the L.S.E., 35.5% are smaller than the optimal size for large-scale manufacturing.

4.2.3 Foreign Investment as a Means of Renovation within the Traditional Sectors

Currently, at the same time as they are increasing their production capacities, southern European countries are trying (within the traditional sectors) to switch to products with higher value added as a means of stimulating further growth. This new specialization is already well established in Spain. In 1981, the Spanish government introduced reconversion programmes in order to modernize production processes and improve product quality in the traditional sectors. Production lines in the clothing and textile industries, for example, have been made more flexible by a unique production process that is constantly evolving and can be adapted to market conditions.[35]

This trend towards specialization is also under way in Portugal and Greece, particularly in the clothing and footwear industries. Thus Portugal - in its trade with member states - seems to have swapped its legendary strength in the standardized production of cloth for complete specialization in fashion clothes. This area requires greater know-how and is a rapidly expanding industry. Two textile technology centres, one in Porto, the other in Lisbon, have been set up as a result.

Investment in the textiles industry is also one of the current priorities of Greece: at 2,800 Ecus, annual investment per year is twice as high as in Spain; and four times higher than in Portugal.[36] In this sector, creativity and design costs, as a proportion of total production costs, in all four countries have increased from 5% in 1979 to 10% in 1988.[37] The same process can be observed in the footwear industry.

Similarly, in Spain and Portugal processing industries such as timber, furniture and paper seem to be marking time on primary activities. Raw materials (wood, paper) are now being imported from Community countries. Such specialization is not easy to put into practice, and many jobs have been lost in these traditional sectors. The number employed in the Spanish textile industry has fallen by 42.5% since 1980. Moreover, the concentration on more sophisticated products requires considerable expenditure on R & D and there are also significant learning costs. The role of foreign investment could prove decisive in this process. The investment capacity of the multinationals, together with the know-how they have accumulated, are major resources.

Farinas and Martin have looked at this question.[38] In particular, their 1988 study confirms the recent trend in Spain towards intra-sector specialization. In other words, this specialization is occurring not at sector level (inter-sector specialization), but rather at a lower level of economic activity - that of relatively homogeneous products manufactured by comparable production processes. Using an econometric study as a basis, the authors clearly identified the main determinants of this type of specialization as expenditure on R & D and foreign investment. This highlights the contribution of foreign investment to the simultaneous development of all the stages of an industry.

The same is true of Portugal:

> the rapid evolution towards high-level models in the textiles industry seems to have been made possible by the design skills of the foreign firms in this sector of the market and the availability of a cheap labour supply to put those skills into practice.[39]

This enhanced specialization is already beginning to bear fruit: the two sectors chiefly concerned, clothing and footwear, have found themselves propelled to leading positions in the Portuguese economy. They were the only two industries to record a surplus in 1987, whereas the other traditional sectors came up against insufficient demand and competition from non-member states. Similarly, the diversification of the Spanish economy is being reflected in its foreign trade: the processing industries are expanding rapidly.

The presence of multinationals has also enabled the Spanish food industry to change over successfully to a new combination of down-market and up-market products. Sharp rises in exports are predicted as a result, which should compensate for the job losses caused by restructuring.[40]

The multinationals have also been responsible for the development of the Spanish motor vehicle industry. This mature sector went through a difficult period during the 1980s, but is now performing well in the export market compared with the same sector in Portugal (see differences in Table 11). However, the locational conditions in Portugal, similar to those in Spain, lead us to believe that foreign investment in this sector should, with the opening up of national frontiers, be divided between the two Iberian countries.

Only Greece seems to be lagging behind in this process of renovation. Its difficulties can be explained partly by inadequate foreign investment in manufacturing industry, as foreign investment is mainly concentrated in tourism and the purchase of land. The trend towards relocation that is expected to emerge with the introduction of the single market may help Greece to specialize more effectively.

This enhanced specialization in the traditional sectors is not a hindrance but rather a complement to the development of the 'high-tech' sectors, where world demand is higher. The new interest of foreign capital in the economies of southern Europe, particularly from countries outside the EC (see section 2.2.2), should assist in the emergence of new poles of competitiveness which cannot always be constructed by internal dynamics alone. We have seen that strategic locational policies adopted by Japanese firms have contributed significantly to the revival of the Spanish electrical and electronics industry. There are also good prospects for the micro-electronics and telecommunications industries in Portugal.

In summary, far from pushing southern European countries into an obsolete and unpromising form of specialization, transfers of activity within the Community by firms in the traditional sectors (identified in Part Two) seem likely, if contrarily, to contribute to the process of specialization on which these countries embarked a short time ago. This process is based on the development of large-scale production in the traditional sectors and a change over to products with greater value added. The advantages are obvious: the economies of southern Europe will be able to compete in these sectors with countries outside the Community, while at the same time concentrating on products for which there is greater world demand. They will also be able to develop an alternative to the advantages of cheap labour that are already beginning to lose some of their attractiveness.

The keen competition between newly industrialized countries nevertheless casts a shadow over this picture. For several years the Asian countries have also been implementing major programmes of product innovation and sophistication, assisted by the technology of the American and Japanese firms that have set up in these regions. This last threat, while confirming the crucial importance of foreign investment in the race towards market segments with greater value added,[41] highlights the need for southern European countries to extract all the competitive advantages that the introduction of the internal market is expected to bring. These are associated with the policy of protection that will be adopted by the Community in relation to non-member states and are the subject of the next section. It is also necessary for the Community to take appropriate measures to ensure that transfers of activity contribute effectively to regional equilibrium.

4.3 Supporting Policies

4.3.1 Community Regional Policy: Preventing New Disequilibria

The regions in which the sectors at high risk of relocation have a strong presence, in both northern and southern Europe, are the ones that will experience the greatest upheavals when the single market is introduced. In the northern European regions dominated by large assembly plants, transfers of activity will lead to considerable job loss.

The consequences of these transfers will be intensified in areas where there are no other industries to fill the gaps. These are generally regions in which previously healthy economies have already been weakened by structural change and where new industries have not been able to create a sufficient number of new jobs. These visibly declining regions include the West Midlands in the UK, Liguria in Italy and certain regions of Belgium.

There is also a high risk of regional disequilibria caused by relocations in southern Europe. Indeed, it seems likely that these transfers of activity will be concentrated in a limited number of developed regions, at the expense of the less favoured areas. Table 12 illustrates this process in the case of Spain.

Table 12. Distribution of foreign investment in the manufacturing sectors in Spain in 1985 and 1986 (%).

	1985	1986
Madrid	32.4	34.3
Barcelona	29.6	31.3
Rest of Spain	38.0	34.4
Total	100.0	100.0

Source: 'Ministerio de economia y de hacienda, Direccion general de transacciones extrangeras', Madrid, 1987.

Almost 66% of foreign investment was located in Madrid and Barcelona, the two main urban centres. According to the report by

Dokopoulou and Hamilton, this concentration can be explained in part by the importance of banks and financial services for foreign investors.[42] It should be noted that more than 50% of manufacturing industry is already concentrated in the two provinces in which these cities are located and the three main provinces of the Basque region. Foreign investment in Portugal is similarly concentrated.[43]

Thus the expected relocations may well further intensify the industrial backwardness of the less developed regions, and may consequently cause more workers to migrate to the more favoured regions. These regional disequilibria are likely to undermine the expected beneficial effects of these transfers of activity. Nevertheless, the anticipated economic growth should help to correct these disequilibria.

The report by Cambridge Economic Consultants[44] shows that firms are considering relocating to peripheral regions against a background of full employment and saturated markets, rather than the other way round. The report concludes that a number of less developed regions will also benefit, when the internal market is completed, from transfers of activities by foreign firms.

These different perspectives, both in the North and the South, highlight the need to develop an appropriate regional policy. The doubling between 1987 and 1993 of the financial resources available to the Structural Funds, and reform of the regulations governing the framework and modalities of their interventions, are part of this problem.[45]

The regions that have been identified as disadvantaged by transfers of activities will be the first to receive support. The reconversion of regions seriously affected by the decline of manufacturing industry and the structural adjustment of underdeveloped regions are the two primary objectives of this new regional policy.[46]

In regions suffering from the decline of manufacturing industry productive investment will be particularly encouraged, through the European Regional Development Fund, with a view to creating jobs to replace those lost in the declining industries. Interventions aimed at improving the infrastructure in these developed zones will focus principally on the rehabilitation of abandoned sites and the redevelopment of declining industrial areas.

The least favoured regions of southern Europe are generally in particular need of improvements to their basic infrastructure. Support for this type of investment will, therefore, continue to account for a significant proportion of the interventions by the European Regional Development Funds in these regions. Transport, telecommunications, vocational training, technological research and development, environment, energy, and rural areas are all categories of infrastructure projects that could be supported. They could encourage better distribution of transfers of activity.

At the same time, 'priority should be given to investment that extends the use of advanced production technologies (in the traditional sectors as well) and contributes to the development of the advanced technology sectors.'[47] Such measures should encourage the enhanced specialization currently favoured by these countries. No doubt measures to attract foreign investment to the least favoured regions could also be worked out.

These measures seem to be heading in the right direction; however, Community regional policy alone cannot bring about the necessary reduction in regional disparities, despite the doubling of its resources. Consequently, the Commission stresses the importance of regional policies implemented at the national level and the complementary relationship that exists between national and Community regional policies. As preconditions for the dynamic evolution that is being sought, it also emphasizes a healthy macro-economic environment and the completion of the single market.

4.3.2 The External Shutter, or the Need for Reciprocal Arrangements

The transfers of activity that are expected to occur with the completion of the single market may, as we have seen, encourage the sectors we have identified to specialize in areas more in tune with the evolution of world demand; however, these sectors are precisely the ones that have benefited until now from considerable national protection (Table 9).

For these sectors, the opening up of frontiers may also signify a reduction in competitiveness and lead to greater penetration of the European market by products from non-member states. While southern European countries enjoy undeniable cost advantages vis-a-vis other member states, this is far from being the case in relation to producers from outside the Community.[48] For example, hourly wages in the Pakistani textiles industry are four times lower than in Portugal.[49]

The footwear industry is important and deserves closer attention. In this sector, imports from countries outside the Community have taken off, with a 15.4% increase between 1984 and 1987. Table 13 shows that the main beneficiaries have been China and the countries of South-East Asia. This flood of products from non-Community countries obviously affects domestic markets in southern Europe, which have hitherto been protected. Table 14 illustrates this process, in the case of Spain, and highlights the current difficulties being experienced by Spain's traditional industries as barriers to trade are removed.

In Greece, imports in this sector already exceed exports, which nevertheless account for 30% of total production. This situation is likely to get worse, since there seems to be some delay in establishing R & D programmes in this sector.[50] In the view of the Greek footwear association, questioned by Booz-Allen, the imposition of temporary import quotas is essential to the industry's survival as it would give firms the time they need to restructure.

Southern European countries are all the more vulnerable to the opening of national frontiers since, simultaneously, they have to develop the production of shoes with higher value added and compete in the same market with other Community countries, particularly Italy. This latter country accounts for 45% of Community production as Italy benefits from well-established distribution networks and produces shoes whose quality and imaginative design put them far ahead of the competition.

The same difficulties are encountered in the other traditional sectors identified in Part Two: ceramics, glass, structural metal products, machinery, drinks, wooden furniture, sports goods and toys. At the same time these industries are also suffering acutely from competition from the newly industrialized countries. For the most part these industries make products over which member states are authorized, under article 115, to apply protective measures.[51] Because of their vulnerability to foreign competition they thus require special treatment.

If the progress of southern European countries were taken into account in the phasing out of national quotas and, in the longer term, of Community-wide protection measures, the industrial fabric of the least favoured regions would be able to develop in a more balanced way. Since it is easy to identify the countries that will benefit from the removal of import quotas (e.g. Taiwan, in the case of shoes), a bilateral framework seems best suited to the negotiation of these reciprocal arrangements (negotiation of self-limitation agreements).

Reciprocal arrangements must also be discussed within the multilateral framework of the GATT. This is particularly true of the textiles sector during the Uruguay round, and the preparation of the regime that will replace the multi-fibre agreement (MFA 4).[52]

The textiles industry is also going through an extremely turbulent period. The rate of penetration for the Community as a whole for products from non-member states increased from 38% in 1985 to 47% in 1987. The situation in the Greek textiles industry is particularly alarming. Competition from the newly industrialized countries can be combatted only with government support, since the prices of exports are well below production costs. In 1987, for example, the Patraiki-Patraiki company recorded a loss of 11 thousand million drachma on sales of 27 thousand million drachma; and in Portugal and Greece as well sustained growth of value added clearly depends on protection from imports from non-member states.[53]

Faced with these prospects, during negotiations on the MFA, the Commission of the European Communities must give priority to the situation of the southern European countries. If such an agreement is not renewed in 1991, 80-90% of producers in the four less well-developed countries would be directly threatened, with significant consequences for employment. It should be remembered that 10% of jobs in the Greek textiles industry have been lost since 1985, and that the corresponding figures for Portugal, Spain and Ireland are 15%, 40% and 35% respectively.

Another fact warrants attention: the recent strong growth in imports from non-member states in the traditional sectors has been a one-way flow.[54] Markets in the developing countries have in effect remained closed, thanks to a whole array of barriers - including restrictions on licences, customs duties, taxes and monetary or administrative measures. In the light of this situation, it seems reasonable to recommend that more systematic requests be made for reciprocity on the part of non-member states, in exchange for reductions in national quotas. In short, they should open up their markets.

It would be ironic if the considerable advantages expected of the single market by non-member states were not accompanied by a widening of access to foreign markets for Community countries. Thus temporary protection measures and requests for reciprocity in opening up markets could be the two facets of the Community's trade policy in the traditional sectors identified.

Table 13. Exports of footwear from non-member states to the EC.(In millions of pairs)

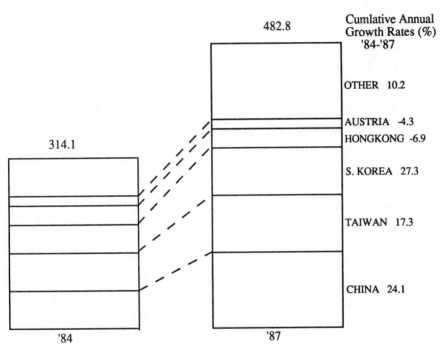

Source: Booze-Allen Analysis

5. Conclusion

The political decision to bring about the single market has turned the spotlight on the European scene and suddenly revealed the many advantages offered by such a vast market without national boundaries.

Actors from outside the Community have no desire at all to miss this opportunity. As a result, they are setting up an increasing number of production units within the Community. The fear of seeing the creation of a 'fortress Europe' only serves to strengthen their view that they will have to manufacture their products within Europe in order to be sure of benefiting from the completion of the single market.

As far as Community firms are concerned, they will be encouraged to seek the most favourable locations within the Community in order to use these locations as platforms to supply the whole of the European market and foreign markets at lower cost. The relocation process studied in this chapter is thus clearly part of the dynamic of optimization of the Community space.

Table 14. Penetration of the Spanish footwear market.

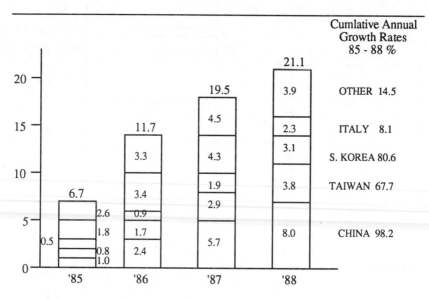

Source: Booz-Allen, INESCOP-FICE.

Our primary aim has been to measure the extent of these trends. Our study leads us to draw new conclusions.

  - On the one hand, there are no grounds for believing there will be a widespread tendency to relocate. Paradoxically, in fact, many of the factors that have traditionally caused firms to relocate their activities, such as tax regimes, the cost of credit and the price of raw materials, will lose their significance with the completion of the single market.
  As far as transfers of activity motivated by wage differentials are concerned, our multi-criteria analysis shows that, in the vast majority of cases (highly internationalized sectors, sectors

primarily serving a national market, high-tech sectors, and sectors in which wage costs are less important), they should be limited in extent.

- On the other hand, this study also clearly indicates the sectors where the risk of relocation, and of consequent social problems, is high. These are traditional sectors, with a poorly paid, low skill work force, that have hitherto benefited from considerable national protection. These industries are currently facing saturated markets and keen competition from the newly industrialized countries.

The adjustments that are required for the completion of the single market may prove problematic in these already threatened sectors. For this reason it is important to, without delay, make available at Community level and in cooperation with both sides of industry, the resources needed to avert the potential regional and sectoral disequilibria identified in this chapter.

In the developed regions, job losses in the sectors identified must be anticipated and serious consideration given to establishing large-scale training programmes for the displaced workers. Grants for restructuring will also help to breathe new life into the declining regions.

In southern Europe, transfers of activity must not have the effect of pushing the economies of that region into an obsolete form of specialization. This study has shown that foreign firms could help these countries to expand by becoming more competitive in the traditional sectors, through large-scale manufacture of products with higher value added and better suitability to the evolution of world demand.

This enhanced traditional specialization cannot, however, be achieved without appropriate supporting measures in the spheres of both regional and trade policy. A policy of investment in infrastructure projects and in R & D should be used to ensure that transfers of activity are equitably distributed between regions.

Above all, temporary protection measures against non-member states seem to be essential in the sectors identified. If the barriers to foreign competition are removed too rapidly, imports from the newly industrialized countries could flood the European market. These sectors would then become even more vulnerable, thus halting the process of renovation within these sectors that is already under way in the less developed countries.

Far from undermining the primary objective of harmonizing trade policy, it is a question of responding to a 'double imperative:' to ensure, on the one hand, the economic development of the least favoured members of the Community, and to preserve a European production capacity in all sectors - including the traditional ones - that is commensurate with the economic power with which it is intended to invest the Community.

Notes

1. Mucchielli and Thuillier, 'Multinationales européennes et investissements croisés,' *Economica*, 1982.
2. Fontagne, L., 'Délocalisation des avantages spécifiques et implantation internationale, le cas de l'industrie automobile,' *Revue d'Economie Industrielle*, No. 36, 2nd quarter 1986, pp. 42-52.
3. Balestrieri, M., 'Recenti sviluppi dei processi di localizzazione dell'industria manifatturiera in Italia,' *Note economiche*, Siena, No. 1, 1983, pp. 136-55.
4. Charron, E., 'Fasa-Renault: un cas d'internationalisation de la production automobile', *Mutations industrielles*, CNRS, Paris, 30 June 1987, pp. 3-53.
5. Lassudrie-Duchêne, B., 'Décomposition internationale des processus productifs et autonomie nationale', in Bourguignat, H., 'Internationalisation et autonomie de décision: le choix français,' *Economica*, 1982.
6. Dunning, J. and Norman, G., 'The Location Choice of Offices of International Companies,' *Environment and Planning*, Vol. 19, 1987, pp. 613-31.
7. This phenomenon is particularly marked in firms seeking to establish themselves in non-EC countries (Latin America and Africa in particular).
8. 'An Empirical Assessment of Factors Shaping Regional Competitiveness in Problem Regions,' first interim report, *IFO (Institute for Economic Research)*, Munich, November 1988.
9. Hoover, E.M., *The Location of Economic Activity*, New York, 1948, p. 48.
10. Bord, P., 'Evaluating Japanese Investments in Europe,' *EGIS*, pp. 136-52.
11. Dhombres, D., 'Honda prend 20% du constructeur automobile britannique Rover,' *Le Monde*, 15 July 1989, p. 27.
12. 'Semiconductors: Fujitsu's End Run around the EC,' *Business Week*, 15 May 1989, p. 53.
13. 'American Firms and Europe: Le défi Is Back,' *The Economist*, 13 May 1989, pp. 80-84.
14. 'Tokyo Claims London as a Colony in Empire of Financial Services,' *Wall Street Journal*, 8 March 1988, pp. 11-12.
15. Decker, W., 'The American Response to Europe 1992, '*European Affairs*, May 1989, pp. 105-10.
16. Scholl, R.B., 'International Investment Position: Component Detail for 1989,' *Survey of Current Business*, 15 June 1990.
17. 'Los Japoneses diverficicaran su inversion en España', *Expansion*, 15 May 1989, p. 3.
18. Le Nail, P., 'Portugal: explosion de l'investissement étranger,' *Eurépargne*, No. 32, May 1989, pp. 43-45.
19. 'Getting Ready: Results Survey EC 1992,' *EC Report*, KPMG International Office, Amsterdam, 1989.
20. Michel, D., 'L'Europe vue de France, d'Italie et d'Espagne,' *L'Entreprise*, July 1989, pp. 57-61.

21. Cittanova, M.L., 'L'Espagne, le nouvel Eldorado de l'Europe,' *Eurépargne*, No. 29, February 1989, pp. 15-17.
22. Dokopoulou, E. and Hamilton, I., 'Development Potential of the Regions of Spain in the Employed EC,' *LSE*, December 1988, pp. 10-11.
23. For example, Balestrieri, M., op. cit., 1983, p. 142.
24. 'Structure des salaires dans 8 pays de la Communauté européenne,' *Centre d'Etudes des Revenus et des Coûts (CERC)*, Chapter III, November 1988, p. 6.
25. Marwick, P., '1992: Getting Ready,' *EC Report*, KPMG, 1988, p. 67.
26. *I.F.O. (Institute for Economic Research)*, op. cit., November 1988, p. 28.
27. 'The differential effects of the adhesion of the European Community on industry in the regions of Spain and Portugal,' *Société internationale pour le Développement (SID)*, November 1987, p. 30.
28. Katseli, L. et al. 'Structural Adjustments of the Greek Economy,' *(CEPR)*, London, 16-17 March 1989.
29. Dunning, J., *International Production and Multinational Enterprises*, Allen & Unwin, 1981.
30. Fishwick, P., *Multinational Companies and Economic Concentration in Europe*, Gower, Aldershot, 1982.
31. Dokopoulou, E. and Hamilton, I., op. cit., December 1988, p. 15
32. Dokopoulou, E. and Hamilton, I., 'Multinationals and Manufactured Exports from an Enlarged EEC Periphery; The Case of Greece', *Industrialisation in Developing and Peripheral Regions*, Croom-Helm, London, 1986, pp. 205-231.
33. *SID*, op. cit., November 1987, p. 32.
34. Source: Instituto Nacional de Estadistica, 1986.
35. *SID.*, op. cit., 1987, p. 45.
36. 'Effects of the Internal Market in Greece, Ireland, Portugal and Spain,' Final report of a study by Booz-Allen and Hamilton for the Commission of the European Communities, DG III, appendices, p. 157, 17 July 1989.
37. Booz-Allen and Hamilton, op. cit., appendices, p. 160, July 1989.
38. Farinas, J. and Martin, C., 'Déterminantes del comercio intraindustrial en Espana, in 'Velarde, J. et al., *El sector exterior de la Economia Espanola*, 1988.
39. *SID*, op. cit., 1987, p. 72.
40. Booz-Allen, op. cit., July 1989, p. 52 of the final report.
41. Scott, A., 'Semiconductor Industry in South-East Asia: organisation, Location and the International Division of Labour,' *Regional Studies*, 1987, pp. 143-60.
42. Dokopoulou, E. and Hamilton, I., op. cit., 1988, pp. 76 and 85.
43 *SID*, op. cit., 1987.
44. Cambridge Economic Consultants, 'The Regional Impact of Policies Implemented in the Context of Completing the Community's Internal Market by 1992', 1987.
45. Politique réalisée de manière coordonnée par le fonds européen du développement régional (FEDER), le Fonds social européen (FSE), le Feoga-orientation, La Banque européenne d'investissement (BEI).
46. See guidance note relating to interventions in underdeveloped regions (objective no. 1) and in regions of industrial decline (objective no. 2), DB XVI/A.2, CEC; document approved by the Commission at its meeting of 15 February 1989.
47. Guidance note, CEC, op. cit., 1989, p. 8.
48. Dokopoulou , E, and Hamilton, I., op. cit., 1988, p. 238.
49. Booz-Allen and Hamilton, appendices, op. cit., July 1989, p. 174.
50. Katseli, L. et al., op. cit., 1989.

51. Article 115 of the Treaty of Rome permits the Commission to authorize a member state to ban and monitor products imported from non-member states and circulating within the Community when that member state places restrictions on direct imports of those products and can provide detailed proof of the difficulties caused by the additional imports.
52. Agreement under the terms of which the EEC has negotiated bilateral agreements with several exporting countries on restricting the import of textiles and clothing by both category and 'region' (member state).
53. Booz-Allen and Hamilton, final report, op. cit., 1989, p. 49.
54. *SID*, op. cit., 1987.

3. European Economic Integration from the Standpoint of Spanish Labour Market Problems

José Luis Malo de Molina and Pilar García Perea

1. Introduction

This chapter analyzes the potential risks of the development of the single market for countries with low wage and productivity levels and high unemployment, and offers some proposals relating to economic policy and the development of the future European wage structure. To this end the prospect of European economic integration is analyzed from the standpoint of Spanish labour market problems.

With regard to unemployment and productivity, the Spanish economy, among Community countries facing European economic integration, is in a position of comparative disadvantage vis-à-vis central European countries. Accordingly, the success of Community-wide integration requires the attainment of two objectives which have not proved readily compatible in the past. First, to reduce the productivity differential and in turn absorb accumulated unemployment, growth rates higher than average Community levels must be sustained on a lasting basis. Second, however, a reasonable degree of Community-wide economic policy convergence must concurrently be attained in order to obtain similar levels of stability and equilibrium.

The comparative advantages arising from the position of Spanish wages within the European wage structure are fundamental to attaining these dual objectives. Countries such as Ireland, Greece and Portugal, which have a low level of productivity, should also try to take advantage from their position in the European wage structure.

The loss of competitiveness that may ensue from unfavourable wage trends, which might result from some of the very mechanisms associated with European integration, could severely and adversely affect not only the Spanish economy but also all those countries which face a similar situation.

Given the high degree of international capital mobility which the development of Single Market projects will facilitate, exchange rate stability – as required by integration – greatly restricts the possibility of implementing economic policies that diverge from those of other member states and especially those member states that wield greater influence on monetary and exchange-rate mechanisms. In this respect, although integration offers new incentives for maintaining stability, it undoubtedly also entails a substantial reduction in the degree of freedom that national economic authorities enjoy, giving rise to adverse consequences for economic policy formulation.

In order to address these matters, this chapter is structured as follows: the next two sections diagnose the problem of unemployment in the Spanish economy and the employment policy pursued over recent years. Section 4 sets forth the conditioning factors of the Spanish economy at the outset of European integration, notably the high level of unemployment, the technology gap and relative inflationary tendencies. In-depth analysis is made in Section 5 of the factors favouring the Spanish economy and offsetting the disadvantageous conditioning factors – namely: the wage advantage (above all else), capital import capacity and high growth potential. Section 6 assesses the foreseeable impact of integration on the balance of favourable and unfavourable factors and, lastly, Section 7 considers some of the potential implications of employment harmonization projects within the purview of the factors discussed in this chapter.

2. Diagnosis of Unemployment in Spain

The principal constraint on the Spanish economy is the high level of unemployment. Despite rates of growth exceeding 5% in the last three years, unemployment has remained at 17.3% – by far the highest rate among OECD countries. This is why a description of the imbalance of the Spanish labour market should be our starting point.

A thorough diagnosis of unemployment would require in-depth and inevitably controversial analysis of its causes, which would be beyond the scope of this article. Accordingly, this section aims merely to summarize its principal features and to establish the appropriate context for subsequent discussion. Certain issues that are open to debate are summarized here, without subjecting each one to detailed analysis. These have been the subject of a relatively extensive literature.[1]

The gravity of Spain's unemployment cannot be denied, even though there are serious obstacles which prevent its accurate measurement. Traditional labour force and production classifications are ill-adapted to an employment market which has been affected by major changes, which have frequently eroded the stability of industrial relations. However, although there are no reliable figures, everything would indicate that the 'black' economy (the extent of which is unquestionable) does not substantially modify mass unemployment, which in Spain is almost twice the European average.

Various factors have brought this situation about. However, the basis for the particular behaviour of unemployment in Spain lies principally in the exceptional erosion of the demand for labour in the private sector of the economy between 1974 and 1984. Admittedly, demographic trends have played a more unfavourable role in Spain than in other European countries, owing principally to the effects of a delayed baby-boom[2] and to a sharp turnabout in the large labour migration flows. It is also true that the economic crisis discouraged many potential workers from joining the labour market, leading to a sharp fall in the participation rate, offset by the increase in the employable population. If we consider the 20 year period ending in 1985 (when the employment level bottomed out), the population of working age increased by 25% whereas the participation rate fell by 11%. Thus the fall in the participation rate is a key factor in explaining an increase in unemployment of only 2.7 million, despite an increase in the working age population of 5.7 million and a fall in employment of 1.2 million. The foregoing figures clearly demonstrate the weight of demand factors among the causes of high unemployment in Spain.

One of the most controversial issues behind the collapse of labour demand, and one of the most important when designing employment policies, is the part played by technological change. Unquestionably, the decrease in labour demand took place against a background of modernization of the Spanish economy and the incorporation of new labour-saving technology. However, this process should be considered neither in isolation from the adverse behaviour of relative prices and the labour market, nor as the principal cause of mass unemployment. Although this is not the appropriate forum for discussing this matter in depth, reference should be made to some of the arguments supporting this opinion.[3]

The various estimates of productivity gains attributable to technological change show a decline after 1975, the very time at which employment problems began to emerge in the Spanish economy. It thus proves difficult to treat technological change as the principal underlying cause of unemployment when the latter surged at a time when demand stagnated and relative labour costs were rising. These events coincided with a reduction, not a rise, in the labour-saving effects attributable to technological improvements.

This argument is consistent with the behaviour of investment, the main vehicle for incorporating technological progress. The emergence of mass unemployment was parallel to the virtual paralysis of the flow of gross capital formation. This would preclude any description of this period as one of exceptional technological innovation.

The main explanation for the unemployment problem lies in the drive to modernize the Spanish economy in the 1960s, which entailed substantial increases in productivity, and then ran into highly adverse final demand and cost conditions in the mid-1970s. This led to a sharp, long-term collapse in the demand for labour, exacerbated by serious shortcomings in the workings of the labour market.

In Spain as in other countries, the employment crisis arose under the influence of the forceful downturn in aggregate demand, yet there are many indicators that the weakness of aggregate demand did not alone explain the erosion of employment. In many countries the output/employment ratio had shown considerable instability since the early 1960s. In Spain, particularly, the stagnation of production was accompanied by strong average productivity gains in the workplace which caused widespread layoffs,[4] thereby signifying that employment cutbacks were greater than those attributable simply to stagnating demand. This effect was less intense in other countries. International comparisons reveal that the effects in countries with largely similar demand problems were nevertheless markedly different: whereas certain countries recorded only a slight decline in the rate of net job creation, others with major wage and labour market problems were affected by a severe reduction in jobs.[5]

Above and beyond these considerations, however, the slackening of demand was clearly linked to economic stabilization policies which sought to tackle the serious price imbalances prevailing: the public deficit, falling individual savings and the balance-of-payments deficit. In this respect, the weakening of demand was partly a reflection of a reduction of the rate of sustainable stable growth, given the aggregate supply conditions and the working of the labour market. Indeed, this was the main message to be deduced from the estimates of the non-accelerating-inflation rate of unemployment (NAIRU) in the Spanish economy during the period of employment reduction.[6]

Based on these estimates, during the first phase of the oil crisis (1973-79), observed unemployment was clearly below the rate of unemployment required for stable inflation (i.e. below the NAIRU). However, following the second oil crisis (1979-84, which was the last year addressed by Dolado et al. (1986) the observed rate of unemployment, which had climbed spectacularly, was close to the estimated NAIRU. This indicated major rigidities in aggregate real wages and the consequent difficulty of reducing unemployment by expanding aggregate demand without significantly raising inflation.

Thus, the inadequacies of the Spanish labour market, the long period of economic difficulties caused by the oil crisis, and the far-reaching institutional reforms introduced during the political transition, all contributed significantly to major imbalance. The limited adaptability of the labour market was highlighted by several main factors. The first was excessive wage rises during most of the seventies; and the second was adverse wage-structure trends, which entailed a greater burden on production costs in labour-intensive and demand-sensitive industries. Finally, workforce-reduction costs and excessively rigid hiring methods during the main part of the crisis, although initially delaying employment cutbacks, ultimately made it more far-reaching and costly by amplifying the effect of the crisis on corporate profitability and causing, in certain cases, closures and a fall in productive capacity.[7]

In these circumstances, the unfavourable performance of relative prices and the diminished adaptability of the labour market had lasting effects on gross capital formation and led to a shortage of potentially profitable productive capacity. Therefore, the high level of unemployment could not be viewed as a short-term problem of cyclical imbalance; rather, it was caused by imbalances between industrial investment, aggregate labour demand and the increase in the potential workforce. It was, then, a long-term problem which affected the course of growth. Of interest in this connection are the results of the econometric model of the labour market carried out by the Planning Department of the Spanish Ministry of Economy and Finance. These results confirm the significance of the shortage of productive capacity as a cause of the erosion of employment in the Spanish economy.[8]

3. Spanish Employment Policy

Using a similar diagnosis to that outlined above, Spanish employment policy was based on a mid-term strategy to contain the basic imbalances, underpinned by disciplined, consistent financial policies and by the abolition of wage indexation mechanisms. Recovery of employment would be the outcome of industrial rationalization, an increase in forecast returns on investment, labour cost (wage and non-wage) moderation and the introduction of institutional reforms in the labour market to improve flexibility. However, the implementation of this policy, outlined after the Moncloa pacts in 1977, was not consistent until 1982 when a majority government gained sufficient freedom of manoeuvre to articulate the interests of the different social actors and abandon the policy of protecting ailing industries and postponing manpower reductions.

The design of employment policies required for integration into the European Economic Community (EEC) should take account of the results of the restructuring and adjustment policies pursued over recent years. Hence, a schematic outline for evaluating this strategy must be formulated. This strategic approach, which has demanded considerable costs and effort, has nevertheless brought about satisfactory results with regard to price stability and the recovery of profitability and investment, enabling the attainment of rapid growth to be.

Figure 1 depicts some of the most significant indicators in this major change. Output growth rose from a cumulative rate of 1.2% in the period 1979-84 to 4% in the period 1984-89, reaching an annual rate of 5% for the last three years. Gross capital formation, which underwent a cumulative fall of 2.8% per year between, grew at an average rate of 13% in the second five-year period. As a result, in the last three years alone, investment grew by 53% in real terms. In turn, the inflation rate, at an average rate of 13.6% in the 1979-84 period, was reduced to 6.5% in the period 1984-89.

The most outstanding results were in the area of employment, reflecting the priorities formally established when this economic policy was designed.

Figure 2 plots the changes in employment for different sectors of the Spanish economy over the two periods. Between 1977 and 1984 – when net job losses were predominant – total employment in the economy fell by 1.8 million; whereas between the second quarter of 1985 – which marked the reversal of this trend – and the fourth quarter of 1989, the net increase in jobs was 1.6 million. This reversal is all the more striking if we exclude agriculture, where an excessive amount of the working population is retained and which, logically, has been reducing its level of employment.

Figure 1. Indicators of changes in the Spanish economy.

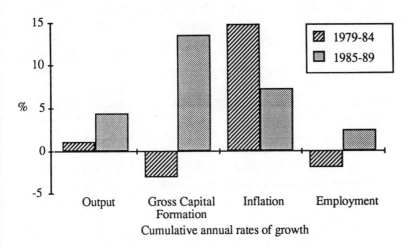

Cumulative annual rates of growth

Figure 2. Changes in employment 1977-1989.

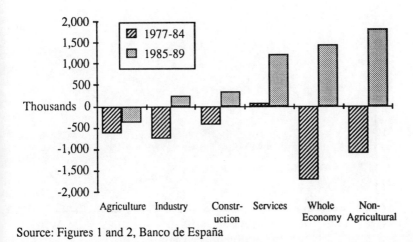

Source: Figures 1 and 2, Banco de España

Net job creation in the non-agricultural sector totalled 2.6 million over this last period, which significantly outpaced the net reduction of 1.1 million recorded over the previous seven years. This aggregate performance was the result of different trends in different sectors. Large scale employment cuts in industry (0.8 million jobs in the first period analyzed) gave way to moderate employment growth, whereas in construction the recovery was more pronounced. The services sector witnessed the beginnings of a major employment expansion, and 1.4 million net jobs were created in the second period. The foregoing comments refer exclusively to overall employment data; however, if detailed analysis is made by occupational category, the difference between trends is more stark, since recovery was much stronger in the wage-earners, where employment cutbacks had initially made most impact.

Nevertheless, despite the employment recovery in the latter period, the degree of accumulated imbalance was so great that the outlook appears uncertain. Recent experience clearly illustrates the nature of these difficulties. Employment growth in recent years, at rates that cannot be projected to the near future, has been accompanied by a notable recovery in participation rates. This has confirmed the scale of the discouragement engendered during the crisis (see Figure 3), and the resulting reduction in the unemployment rate from its peak has been a modest 4.9%, after more than three years of buoyant job creation.[9]

Figure 3. Changes in the participation rate.

Spanish Economy

Source: Banco de España

With the previous information as a starting point, one can expect that completion of the process of the Spanish economy's integration into Europe will impose severe demands on employment policy. Forecast demographic growth for the coming decade, combined with the upswing in the participation rate (which should be accompanied by improved labour market conditions) require high, sustained employment growth. This is needed in order to absorb both the accumulated and the discouraged unemployment, which resulted from the fall in the participation rates ensuing from the crisis. Estimates for potential labour supply are uncertain since, although demographic projections are relatively well-defined for the next ten years,[10] estimates for the participation rate are subject to much uncertainty in view of their strong dependence on the economic cycle. There is extensive empirical evidence of the cyclical component of the participation rate but, regrettably, there are no reliable quantitative estimates of its scale. However, the extent of the problem may be illustrated by the many examples given in the final report of the Experts Commission on Unemployment, which are summarized in Table 1.

Table 1. Estimates of job creation requirements up to the year 2000.

	Assumption for the year 2000		Job creation requirement		
	Rate of activity %	Rate of unemployment %	Total (000) %	Annual average %	Annual rate of growth %
1	52	20	1,601	119	1.0
2	52	10	3,058	227	1.9
3	52	5	4,099	304	2.3
4	54	5	4,641	344	2.5

Source data: 1987; activity rate 50.0%; unemployment rate 20.0%.
Source: Experts' Commission on Unemployment (1988).

It may be deduced from the examples in Table 1 that the virtual elimination of unemployment by the end of the century (i.e. a rate of 5% that may be considered as equivalent to the former concept of frictional unemployment), and restoration of the rate of participation prevailing prior to the crisis (between 52% and 54%), will require the net creation of 4.5 million jobs, signifying an annual average of more than 300,000 jobs. The true extent of the challenge implied is shown by the fact that employment would need to grow as dynamically over the next 12 years as it has recently, when demand and cost conditions have been exceptionally favourable.

4. The Constraints on Integration of the Spanish Economy into the EEC

At the start of the 1980s the prospect of the Spanish and Portuguese economies being incorporated into the EEC was viewed by most observers with justified concern and uncertainty, owing to the seriousness of the economic crisis and the lack of flexibility and adaptability of the economies of both countries. The effectiveness of the adjustment policies pursued, and a favourable international climate have ensured the relative success of the first phase of the timetable for gradual integration envisaged in the Treaty of Accession.

As previously stated, the Spanish economy has expanded strongly in recent years, followed closely by the Portuguese economy. Both have recorded consistently higher rates of growth than other EEC member states. Spanish economic recovery, initiated in mid-1985, has mainly been impelled by a strong investment drive, instrumental to which was the challenge posed by EEC entry and the resulting increased competitiveness. Gross capital formation, at barely 19% of GDP at the outset of the recovery, has been growing at about 14% over the last three years up to a level close to 25% of GDP. The latter figure is similar to that recorded in most past phases of major growth, and is notably higher than that in other Community economies, except Portugal, which (as in Spain since 1986) has also experienced fast investment-led growth.

As concerns gross capital formation, investment in machinery and capital goods increased, over the same period, from 7% of GDP at the outset to 9.5% in 1989. In short, the Spanish economy has made a forceful investment drive which will facilitate its adaptation to full EEC integration.

This investment process, however, is not taking place against a background free of serious imbalances. The dramatic advance of capital formation has not been accompanied by an increase in national savings, and the Spanish economy has come up against a net borrowing requirement which has taken the form of a rapid deterioration in the balance of payments current account, the balance of which has dropped from a surplus (1.5% of GDP) in 1985 to a deficit of 3.2% (in the same terms) in 1990.

Under these conditions, the fulfilment of the commitments undertaken on accession to the Community and of the new European integration plans presents new challenges that may be summarized as follows:

1. In view of Spanish labour market developments since the 1970s, the low participation rate recorded and demographic forecasts, European integration will be constrained by the need to absorb a level of unemployment higher than that in other European countries. This will affect the relationship between the labour market in Spain and that in Europe, and will restrict the design of domestic economic policies.

2. Despite profound industrial restructuring which accompanied the crisis and subsequent years of sluggish development, the industrial sector has imbalances and shortcomings which make it vulnerable to the increase in foreign competition. Notable among these are a sizeable technology gap (compared with the mainstream EEC and future Single Market economies), comparatively low levels of productivity and a marked dependence on capital goods imports. Although international productivity comparisons are the subject of debate as to methodology, output per employee (measured in terms of purchasing power parity as depicted in Figure 4) gives an idea of the problem. According to these data, the Spanish economy is at approximately 80% of the average Community level and there is no clear tendency for it to bridge the gap. This productivity gap is particularly wide in the case of Greece and Portugal.

3. The Spanish economy has substantially reduced inflation. This has enabled the rates prevailing in the early 1980s to be halved. However, the rigidity and restrictive parameters of certain markets, the inadequate development of competition in others, and the remains of heavy state intervention have fostered persistent inflationary tendencies which hamper the sustaining of long-term, high growth rates. In recent years, the increase in the current-account balance of payments deficit (as yet readily manageable in terms of financing) has acted as a safety valve, enabling a high level of demand – increasingly oriented towards investment – to be created, without exerting excessive pressure on prices. However, these trends are not sustainable; accordingly,

the gap between national demand and national output which has widened as expansion has advanced, will give rise to inflationary tensions and the worsening of the already high deficit on the current-account.

Figure 4. Productivity levels. (EUR 12 = 100)

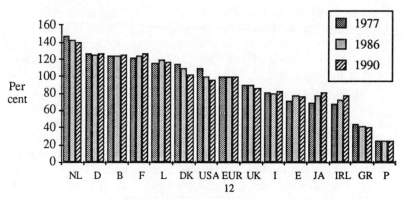

Per cent

GDP at market prices per person employed at
1980 prices and exchange rates (Ecu)

Source: Eurostat

The problems posed by European integration of the Spanish economy are shared by the less developed countries of the Community, such as Greece, Ireland and Portugal. In all these countries it has been necessary to undertake adjustment policies aimed at reducing the basic imbalances – mainly inflation and the budget deficit. Except in the case of Greece (in which poor results have been achieved with regard to European integration), the rest of the countries have been fairly successful. The adjustment policies adopted by Spain and Portugal have enabled higher growth than among the other European countries.

Thus, the challenge of European integration for an economy such as Spain's involves the simultaneous reduction of the productivity gap and absorption of accumulated unemployment. Both objectives, which are not wholly compatible, may only be achieved by sustained rapid growth over a long period of time. This challenge is also confronted by the less developed countries of the Community. The economic policy implications of maintaining a long-term, advantageous growth differential, in relation to the Community as a whole, are unquestionably numerous and demanding. This is especially so if we consider that these countries, even with the progress they have achieved, suffer basic imbalances such as current account deficits, inflationary tendencies and budgetary deficits. All of these imply a serious handicap.

5. Factors Favouring the Relative Position of the Spanish Economy

The high level of unemployment, the technology gap evident in the industrial structure and the problems of inflation shared by the less developed countries of the EEC, reduce their ability to address the challenges of integration. In Spain, however, these relative disadvantages – as compared with average Community levels – are offset by several factors which favour Spain's position. These are: the greater growth potential of the Spanish economy and therefore the better investment and expansion opportunities for domestic markets, the comparative advantage in terms of lower relative labour costs and as a result, the strong capacity to attract foreign capital. These compensatory factors have meant that the first phase of integration has been successful for the Spanish economy, especially as compared with the other less developed countries of the Community.

The Spanish economy has succeeded because it has been able to take greater advantage of its strengths than other countries. Spain's severe adjustment policies have brought greater control over the budget deficit and inflation. This, together with the great productivity increases obtained, has helped control unit labour costs. Comparing the Spanish situation with that of Greece and Portugal reveals that, although Spain experienced faster wage growth, the relative level of unit labour costs remains favourable because of the dynamism of Spanish productivity.

The discrepancy between wages and unit labour costs in Greece and Portugal is manifest in their very low productivity levels, as can be seen in Figure 4. This heralds adjustment problems in the labour markets of these countries, similar to those endured by the Spanish economy in earlier years.

In principle, the construction of the Single Market offers the opportunity for the less developed areas of the Community (where the scope for productivity growth is greater and wages are comparatively lower) to step up foreign investment inflows. This would alleviate the shortage of domestic savings in relation to investment opportunities and would help finance necessary imports of capital goods. Both issues are of critical importance for taking advantage of the opportunities for growth and catching up with the economies of more advanced member countries.

The balance between favourable and unfavourable factors may be affected by integration projects. To assess potential developments here, brief reference should be made to the role of foreign investment, in relation to the wage advantage offered by the Spanish economy.

After a surplus in its foreign trade for each of the four years between 1984 and 1987, the Spanish economy's current-account showed a deficit of US$ 3,110 million (1% of GDP) in 1988, and the deficit remained at 3.2% of GDP in the following two years. Hitherto, the intensity of capital inflows, which pushed the peseta firmly upwards (compounding the difficulty of implementing economic policy), made the financing of these deficits relatively easy. Indeed, foreign currency reserves have continued to rise faster than is desirable. However, the scale of the estimated deficits casts doubt on the Spanish economy's future capacity to attract enough funds to finance them, given an increasingly liberalized climate for the free movements of capital.

The factors underpinning the size and stability of these capital flows (namely, the greater growth potential of the Spanish economy and the comparative advantage in terms of lower relative labour cost) are of strategic importance for the maintenance of a growth rate above that in the rest of the Community. These factors, together with stable inflation and external balance, consequently enable both unemployment and the technology gap to be reduced.

As can be seen in Figure 5, there has been a sustained increase in foreign investment in Spain since the mid-1970s. As Figure 6 reflects, such investment has become the chief cause for the heavy basic balance of payments (current account plus long-term capital) deficits of recent years. This process has increased drastically since 1986, coinciding with two distinct factors which had highly diverse consequences: Spain's accession to the EEC, and the outset of a period of very high interest rates. Both factors have boosted capital inflows into Spain. Presumably, however, the specific investments induced by each factor have widely differing degrees of permanence. For deficit financing, a distinction must be drawn between capital inflows which result from the investment and growing-market opportunities offered by the Spanish economy – for which high stability may be presumed – and those arising from the high interest rates that have accompanied taxation and monetary policy. In principle, these capital inflows appear more responsive to domestic stability and the credibility of economic policy, and may therefore be more vulnerable to downturns.

Figure 5. Foreign investment in Spain. (billions of US$)

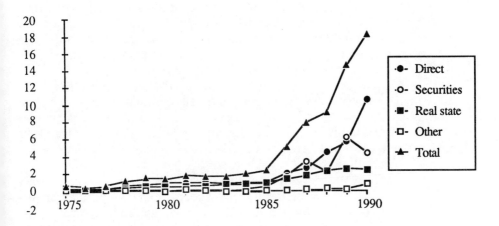

Figure 6. Basic balance. (thousand million US$)

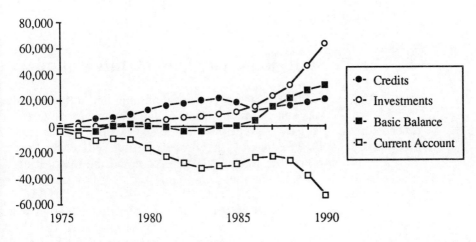

Source: Figures 5 and 6, Banco de España

113

Although studies using highly detailed information (e.g. pinpointing different types of investment, countries of origin, recipient industries, etc.) reflect the recent existence of relatively sizable, speculative capital movements, they also suggest the pre-eminence of structural factors principally associated with investment opportunities brought about by EEC entry.

Historically, the relatively low level of labour cost was one of the most significant variables explaining Spain's capacity to attract foreign capital. This advantage subsided appreciably during the period of wage inflation, but it re-emerged strongly after 1980, once wage moderation prevailed anew and after major reforms in the workings of the labour market had occurred (see Figures 7 and 8). Exchange-rate-adjusted (between Spain and the EEC and industrialized countries as a whole) relative industrial labour costs have once more tended moderately downwards in recent years (see Figure 9). It should be remembered, however, that cost advantages become more marked when markets are liberalized and the peseta belongs to the ERM.

A favourable movement in the unit labour costs is not the only requirement to attract foreign investment. Other important factors include: labour force qualifications, raw materials costs, energy costs, the infrastructure endowment and the technological level. Special effort should be made to improve labour force qualifications in those countries which face a comparative disadvantage. The progress recorded in this field, thus increasing productivity, creates a margin for the growth of real wages compatible with the employment growth.

6. The Possible Repercussions of Integration

Having described the balance between favourable and unfavourable factors which has seen the completion of the first phase of Spain's accession to the EEC, attention now turns to how the Spanish economy may be affected by the processes that will ensue from European integration. From Spain's point of view, the main effects of the process of integration may be summarized as follows:

1. The anticipated increase in competition in the Single Market will be compounded in Spain by the gradual elimination of tariffs pursuant to the Accession Treaty. The lowering of tariff barriers is well under way, but there remains a significant amount of protection that must be dismantled gradually. To date, progress

in this area includes major improvements in the effective allocation of resources and greater price and wage-setting discipline. As on previous occasions, the stimulus of economic liberalization has been invigorating and the industrial structure has responded more strongly than was expected, although imports have grown very rapidly and the current-account deficit has deteriorated abruptly. Thus, the completion of the schedule for tariff reductions and the simultaneous implementation of liberalization projects throughout Europe reinforce the importance of the factors underpinning the competitiveness of Spanish industry which are the wage advantage, in particular, and the ability to attract foreign investment. Harnessed by the EMS exchange-rate mechanism, the incentives for competition are greater, but the defence of comparative advantages becomes more difficult. Exchange-rate policy cannot be looked to for help; enhanced competitiveness depends more substantially on productivity and price-setting in the factor markets. These changes prove particularly difficult for countries without a long tradition of free market competition and with severe rigidities in their labour markets.

Figure 7. Changes in real unit labour costs. (1960=100)

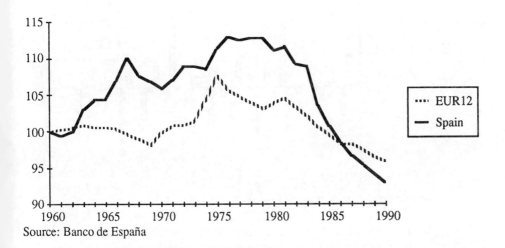

Source: Banco de España

2. The increase in capital mobility which will arise pursuant to the implementation of the Single European Act will bolster the relative attractiveness of investment opportunities in Spain and, accordingly, it is to be expected that the country's ability to attract stable or permanent capital will become greater. In turn, this would offset the adverse effect of increased competition on the current account. However, this will depend increasingly – and crucially – on maintaining a favourable labour cost ratio and economic stability. The commitment to exchange-rate stability (a condition of the peseta's inclusion in the EMS) and to progress in the field of monetary union, entails a fall in the strong risk premium that has traditionally characterized investment in Spanish assets, and which will promote the in-flow of capital. Parallel to this, however, the abolishing of capital controls and the rapid development of new international financial instruments tend to eradicate the boundaries between permanent investments and other types of capital flows, thereby greatly increasing the volatility of capital movements as a whole.

Figure 8. Real unit labour costs. (compound annual rates of growth)

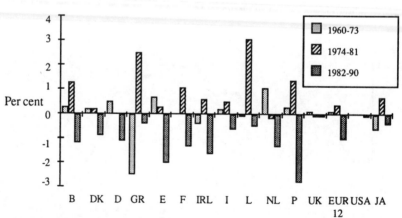

Source: Eurostat and Banco de España

3. In relation to labour mobility, although there are many barriers to a substantial increase in international labour flows, once the transition periods envisaged in this area elapse, and the measures envisaged under the Single Act are applied, the Spanish economy

can be expected to step up the export of medium and low-skilled labour and the import of high-qualified labour. These movements will tend to benefit both the labour market and corporate modernization.

Figure 9. Relative labour cost.

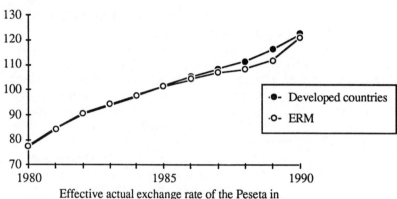

Effective actual exchange rate of the Peseta in
relation to developed and ERM countries (using
unit labour costs as relative prices)

Source: Banco de España

4. The growing interdependence of the Single Market and the advance towards monetary union reduces the margin for diversity of economic policy among the mainstream EMS countries. For countries with higher levels of inflation, the erosion of sovereignty in the management of domestic economic policy entails the greater cost of foregone potential growth and of unemployment in order to restore macroeconomic equilibrium.

Progress towards European integration highlights the significance of those factors that have been supporting the economic equilibrium of recent years. If, over the coming years, the same conditions continue which have enabled the wage advantage to be retained and reasonable levels of internal stability and balance of payment results to be achieved, it is to be expected that Spain will take full advantage of the opportunities offered by the Single Market. However, if such conditions are adversely altered, the outcome may be very bad. It is instructive to study both alternative courses of events in depth (see Oliver Blanchard and Samuel Bentolila 1989).[11]

6.1 The Optimistic Scenario

It is assumed that stable growth above the Community average can be sustained and that the current imbalances (inflation and foreign deficit) can be kept within controllable limits. This will require a pattern of export-driven, job-generating growth.

Wage moderation and flexibility – with rises pegged to labour productivity – will be vital to Spain's ability to meet these requirements. In the course of events which would allow these requirements to be met, economic growth may be accompanied by a large number of new jobs and the gradual reduction of unemployment. This would be of unquestionable benefit for the labour market. Increased demand for jobs will promote labour mobility, which will particularly benefit the most depressed regions. Greater mobility will ease the way for greater wage differentiation in line with labour productivity increases. Accordingly, it will be possible to introduce progressively higher levels of technological development, gaining gradual access to leading-edge technology without exacerbating the imbalances of the economy. However, this would require improvements in vocational training and more highly qualified labour.

Healthy growth, with moderate labour costs, will promote foreign investment and the introduction of new technology, enable Spain to finance borrowing and ensure a growth rate above that in the most developed EEC countries.

6.2 The Pessimistic Scenario

If the economy's basic imbalances (inflation and the foreign deficit) are not controlled, a new phase of long-term deep recession will ensue.

Persistent excessive consumer demand will tend to exert greater pressure on prices, and it will prove very difficult to sustain wage moderation, especially in view of the high popularity of wage-indexing mechanisms in Spanish industrial relations.

Demand pressure will be accompanied by wage growth and a climate of social confrontation, triggering an inflationary spiral. Price increases will reduce competitiveness and will worsen the trade balance, discourage capital inflows and, consequently, slow investment and the bridging of the technology gap.

To avoid these adverse effects, it will be necessary to adopt a restrictive economic policy geared to eliminating the pressure of demand. This option may prove more costly within the confines of the EMS whose adjustment mechanisms, although exerting tighter control on inflation, cannot prevent a recession in the face of an upsurge of inflation.

If the foregoing situation should prevail in 1992, the results of European integration will be a step in the wrong direction as the Spanish economy will gradually lose its comparative advantage, i.e. moderate labour costs. The simultaneous impact of heightened competition and an increase in nominal labour costs and in prices will tend to drive out those industries with productivity levels below those of other EEC countries. Under these circumstances unemployment will rise again and foreign investment flows will rapidly dry up. This will increase problems of financing the foreign-deficit and will rule out the possibility of compliance with the exchange-rate stability commitments undertaken.

7. Certain Implications of Labour Harmonization Projects

One of the most debated issues in the European integration project is the scope of the European 'social space.' The ultimate aim of a united Europe is to attain a high, uniform degree of social well-being in all EEC member states. From this perspective, the construction of a European social space is presented as a proposal to reach these goals through a series of commitments and actions that lead to increasing harmonization with regard to employee welfare and social benefits.

However, institutional uniformity and the harmonization of working conditions, applied to countries with widely differing degrees of modernization against a background of virtually full market integration, may cause severe imbalances that harm countries with lower levels of technology and capital stock.

In a situation of full labour and capital mobility and high-level competition, one of the few means at the disposal of less-developed member states to maintain their comparative advantage while the technology gap is being reduced is to retain sufficient flexibility in their labour markets so that labour costs move in unison with productivity and allow the disadvantage arising from the lower technological level to be offset.

If this adjustment mechanism is obstructed through the imposition of a policy of nominal wage uniformity, industries with low levels of productivity will see their unit labour costs rise and will rapidly lose their competitive advantage. Factors of production will gravitate towards more competitive companies, transferring wealth to centres which started from a higher level of development. This will thus accentuate the intra-Community differences and social hardship arising from the forced mobility of labour due to lack of work in the most depressed areas. Pushing this argument to its limit, we would witness the creation of a rich, densely populated Europe in the currently more advanced northern countries, and a discarded Europe under the burden of massive unemployment made up of those groups facing the highest obstacles to entry onto the job market (poorly qualified labour, the young and women) who would have ever fewer chances of finding work. Further, a situation of this nature would tend to increase the level of unemployment at Community level since there would be a bias towards using capital at the expense of labour as the only means of defending comparative advantage.

The repercussions of an excessively rapid move towards wage uniformity and a common institutional framework among the different member states are so serious that rapid moves on this direction are not to be expected. Indeed, there is a generally accepted consensus across the Community as to the need for the integration not to rely excessively on attempts to harmonize the different labour institutions. This does not imply that we should not seek progressive wages harmonization, especially in those countries with great potential growth in productivity, but the harmonization process must be compatible with moderate unit labour costs. Both aims can be pursued because the potential growth of productivity in the less developed countries is much higher than in those countries which are technologically more advanced.

As indicated by Begg and Wyplosz,[12] the immediate effects of the development of the Single Market should, given the trade union structure at the outset, be a fall in the degree of centralized wage bargaining at European level owing to the increase in the size of the market and the degree of competitiveness. In these circumstances, it is in unions' interest to pursue a strategy of extending the wage gains and benefits from countries with high wage levels and social welfare benefits to the rest of the Community. However, it would be unreasonable that projects for harmonization of employment conditions should prevent the necessary differentiation among the institutional frameworks for preserving the degree of flexibility desirable in the European wage structure.

Notes

1. An adequate summary of the various approaches can be found in Paper 26 of *Papeles de Economía Española (Papers on the Spanish Economy)*, which deals monographically with the subject of unemployment in Spain. The work of Dolado, J.J., 'Valoración crítica de las estimaciones econométricas disponibles de la relación entre los precios relativos y el empleo' ('Critical evaluation of available econometric estimates of the relationship between relative prices and employment'); and of Viñals, J., 'La importancia de la evolución agregada del coste salarial real en el comportamiento del empleo en España' ('The significance of aggregate changes in real wage costs for employment behaviour in Spain') – commissioned by the Experts' Commission on Unemployment – also provide an overview of the various explanations and causes of unemployment.

2. As stated by Agüero, I. and Olano, A. in *Oferta de trabajo de jóvenes: aspectos demográficos y económicos (Labour Supply among the Young: Demographic and Economic Aspects)*; 'En España hay ahora más jóvenes que nunca' ('Today the Young Are More Numerous than Ever Before'), *Economía y Sociología del trabajo (Labour Economics and Sociology)*, No. 1/2, December 1988.

3. The basis of an opinion, contrary to that subscribed to in this article, on the importance of technical progress in explaining the fall in the demand for labour, can be found in: Jaumandreu, J., 'Produción, empleo, cambio técnico y costes relativos en la industria española, 1964-85' ('Output, Employment, Technical Change and Relative Costs in Spanish Industry, 1964-85'), *Investigaciones Económicas (Economic Research)*, 1987; Rodríguez Romero, L.: 'Elasticidad de sustitución entre inputs primarios en las grandes empresas industriales españolas' ('Elasticity of Substitution among Primary Inputs in Large Spanish Industrial Companies'), *Investigaciones Económicas (Economic Research)*, 1987, and: Segura, J. and Restoy, F., 'Una explotación de las tablas Input-Output de la economía española para 1975 y 1980' ('Putting the Spanish Economy Input-Output Tables for 1975 and 1980 to Use'), *Fundación Empresa Pública (Public Sector Foundation)*, 1986.

4. This argument was voiced for the first time in Rojo, L.A.: 'Desempleo y factores reales' ('Unemployment and Real Factors'), *Papeles de Economía Española no. 6 (Papers on Spanish Economy)*. Pilar García Perea's doctoral thesis, 'Análisis desagregado de la productividad del ttrabajo y de los costes laborales en la industria española 1964-1984' ('Disaggregated Analysis of Labour Productivity and Labour Costs in Spanish Industry: 1964-1984'), furnishes ample empirical evidence of this factor.

5. Among the many studies addressing this approach are: Coe, D.T., 'Nominal Wages: The Nairu and Wage Flexibility,' *OECD Economic Studies*, 1985; Coe, D.T. and Gagliardi, F. 'Nominal Wage Determination in Ten OECD Economies,' *OECD Working Papers*, 1985; Klan, F. and Mittelstadt, A., 'Labour Market Flexibility and External Price Shock,' *OECD Working Papers*, 1985 and Grubb, D., Jackman, R. and Layard, R., 'Wage Rigidity and Unemployment in OECD Countries,' *European Economic Review*, 1983. The inclusion of Spain in such comparative studies can be found in Dolado, J.J., and Malo de Molina, J.L., 'Desempleo y rigidez del mercado de trabajo en España' ('Unemployment and Labour Market Rigidity in Spain'), *Banco de España, Boletín Económico (Bank of Spain Economic Bulletin)*, 1985.

6. See: Dolado, J. J. and Malo de Molina, J. L., and Zabalza, A., 'El desempleo en el sector industrial español: algunos factores explicativos,' *Bank of Spain Working Paper 8508*. Subsequently published in *Papeles de Economía Española (Papers on the Spanish Economy)*, No. 26 and as 'Spanish Industrial Unemployment: Some Explanatory Factors,' 1986.

7. This latter aspect was highlighted in the FEDEA report on the labour market: Novales, A., Sebastián, C. and Servén, L.: 'El paro en España: características, causas y medidas' (Unemployment in Spain: Characteristics, Causes and Measures), *FEDEA*, 1989.

8. See: Andrés, J. and Molinas, C., 'Una modelización del mercado de trabajo en España' ('A model of the Spanish Labour Market'), *Directorate General of Planning of the Spanish Ministry of Economy and Finance*, 1987; and Andrés, J., Molinas, C., Sebastián, M. and Zabalza, A., 'The Influence of Demand and Capital Constraints on Spanish Unemployment', *Directorate General of Planning of the Spanish Ministry of Economy and Finance*, 1988, and Andrés, J., 'Políticas selectivas de estímulo y medidas específicas para la reducción del paro en España' ('Selective Incentive Policies and Specific Measures for Reducing Unemployment in Spain'), paper prepared for the Experts' Committee on Unemployment, 1988.

9. An analysis of recent trends in economic activity can be found in the work of de Miguel, C., 'La participación femenina en la actividad económica. Estructura y tendencias' ('Women at Work: Structure and Trends') and 'Tendencias de cambio de la población activa' ('Changing Working Population Trends'), part of the Spanish Socialist Worker Party's *Programme 2000*. Documents by the Experts' Committee on Unemployment can also be consulted; see: San Juan, C., 'La población como condicionante de la oferta de trabajo' ('The Population as a Conditioning Factor in the Supply of Labour') and Fernández, F., 'Tasas de actividad con especial referencia ala caso de las mujeres' ('Participation Rates with Special Reference to Women').

10. See, for example, del Hoyo, J. and García Ferrer, A., 'Análisis y predicción de la población española (1910-2000),' ('The Spanish Population: Analysis and Forecast (1910-2000)'). *FEDEA*, 1988.

11. Blanchard, O. and Bentolila, S., 'Spanish Unemployment,' paper presented at the Economic Policy Panel, Fall 1989.

12. Begg, D. and Wyplosz, C., 'Labour Markets and Wage Setting after 1992' mimeo.

4. Wage Structures, Employment Problems and Economic Policy in Europe[1]

Felix R. FitzRoy

1. Introduction: Macro- and Microeconomics of Wages and Employment

The threat of world-wide recession and inflation induced by the Gulf crisis and the latest oil-price shock has overshadowed long-standing concerns. Yet, persistently high unemployment throughout the recent period has remained one of the major economic problems in Europe, and generated equally persistent controversy in macroeconomics on both sides of the Atlantic. Keynesians routinely provide evidence of inadequate aggregate demand, while more classical economists find excessive wages to be the main cause of excess supply in the labour market.

In contrast to much policy and academic discussion, the main thrust of the present chapter is that the macroeconomic framework of aggregate wages and employment is not sufficient for an adequate understanding of current employment problems and the formulation of effective policy measures against inflation and recession. As Blanchard and Summers (1988 p. 182) put it, 'European experience of the 1980s poses a profound challenge to standard Keynesian and Classical theories of economic fluctuations.'

However, there are some important 'stylized facts' about comparative macroeconomic performance which form a useful background and departure point for further, micro economic analysis. Perhaps the most useful is Freeman's (1988) short, insightful comparison of European-American employment performance. Aggregate European employment (as hours-adjusted per cent of labour force) declined drastically, compared with steady growth in the US in the 1970s and 1980s. According to Freeman (1988b p. 296):

> Countries with large increases in real wages...had smaller growth in employment or total hours than countries with small wage increases...There is a parallel inverse relation between employment and productivity growth, with, for example wages and productivity growing slowly and employment rapidly in the United States and Sweden and the converse occurring in Belgium, Spain and in the 1980s the United Kingdom, among others.

Freeman is duly cautious about how to interpret these correlations, in contrast to some macroeconomists. He discusses issues of flexibility and causality which will concern us later, and notes finally (pp. 298-9) that in Europe and the US *per capita GDP grew at the same 1.3 per cent rate. From this perspective Americans worked harder for the same gain in living standards as Europeans.'* But for many Europeans, lower-paid and part-time work to augment family income seemed to be unavailable, while the proportion of long-term unemployment has increased until recently.

With this background we focus in the rest of the chapter on the microeconomics of employment and wages, and in particular on the recent developments in these areas which have overturned many of the traditional text-book notions on which much official doctrine and policy is still based.

The plan of the chapter is to discuss the allocative role of relative wages in response to structural change in Section 2. Since firm- and location-specific investments of various kinds limit the mobility of many workers, adjustment may be slow. In Section 3 we turn to the problem of sharing the firm-specific rents created by specific investments. This leads naturally to the important issues of efficiency wages and profit sharing and their relationship to employment. In Section 4 we review the growing evidence for widespread monopolistic competition in product markets, and the consequences thereof for employment. This leads to issues of industrial policy, and particularly the very different behaviour of large and small firms, and the importance of new entrants for competition and employment. Working time is discussed in Section 5 and conclusions are summarized in the final part, Section 6.

2. Relative Wages and the Allocation of Labour

Aggregate statistics mask the concentration of unemployment among the unskilled, youth, and in declining or depressed industries or areas. The traditional text-book response to 'disequilibrium' or imbalance between demand and supply in labour (and other) markets is that relative prices or wage differentials between occupations, regions or skills should adjust until 'equilibrium' is attained or markets clear. In practice, European unions are strongly committed to 'wage solidarity' or uniform pay for the same job, irrespective of local conditions; and they have also generally attempted to reduce differentials in the interests of equity or a more egalitarian distribution of income. Various other factors discussed below also suggest obstacles to improving allocation through more flexible wages. In the next subsections we first review the evidence on relative wages, and then consider these factors in more detail.

2.1 Wage Differentials, Factor Mobility and Structural Change

Much evidence from several countries on the role of differentials has been summarized in Marsden (1988), and OECD (1985, 1987). Marsden concludes 'that wage differentials are not very responsive to supply and demand pressures'(p. 33). A systematic quantitative study of relative wages and blue-collar employment in 21 West German manufacturing industries has been done by FitzRoy and Funke (1988a). They found that unskilled employment has rapidly declined from 1965 to 1985, both absolutely and relatively, while skill differentials have also decreased in most industries. The relative employment position of the unskilled has also worsened over time, all of which suggests a permanent 'disequilibrium' and a primarily redistributive response of relative wages.

FitzRoy and Funke estimate labour demand for various classifications, but they find a systematic negative response to relative wages, as suggested by theory, only for unskilled female employment. Estimation problems are severe, however, because relative wages only change slowly over time. In other estimates of disaggregate labour demand, the own wage has a significant negative effect (FitzRoy and Funke, 1988b, 1989). For the UK, there is little evidence that rapidly widening differentials or growing inequality of pay has improved allocation or motivation.

125

Burda and Sachs (1987) provide interesting evidence on service sector employment in Germany and the US. Relatively high service wages in Germany have followed manufacturing pay more closely than in the US and appear to have induced a much higher capital intensity and productivity growth, as well as correspondingly slow service employment growth, in Germany as compared to the US. In addition, almost medieval occupational licensing laws and regulations seem to have complemented egalitarian and uniformly high wage structures to help restrict the entry of the low-pay service and secondary sector employers who have created many of the new jobs in the US in recent years.

While vocational training in Germany is the envy of most other countries, craft and trade associations and their unions maintain formidable barriers to entry with guild-like restrictions, which primarily maintain monopoly rents for members by excluding competition under the usual pretext of 'protecting' consumers from 'low-quality' suppliers. Supply of low-cost services, self-employment, consumer choice and entry of new firms are all severely handicapped by this blatant and dysfunctional system of legal monopolies that is a major cause of high unemployment and a relatively low 'quality of life' in a very wealthy country, as Brunowsky (1988) has developed in detail in his excellent book. On the other hand, investment in environmental protection, which is urgently needed to protect consumers, is generally labour intensive and so could also generate much additional employment but is hindered by producers' lobbies and EC wrangling (Porritt 1990).

Technological and structural change and international competition have undoubtedly shifted demand towards more skilled employment in manufacturing and elsewhere; however, innovation and technological change are also in part a function of relative prices, and the rapid growth of unskilled wages has probably stimulated much investment in labour-saving capital equipment. This investment maintains productivity growth which in turn allows only a dwindling labour force to enjoy their higher wages. Many services in Germany and other European countries are not only inordinately expensive but also are in short supply or rationed in classical disequilibrium, with major welfare losses in consequence, both among deprived consumers as well as unemployed, potential workers.

The very low participation rate of women in the German labour force is noteworthy in this connection, and contrasts with extensive and often part-time employment of women in the state-run part of the Swedish service sector, which performs many of the functions of privately supplied services in the US. The costs of state service employment on the Swedish scale would be hard to bear for other countries, so greater wage flexibility, deregulation of the labour market, and consequent expansion of private service employment should be high on the policy agenda in the rest of Europe. Such measures would of course also reduce the inflationary dangers involved in more expansive macropolicy.

2.2 Costs of Mobility

A major question in labour economics remains the slow response of (relative) wages in declining industries and regions, and the immobility of displaced workers. As Blinder (1988 p. 4) asks, 'why don't unemployed steelworkers go to work at McDonalds?' In this and following sections we consider some of the main hypotheses which have been advanced to explain these puzzles.

While regional wage differentials are usually small in nominal terms, major differences in housing costs must be considered to compare realistic real wages. The dramatic increase in house prices in many prosperous areas in recent years has provided windfall gains for existing owners, but also an important deterrent to mobility of workers from depressed areas. Disruption of personal and family relationships add substantial non-pecuniary costs to mobility, while social security and unemployment benefits increase the incentive to delay any move, particularly to lower-paid employment. The rapid growth of occupational differentials and pay-inequality in the UK during the 1980s seems to have done less to reduce official unemployment than the numerous redefinitions that exclude certain categories of individuals and thus lower the published figures.

The simple theory of 'wait-unemployment' as a rational response to loss of highly paid, primary sector jobs has received strong support from Burda (1988). A measure of the level and duration of unemployment benefits has considerable explanatory power in his cross-country estimates of unemployment rates. As usual in quantitative studies, however, causality is difficult to establish. There is also evidence that more generous benefits in some countries represent in part a response to the increasing duration of unemployment spells following OPEC energy-price shocks and recessions. Of course, these supply shocks would have been much less disruptive if Western unions had accepted large scale work sharing or shorter weeks in response, as in Japan, and reduced their wage claims, as in Sweden (FitzRoy 1981).

Sweden also offers major lessons to other countries for encouraging occupational mobility as an alternative to long term unemployment in response to structural change. Extended unemployment benefits in Sweden are typically conditional upon participation in appropriate state-funded retraining schemes and reallocation if required by subsequent job availability. This programme has been extraordinarily successful in a country without substantial reserves of energy or other natural resources, and imitation should become a political priority in the rest of Europe. For, as Layard and Bean (1988) emphasize, the very rapid growth of long term unemployment in most of Europe not only represents destruction of individual human capital, but also fails to restrain wage claims by employed workers because the long term jobless are effectively removed from the labour market and immobilized for the various reasons discussed above.

Layard (1989) argues convincingly that Swedish-type retraining and active labour market policies represent the most promising response to current European problems. In the UK not only retraining but even basic vocational training have been disastrously neglected in recent years, leaving Britain with lower skill levels than most other European countries.

3. Rent Sharing and Collective Bargaining

In this section we turn to recent explanations for the stickiness or unresponsiveness of wages to external pressures of unemployment. However, sticky wages are not the only phenomenon incompatible with traditional competitive models of the labour market. Recent research with individual panel data in the US shows large inter-industry wage differentials for both union and non-union employees, which are correlated with industry concentration, capital intensity, and profitability. Unobserved personal characteristics cannot plausibly explain these results (Krueger and Summers 1988, Dickens and Katz 1987). Related results for the UK are summarized by Blanchflower et al. (1990), and direct evidence on union rent sharing in concentrated industries is in Belman (1988) and Karier (1988).

The importance of rent sharing had long been emphasized in the industrial relations literature, and in the older, institutional tradition of labour economics, though these insights were largely forgotten in the excitement generated by human capital theory. And only recently has sufficiently detailed personal data become available to convincingly refute explanations for observed differentials in terms of unobserved characteristics. Recent research on profit sharing surveyed in Blinder (1990) has not, however, been related to the rent sharing literature, in spite of basic connections (FitzRoy 1990).

3.1 Specific Investment and Rent Sharing

In addition to the mobility costs described above, most employees acquire skills which are specific to their job or their firm. Purely specific knowledge and abilities are lost on moving to a new job, so productivity may decline unless a generally better opportunity or match with a worker's non-specific abilities can be found elsewhere. Clearly, an employee's willingness to invest in specific training, say by accepting initially low pay, depends on expected subsequent rewards. Mobility costs generally increase with age, so seniority benefits in the form of increased earnings and protection against lay-off are widely used incentives for workers to assume the risks of immobilizing themselves by specialization.

Much tangible capital investment is also firm-specific in the sense that resale may involve substantial loss, so it follows that rents from specific assets or (partial) immobility are a general feature of productive organization (FitzRoy and Mueller 1984; Williamson 1985). The necessity of sharing rents, and minimizing the losses which distributive conflict can inflict on all parties, have helped to generate the complex structures of collective bargaining, regulation and codetermination which dominate European labour markets.

Recognition that most wages represent a 'bargain' for sharing the returns or rents from some joint activity or enterprise helps one to understand why wages and wage scales are sticky. Bargaining is costly and conflict or disagreement can be destructive. Wages have a distributive as well as an allocation function, so it is rational to maintain an agreement once accepted until pressures for change become substantial and 'permanent' rather than probably merely transitory. There is also much evidence that strongly held notions of fairness and equity play a major role, inhibiting classical competition and 'clearing' of the labour market (Solow 1990).

Collective bargains have to be enforceable or at least amenable to arbitration by third parties, and this has led to detailed and precisely defined job-classifications and pay scales which also, however, represent serious impediments to flexibility of work organization and allocation in the firm. Structures of codetermination and legal regulations, originally designed to protect workers from arbitrary or unfair treatment, have also delayed the introduction of flexible team work as practiced in Japan, and increasingly required by rapid technological and market change everywhere (Acs and FitzRoy 1989, FitzRoy and Acs 1989).

In the US, non-union firms are pioneering the use of flexible team production, fewer job-classifications and other features of the 'J-firm' (Aoki 1988), with substantial productivity benefits (Kochan et al. 1987). In Europe the famous and successful Volvo plants at Kalmar and Uddevalla, Sweden, are among the few experiments on these lines. A similar organization of work in a small German firm studied by FitzRoy and Kraft (1985) was essentially independent of unions and the formal institutions of codetermination.

3.2 Efficiency Wage Theories

Economists have recently been developing the old idea that employees are concerned with equity, or the perceived fairness, of pay-scales in their organization (Frank 1984, Solow 1990, Akerlof and Yellen 1988). Since unemployed 'outsiders' are not directly involved in bargaining, equity considerations can help to explain why differentials remain unresponsive to unemployment. Attempts to reduce wages may lead employees who feel unfairly treated to shirk their duties and generate costs in excess of the expected saving when supervisors cannot evaluate and reward individual performance precisely.

Conversely and more generally, payment above the feasible minimum or 'market rate' for a particular job may improve the quality of applicants, and motivate incumbents to greater effort out of gratitude, or perhaps fear of losing the additional rent attached to the job. Such 'efficiency wages' may be paid even without the presence of unions, and in spite of persistent unemployment which should put downward pressure on earnings according to traditional competitive theories. On these lines higher pay should represent an alternative to close supervision, and thus reduce overheads as well as turnover and malfeasance. Empirical tests of these specific predictions of efficiency wage theory are difficult because the relevant microdata are not usually available. However FitzRoy and Vaughan-Whitehead (1989), using French microdata, obtained results which were consistent with the theory.

Numerous studies of incentive pay schemes have found that individual earnings are often little or unrelated to even easily observable individual performance at all levels of firm organization, from CEO to junior sales people and unskilled production workers. Baker, Jensen and Murphy (1988) express the puzzlement felt by most neoclassical economists in the face of these anomalies, but they make no mention of the theories of fairness and equity cited above which do at least begin to provide an explanation.

It is also often overlooked that current pay and performance need not be closely related in order to provide adequate incentives in long term employment relationships. Japanese experience with very steep age-earnings profiles and long term employment suggests that promotion possibilities and peer-group pressure are powerful motivating forces in an interactive and cohesive work organization (Aoki 1988).

In an interesting and original study, Rebitzer (1988) provides empirical evidence from the US for the importance of long term employment relationships in providing alternative incentives to current market pressures, and thus mitigating the adverse consequences of low unemployment on motivation and wage inflation:

> As the economy approaches full employment, the tightening of labour markets causes wage growth to increase and productivity growth to slow. However, these adverse effects of low unemployment are considerably reduced where firms have established long-term employment relations with their employees (Rebitzer 1988 p. 393).

3.3 Profit Sharing, Efficiency and Employment

Profit sharing and employee ownership schemes have been multiplying rapidly in recent years in the US and Europe, though not for the macroeconomic reasons put forward by Weitzman (1984), who claimed that extensive profit sharing in place of rigid wages could abolish both inflation and unemployment. Economists such as Baker, Jensen and Murphy (1988) have been puzzled by the success of these schemes, since the free-rider effect or the inability of most individuals to have much influence on the profitability of their firm would seem to exclude any direct incentive effect. This argument again ignores the importance of fairness considerations. While wages can and do adjust in the long run to share firm-specific rents, profit sharing provides an automatic and immediate adjustment mechanism without bargaining costs, which can plausibly improve employee perceptions of welfare and fair treatment.

Extensive research from many countries surveyed by Weitzman and Kruse (1990) shows a strongly consistent association between profit sharing and productivity though, as usual, causality is difficult to untangle from the data. FitzRoy and Kraft (1985, 1986, 1987) argue that sharing provides a group incentive for cooperation and productive interaction, and is likely to be most effective where team work and cooperative effort are important but difficult to observe and reward on an individual basis.

Much evidence summarized in Blinder (1990) suggests that profit sharing is most effective in conjunction with team-work and job-related participation. For profit shares as an alternative to part of the fixed wage, which is rarely observed in practice, Weitzman (1984) and others have argued that firms will expand employment, thus reducing earnings and profits per employee. This is implausible, because employees strongly resist pay cuts unless bankruptcy and the survival of all their jobs are threatened. Efficiency wage theories predict that reduced earnings would lower motivation and increase turnover, particularly of the most skilled and mobile employees.

On the other hand, it is probable that employees would accept the increased variability of profit related pay, provided that average or expected earnings were maintained and the variation of employment (the probability of lay-off or short weeks) were reduced. About half the European employees surveyed recently expressed willingness to accept temporary pay reductions under profit sharing (Nerb 1986).

It is true that European unions have generally opposed the flexibility of this, and most other kinds – including decentralized or firm-level – of profit sharing. However, this opposition is probably based on union officials' concern to maintain control over all aspects of centralized bargaining, including uniform wages and working time. Survey evidence suggests a strong preference for more part-time work and flexible hours. Indeed, about a quarter of European employees would prefer fewer hours at the same hourly wage (Nerb 1986), but unions have resisted these demands in order to maintain 'proletarian solidarity' and class consciousness under uniform working time.

A few studies have found a relationship between profit sharing and employment, but data problems are usually severe. In a large sample of US manufacturing firms, Kruse (1988) finds that employment is more stable in deferred-profit sharing firms, and that stability increases upon introduction of the scheme. This result does not appear to be due to wage effects or simultaneous adoption of new management or personnel policies. Related results were also obtained by Finseth (1988). FitzRoy and Vaughan-Whitehead (1989) found some evidence for a positive employment effect of current profit sharing in a sample of French manufacturing firms, but no effects of deferred sharing.

If it were only the case that the most successful or best managed firms shared profits to avoid negative reactions by workers it would be hard to explain the rapid growth of such schemes in recent years. On the other hand, if tax-inducements were the main explanation, the various beneficial effects which have been found would be surprising. An argument for encouraging sharing in the West has been the importance of bonus payments in association with widespread work sharing and low aggregate unemployment in Japan. However, this evidence needs more careful interpretation.

FitzRoy and Hart (1990) show that wage components are also very flexible, or responsive to industry-level cyclical indicators in Japan, while the share of bonus pay in total labour cost remained constant over time. This does not support anything like a mechanical profit share and a fixed wage, à la Weitzman, and indeed Aoki (1988) and others emphasize that both bonus and standard wage payments are related to firm performance as well as individual incentive considerations in Japan. Policy measures to encourage profit sharing make most sense for small firms which are often short of investment funds, as will be emphasized below. European experience and institutions of profit sharing are reviewed in detail by Uvalic (1990); and Vaughan-Whitehead (1990) provides much background and new evidence from France. The relation between explicit profit sharing and rent sharing through profit-related wages has been neglected in the literature, though both are probably related to fairness theories of efficiency wages (FitzRoy 1990).

4. Monopolistic Competition, Firm Size and Employment

Producers with market power due to product differentiation, technical monopoly or informational imperfections, and who face downward sloping demand curves will set prices above competitive levels. Production and employment will then remain below competitive levels and welfare losses result. The growth of import penetration and the threat of potential competition even in concentrated markets have led many economists in recent years to accept the competitive model of price-taking firms as at least a useful approximation to real world complexity, but recent empirical and theoretical work reviewed in the next subsection below casts serious doubt on this position.

If competition among existing producers is generally imperfect, policy to stimulate competition and employment growth through new entry assumes considerable importance. This leads to discussion of economies of scale in the following subsection, where again long-standing views which have formed the basis of much of industrial policy in Europe are collapsing in the light of current research. In the final subsection, 4.3, the important questions of new entry, firm size and employment are discussed.

4.1 Evidence for Monopolistic Competition

By examining the behaviour of price-cost margins over the business cycle, Hall (1988) and Domowitz et al. (1988) have recently provided striking evidence for monopolistic competition in many industries in the US. The theoretical basis for 'contestable' markets or potential competition to ensure competitive pricing has also been demolished by Stiglitz (1987), who shows that even small sunk costs destroy the efficiency properties of potential competition.

It should be emphasized that imperfect competition does not imply excessive profits. Fixed costs and overheads of production are assumed away in the competitive model of constant returns to scale, but in practice may offset the rents from sales at price above marginal cost. Since price-cost margins depend on the degree of product differentiation perceived by consumers, marketing efforts aim to foster 'brand-name reputations' and hinder rational comparison of products which may be essentially identical.

From a social viewpoint, much advertising of this kind appears wasteful, and indeed anticompetitive, in as far as it hinders introduction of improved products by maintaining irrational 'brand loyalty' among consumers. Since advertising expenditure represents a fixed cost, not dependent on sales or production, larger firms benefit from lower unit costs of production. This property of advertising forms an important barrier to entry by new or small firms in monopolistic markets, even when the incumbents are relatively inefficient in other ways. This has serious consequences for welfare and employment, as we develop further in the next subsection.

4.2 Economies of Scale

Belief in economies of scale, or lower unit costs of research, development, marketing and production in large organizations, has long been almost an article of faith among economists and especially policy makers. This belief was never based on much hard evidence, and more recently, evidence on decreasing returns or the diseconomies of large-scale operations has been accumulating. At the same time, two developments have taken place which undoubtedly favour smaller scale production (Best 1990).

The first is the shift from standardized, mass-produced items to customized and batch production described by Piore and Sabel (1984) as a move to 'flexible specialization.' The second (related) development is the new technology of automation and data processing which facilitates flexible production and reduces the cost-advantages of standardization and large plants (Acs and Audretsch 1989a).

With this background, it is noteworthy that the small-firm share of US manufacturing has increased substantially in the last decade, but slightly decreased in Germany. Recent research has established that large firms are not generally more effective innovators, as is still widely believed (Acs and Audretsch 1988, 1989a). On the other hand, small firms face serious disadvantages in the capital market even in the US. Individuals switching to self employment, as well as smaller firms, often 'face binding liquidity constraints' (Brock and Evans 1989 p. 14), due to the information costs in credit markets discussed by Stiglitz (1985), which penalize smaller transactions.

A fundamental reason for the relative inefficiency of many large corporations is the fact that top managerial compensation depends mainly on size and only very weakly on profitability or efficiency (Baker, Jensen and Murphy 1988, FitzRoy and Schwalbach 1990). This creates an incentive for unprofitable investment of 'free cash flow' instead of payout to shareholders, and 'could explain some of the vast amount of inefficient expenditures of corporate resources on diversification programs that have created large conglomerate organizations over the last 20 years.' (Baker et al. p. 609). The growth of large firms mainly for the benefit of their managers thus diverts funds away from the capital market and more valuable investment by liquidity-constrained smaller firms.

Larger firms are also less subject to discipline by takeover, particularly in Europe where company law often creates obstacles to hostile acquisition, and in any case takeovers in the US are far from exclusively efficiency-promoting. Redistributive capital gains, often based on insider trading, are a frequent motive, and the breaking of implicit agreements with customers or employees are one negative consequence. The main benefits seem to arise from the breakup of inefficient conglomerates in leveraged or managerial buyouts (LBO) which, however, risk-aversion by all parties rarely permit in Europe (Schleifer and Vishny 1988).

4.3 Small Firms, New Entry, and Employment

One of the most remarkable findings in the growing literature on small firms is that their share of employment in US manufacturing has increased substantially in recent years, while shares have remained constant in Germany (Acs and Audretsch 1989b). This suggests that rapid employment growth in the US, and decline or stagnation in the main European economies, may be related to the more dynamic small firm sector in the US, with its generally lower barriers to new entry. These differences stem not only from misguided government policies in support of large firms in Europe, but also from the much larger venture capital market in the US and from the much greater willingness of experienced managers and scientists to quit secure jobs and share the entrepreneurial risks in new enterprises.

Small high-tech firms in the US are responsible for much of the product innovation which has compensated for the decline of traditional industries. Unions are weak in the innovative new areas, while profit sharing and employee shareholding are most prevalent there (Smith 1988). However, most small-firm employment is not in high-tech manufacturing or related services, but in lower paid manufacturing and service occupations, and this has led to critique of job creation in the small-firm sector as a solution to unemployment problems.

It is true that workers with the same skills and other personal characteristics may sometimes be paid more in large firms, though the evidence is mixed (Brock and Evans 1989). However, workers also express greater dissatisfaction with jobs in the more bureaucratic and regimented conditions of a large organization and are much more prone to strike (Prais 1981). Higher pay may thus include a compensating differential for inferior working conditions and reduced job satisfaction as well as a share of any monopoly rents. In any case, a low-paid job may be preferred to no job at all, especially by those not receiving generous unemployment benefits.

From a social point of view, a job that is acceptable for some workers is preferable to lengthy subsidized unemployment for the same persons. There is much evidence that prolonged unemployment erodes human capital and motivation, and ultimately leads to exclusion from the labour market. There is little evidence that search for new employment is facilitated by unemployment, and indeed lack of social contacts at the workplace may handicap job search by the unemployed (Layard and Bean 1988).

Small and new firm entry and job creation in Europe is severely handicapped by decades of government policy in support of large corporations and quasi-monopolistic suppliers of state industries (Geroski and Jacquemin 1985). Overcapacity in declining sectors such as steel and shipbuilding is maintained by price support and other subsidies to protect jobs at enormous cost to the taxpayer, instead of retraining redundant employees and reducing excess capacity along Swedish lines. It is far from obvious that market integration by 1992 will favour new entry and job creation rather than wasteful conglomerate empire building and speculative takeover of the kinds long practiced in the integrated US market. Finally, the attitude of European trade unions is generally inimical to small-firm employment expansion because union organization is everywhere strongest in large firms, and union leaders fear loss of influence in the less impersonal small businesses, which also encourage profit sharing, direct worker ownership, and participation in job related decision making.

5. Working Time and Labour Demand

Union demands for reduced working time as well as higher wages have been supported in recent years by claims that unemployment could be reduced if the available work were 'redistributed' through a shorter working week. Much research has been devoted to the relationship between working time, wages, non-wage costs and employment, and there is little evidence for employment benefits from further reductions in working time (Hart 1987,1988).

Historically, standard hours have been reduced during boom periods to satisfy an increased demand for leisure, and increased overtime working has often partially compensated for the reductions in standard hours. As a device to reduce unemployment, a blanket reduction of working time has major disadvantages in the current European context.

A fundamental but much neglected point is that uniform working time and leisure is often as anomalous as uniform consumption of any kind. The demand for leisure, part-time work and job-sharing varies greatly according to individual circumstances, and modern technology often allows the combination of flexible individual working time. In one of the few experiments of this kind, a department store in Munich allows employees to choose their desired total weekly hours within a wide range. This flexibility, particularly valuable for women with children to look after, has proved an overwhelming success, with queues of applicants for any vacant position. The rarity of such experiments may be partly due to the weight of tradition, but is also maintained by the bitter opposition of trade unions, whose leaders are determined to keep control of bargaining over total working time as well as wages. Individual or decentralized bargaining over any component is seen as likely to erode union relevance and power in the long run.

Many current full-time employees, particularly second earners in families with small children, would seem to prefer part-time work at the same hourly rate. Flexibility might thus generate a demand for additional employment (Nerb 1986). However, non-wage costs of various kinds penalize employers who offer part-time jobs unless hourly rates are reduced. Even such a trade-off might be acceptable to some second family-wage-earners, but again the unions are vehemently opposed. Clearly, reform of the tax system which imposes substantial and increasing fixed costs of employment should be a major policy priority. This is reinforced by the urgent need to tax pollution and energy use, to avert the major risks from climate change through the 'greenhouse effect' (Porritt 1990).

Another extremely important but little discussed aspect of working-time reduction concerns the differential impact of such reductions on small firms. An employer of 10 workers, each with different tasks and skills, who is faced with a four hour reduction of standard weekly time, can hardly expect to find a new employee who is capable of doing a little bit of everybody else's work. More overtime or less output remains the immediate choice, in contrast to the situation of large firms where substitution possibilities are likely to be greater. In view of the efficiency and job-creation potential of small firms discussed above, the additional handicap represented by mandatory reductions of working time is likely to have negative employment and welfare effects which will counteract any positive substitution effects.

Restrictions on opening and working time in European retailing are a serious obstacle to greater employment, and impose substantial welfare losses on consumers. Opposition to weekend work, which would allow better utilization of costly capital equipment, remains strenuous. On all these and many other related issues, the arguments regularly used by union leaders and politicians reveal profound ignorance of elementary economic principles (Brunowsky 1988).

A more constructive role for the trade unions would require them to reverse their policy of opposition and support the interests of their members in flexible working time at the enterprise level. Such a role is important because individual bargaining always carries some risk for the individual employee whose bargaining power or mobility may be restricted, so fears for the demise of union organization upon abandonment of centralized bargaining would appear to be exaggerated. On the other hand, decentralized organization and bargaining would subject local union or employee representatives to much closer control by their own constituency. Thus fear of loss of power and autonomy by leaders of the existing large centralized unions probably explains much of their current policy stance.

6. Policy Conclusions

This chapter has covered several areas which are not usually regarded as closely interrelated. Policy conclusions have been discussed briefly at various points, and will now be developed more fully in this final section.

As evidence for the interrelatedness of such disparate fields as corporate finance and employment policy, we start from the observation that many large firms are relatively inefficient, particularly at product innovation and flexible organization and employment policies, in part because top managerial compensation depends mainly on size. This creates an incentive for excessive growth and 'empire building,' rather than payment to shareholders of the 'free cash flow' which cannot be profitably invested internally. More appropriate incentives for top management would increase dividend payments, and hence the flow of funds into the capital market available for financing new start-ups and small firms as venture capital. Even in the US the cost of obtaining external capital largely constrains investment in new start-ups to be made out of current cash flow (Fazzari et al. 1988).

Increased entry of new firms would also be encouraged by labour market flexibility and deregulation, as well as reduction of excessive state subsidies and other support for large existing corporations. Enlargement of the small firm sector, in turn, would enhance competition, increase the overall rate of return on capital, and above all expand employment, following experience in the US. An exclusive focus in employment policy on aggregate demand or on wages and the labour market will thus miss important avenues through which welfare, competitiveness and employment can all be influenced simultaneously without additional public expenditure (FitzRoy 1989).

The integrated view espoused here is also important in assessing the consequences of removing direct barriers to trade within the EC by 1992. Much official thought assumes that competitiveness and efficiency will automatically be increased by these developments, with consequent employment gains to follow. However, as usual in economics, there are countervailing tendencies which deserve emphasis (Kay 1989). In particular, liberalization of capital markets without improvement of the incentives provided to top management of large corporations is likely to generate a substantial increase of takeover activity.

The experience in the US in recent years, summarized above, casts doubt on the efficiency-enhancing effects of unrestricted takeovers. Pursuit of speculative capital gains, insider trading, which is hardly sanctioned in many contexts in Europe, and excessive pursuit of growth by the managers of 'free cash flows' are likely results. The LBO operations which are most likely to increase efficiency are inhibited in Europe by the risk-aversion of senior managers. Top-heavy conglomerates, ultimately increased market power, and negative effects on employment and consumer welfare are by no means implausible unless policy makers abandon their cherished but unrealistic faith in economies of scale, and institute a thoroughgoing reversal of current policy towards large firms, preferably coupled with support for venture capital for new start-ups and small firms.

Tax policy is a traditional method for achieving specific allocative goals, but one which is currently providing perverse rather than positive incentives for employment growth. The rapid increase of non-wage labour costs in the form of pay-roll and other related taxes largely to fund a pay-as-you-go system of social security benefits represents a tax on employment which accelerates the substitution of labour by capital equipment. The major obstacle to replacing these perverse taxes by less distorting consumption or value-added taxes (VAT) is the distributive consequence of such change.

Similar arguments are advanced against abolition of the double taxation of dividends, which encourages wasteful investment by large corporations, and against introduction of urgently needed environmental taxes on energy use and toxic emissions. A simplified 'negative income tax' or support for low income recipients would in fact remove the hardship from the redistributive consequences of tax reform, but the political obstacles seem to be currently insurmountable. At the very least, however, these problems deserve much more intensive discussion and wider recognition than they have hitherto received.

A major extension of adult retraining schemes, following the example of Sweden, seems to be the policy measure with the highest chances of realization, in part because the direct costs in the short run are relatively small, and also involve job creation. Removal of tax penalties for part-time work should also be feasible without substantial distributive effects, and would represent a first step towards general flexibility of working according to individual preferences. Clearly, the state sector – still a major employer – could usefully lead the way instead of generally lagging behind the private sector. Overcoming ideological and sectarian opposition by organized labour leaders offers a challenge to public authorities and educational channels. Labour-intensive investment in environmental protection and urban renewal is urgently needed for its own sake, and could generate substantial employment, as Brunowsky (1988) has emphasized.

A move to more flexible, decentralized wage bargaining and deregulation of the more archaic institutions of labour markets to facilitate entry by the self-employed and new firms should arguably be the ultimate goal for policy towards non-inflationary full employment. While benefits from centralized or 'corporatist' bargaining structures are sometimes claimed, the importance of new firm entry for employment and competition would appear to shift the weight of the evidence in favour of decentralization. However, the political obstacles in most European countries are formidable, and promise only glacially slow progress.

It is often pointed out that the UK seems to have the worst combination of decentralized bargaining, uncooperative labour relations and sufficient market power in many sectors. This allows employers to pass on excessive wage increases, which then set the pattern even in more competitive sectors, or contribute to the steadily widening pay differentials and income inequality of the past decade. At the same time, deregulation of credit and housing markets and commitment to an over-valued pound as well as tax-reductions for the high-earners generated an import- and consumption-boom at the cost of both public and private investment and savings.

The high-interest rate policy has then hit the small-firm sector hardest, and destroyed most of the potential benefits of flexibility.

Centralized bargaining with socially responsible union organizations in Germany and Sweden may have contributed to macroeconomic stability, but the costs in terms of universally high wages and low rates of participation in the labour force in Germany will exacerbate problems of adjustment to unification and any future recession.

In view of evidence for failure of the capital market for small business in the US, noted above, a case could be made for state support and extension of the much less developed European venture capital market. Existing state grants and other systems are usually too cumbersome and bureaucratic. The paperwork involved often represents a major deterrent for small enterprises or new start-ups, and the time lags involved are particularly damaging to high-tech prospects where new ideas can quickly become obsolescent.

It is quite conceivable that state funded venture capital suppliers, efficiently organized as independent local units, could develop into profitable going concerns able to repay their loan capital in the long run. To maximize the employment impact it is important to go beyond high tech, and offer funds in any promising service or manufacturing area, according to the available expertise of specialized personnel and institutions. A precondition for success is that staff should be profit sharing professionals rather than salaried civil servants. Similarly, employees should be encouraged to accept shares in future profits rather than initially high wages, to reduce the liquidity constraints on new businesses.

The combination of flexible team-work, unconstrained by formal work-rules and collective bargains, with worker participation in job-related decision-making and enterprise profits, is required both for motivation and adaptation to technological and market change. Isolated, piecemeal policy measures such as tax benefits for employee share ownership currently favoured, do not recognize interactions emphasized here and are unlikely to be effective.

While the emphasis here has been on microeconomic measures, it should be noted finally that none of the policies discussed above can be effective in the long run without adequate public investment in the infrastructure of education, training, health services, transport and environmental protection required by a modern society. Gross neglect of these public goods and services in the last decade in the UK and US have contributed much to their relative industrial and competitive decline, and cannot be compensated by private-sector flexibility or deregulation.

Aschauer (1989) shows that public investment is strongly correlated with economy-wide productivity growth both over time and across countries, with the UK and US trailing their competitors. In vocational training alone, Britain is lagging even further behind all her major European competitors, and so, without the foundation of an adequately skilled labour force, is almost certainly condemned to further relative decline.

It has been argued at length in this chapter that employment and industrial policy are closely interrelated, and should thus be coordinated in the light of recent research in these fields. This requires both academics and policy makers to cross conventional boundaries and take a broader view of the economy than is customary under the specialization that severely restricts much of the relevant debate. Current piecemeal policies, even with the help of the longest postwar boom, have hardly dented the problem of long run unemployment to date, and are unlikely to do so after 1992 without fundamental reorientation, particularly in view of the higher energy prices that dwindling US reserves were making likely even before the Gulf crisis.

Note

1. This chapter is a development of earlier works: 'Employment, Entrepreneurship and 1992: Microeconomic Policy and European Problems,' presented at the CEC Conference, Nice, June 1990, published in *Small Business Economics* 2, 1990 pp. 11-23; and a draft paper prepared for the working group meeting of The Commission of the European Communities, Brussels, 10 April 1989. The author would like to thank David Audretsch, Michael Funke and David Marsden, as well as other members and participants in the working group meetings, for helpful discussions and comments, but retains responsibility for opinions expressed. Reprinted by kind permission of Kluwer Academic Publishers.

5. The Pay Policies of Large Firms in Europe

David Shonfield

1. Flexibility and Decentralization: Change and Continuity

Since the recession of the early 1980s, major employers throughout Europe have faced the associated challenges of growing international competition, an almost unprecedented rate of technological change, and deregulation of both product and labour markets. In these circumstances it would be surprising if many businesses were not to examine and change employment policies.

The changes which have been taking place are often loosely described under the heading 'flexibility.' The term has been used to cover a range of policies and practices, from the annualization of working time to the deployment of temporary workers and the use of sub-contractors. We are said to be moving into a new era – the age of the 'flexible firm.'

It is certainly true that manufacturing industry in particular needs to be able to respond much faster to changes in markets, competition and not least economic circumstances than was the case even 10 years ago. But the danger with a term such as flexibility is that it blurs the considerable differences between the strategies firms adopt. Profit sharing, merit pay and piecework are, for example, all 'flexible' payment systems. Yet they work in quite different ways and some employers are replacing one with another.

There is also a risk of presuming that outcomes are the result of choice rather than necessity. The use of temporary workers, for example, is often a (costly) response to tight labour markets rather than a carefully worked out strategy to cope with market fluctuations or reduce overheads.

There is thus a need for some precision about 'flexibility,' especially when it comes to pay. The aim of this chapter is to assess the dimensions, the scope and the direction of current developments in the wage and salary policies of large firms. We focus in particular on two tendencies which appear to be becoming more widespread in several countries – moves towards payment systems based on individual merit or performance and moves to link pay more directly than in the past to the fortunes of the enterprise. Both developments need to be seen in the context of moves towards decentralization – making units within the firm more responsive and accountable for profit.

How far has this pay 'flexibility' gone and how far can it go? Is the tendency all in one direction? What sort of problems and contradictions are emerging? Is there a convergence between the wage and salary policies of large firms within the European Community? Can one discern a 'European model' for pay, industrial relations and the social policy of business emerging in the context of the Single Market?

These are large issues and the present chapter is in many respects an interim report. It builds on the research on the human resources implications of 1992 conducted by Incomes Data Services in cooperation with the Institute of Personnel Management in Britain during 1988.[1] The main focus is on developments in three countries – France, Britain and Italy – but there is inevitably an 'Anglo-Saxon' bias in the views expressed here. The current situation in Germany is discussed briefly, but developments elsewhere remain outside the scope of this study. However, it needs to be said that the fascination with new company pay policies – in particular individualization and profit sharing – which exists in France and, to a lesser extent, in Italy and Britain, is not necessarily reflected in other countries.

Apart from the national bias two other major caveats need stating. The first is that most of the companies discussed here are in two broad industrial sectors – chemicals and engineering (the latter category is used here in the British sense, to include sectors as diverse as telecommunications and cars). The conclusions are thus heavily influenced by the policies and practice of capital-intensive manufacturing industry. As one of the contentions of this chapter is that the policy issues in different sectors and in different countries are quite distinct, this bias needs to be borne in mind.

Secondly, almost all the companies we look at are transnationals. This has the virtue that one can compare the policies of the same company in quite different national environments but it also means that distinctive national differences – for example in management pay determination – tend to be blurred. The policies and practice of transnational firms, whether British, French, German, American or Italian, are converging at a much faster rate than in large nationally based companies.

The reasons are fairly obvious. Transnational firms tend to be in the same market for senior executives. They recruit from the same business schools. They use the same consultants and they join the same salary clubs. Thus although there are clear differences in the philosophy and the policies of major chemical firms such as Solvay, Rhône-Poulenc, Henkel and ICI, the differences are becoming more blurred as they imitate each other. Generally this is not the case in firms whose operations are wholly or very largely confined to a single country.

The pay policies of large multinationals are usually more innovative than those of large national firms, for similar reasons. There is the further factor that many 'national champions' are in the state-owned sector, or have only been de-nationalized in recent years. Their pay structures and policies are generally more centralized and slower to change. There are of course exceptions to any rule, but these are generally where drastic change has been forced through as part of a survival plan, as in the British steel industry. The continuing centralized policies of the major European airlines provide a salutary balance to the assumptions about wholesale change which are usually made.

Although we are undoubtedly going through a period of flux, with intensive debate about the relationship of wage and salary policies to business needs, there is far more continuity in the policies and practices of most firms – large and small.

In Britain, for example, many companies continue to operate that very traditional form of performance pay, piecework. A large number of firms have incentive bonus arrangements that have remained largely unchanged for years. Few firms have introduced merit pay for manual workers. Progression through pay scales based on performance rather than length of service has become much more widespread for office staff. But such systems usually guarantee a basic annual pay increase which covers inflation. Given the extent of decentralized bargaining in British manufacturing[2] this relative inertia is all the more striking.

While the rate of change can thus easily be exaggerated out of all proportion to reality, and there are important differences between developments in the various countries, it is possible to distinguish the two broad tendencies we noted earlier – the linking of pay to individual performance or the performance of a business unit –

within an overall framework of decentralization of responsibility for management and profit within large firms.

There are, however, important countervailing tendencies. There are signs of a backlash against too much diversification because of loss of control. There is concern about the arbitrary nature of merit pay. There is the need within the context of the single market for transnationals to exert a greater central authority over some elements of pay determination. And many of the most successful enterprises operating within Europe cannot easily be fitted in to a 'decentralizing/individualizing' model – most of the large German companies, as well as the Japanese.

We look both at how these different and somewhat contradictory tendencies are manifesting themselves in different countries and at some tendencies towards convergence within individual transnational firms, before drawing some conclusions on prospects for the next few years.

We start with recent developments in France in particular because it is there that some of these tendencies can be seen most clearly. We do not regard France as a paradigm for the rest of the Community (there is no such thing), but recent developments in French industry can serve as a reference point for the assessment of change in other countries.

2. New Pay Policies in France

The most striking change in France over the last few years is the extraordinary growth in the number of company agreements. As the main French employers' confederation, the CNPF, noted in its recent review of bargaining trends 'from around 2,000 agreements in 1982 the number of agreements grew to nearly 6,400 in 1988.'[3]

There has been a somewhat similar increase in company or plant bargaining in Italy over the past two years (see below). But while the Italian situation to some extent reflects a revival in grass roots trade union activity, in France the growth in local agreements reflects a significant shift of emphasis by employers. Since 1984, in fact, the CNPF has refrained from issuing any central pay guidelines, advocating a 'flexible and diversified' policy. The recommendations for both the 1989 and 1990 bargaining rounds, for example, focus on three elements: increases in accordance with economic progress in the sector and the enterprise, individual performance pay, and collective profit sharing.

2.1 Decentralization at Sectoral Level

The change of tack by the CNPF has been followed through more recently by key sectoral employers' associations, notably the UIMM (engineering employers), which has been in the forefront of promoting both merit pay (*'individualisation'*) and payments tied to profits or productivity (*'intéressement'*).

In the 1987 bargaining round, for the first time in many years, the UIMM decided against naming a pay target, 'the broad consensus being that, given the political and economic situation, such advice no longer made sense, and that firms ought to have the same freedom to manage salaries that they had recovered over prices. In addition to name a standard figure would have been in contradiction with policies aimed at linking pay movements more closely to company results.'[4]. The same policy has been adopted in the three subsequent years.

Sectoral bargaining (conducted regionally in the engineering industry), which was already of marginal importance for larger employers, is now irrelevant for all but the smallest firms. Regional employers' groups have been encouraged by the national federation to draw up two-tier scales of rates. Minimum rates which act as the calculators for service-related pay have been frozen or increased only marginally, while monthly or annual scales of guaranteed minimum earnings have been introduced which are intended to increase more or less in line with changes in actual wages.

The result is that the influence of the industry-wide pay arrangements in French engineering is probably at an all-time low. Pay scales in larger firms are typically 30% or more above the minimum rates and the hierarchy of coefficients for non-managerial posts serves more as a reference point for advertising jobs than anything else. The industry rates, which cover 'shop floor' and office workers, (including supervisors) are 'a fiction with which we can go along happily in the context of weak trade unions,' in the words of one leading French manager.

However, it is notable that the engineering employers have continued with an annual review of their national agreement for executive grades, which lays down minimum salaries and an incremental structure related to service, along with three 'reference points' for more senior management posts.

The continuation of this system is perhaps surprising in view of the determined push towards decentralization from leading French employers and the widespread adoption of merit pay for executives.

It suggests that the rather stratified approach to executive pay which is traditional in many French companies, linking reward to educational background, age and service, may be more resilient than many imagine.

The approach of the CNPF and the UIMM has not necessarily been followed in other sectors. But even the few sectors which have retained the practice of a general salary recommendation, such as the chemical industry, have proposed very limited movements in the form of unilateral guidelines. But here too the industry arrangements have at most a marginal impact on pay policies in large firms.

2.2 The Development of *Intéressement*

In conditions of low inflation and acknowledged trade union weakness, basic pay rises in the private sector over the past three years have in many cases been held below the increase in the cost of living. It is against this background that there has been a significant growth of both merit pay and profit sharing.

Profit sharing in France is by no means new but the existing legislative constraints were significantly loosened by the 1986 Ordonnance on *intéressement*. Firms are, for example, no longer required to obtain official approval for their schemes, nor to have had an agreement on pay in the two years preceding the introduction of the scheme. Different schemes can also now be introduced within the same enterprise. Along with limited tax measures designed to make profit sharing more attractive to employees and some relaxation of other controls, these changes have led to a sustained rise in *intéressement* agreements.

The number of such agreements doubled to just over 2,600 between 1985 and 1987. The number is still rising, if at a slower rate, and it is likely that around one million workers were covered by such arrangements in 1990.

We refer here to *intéressement* as profit sharing, but in fact this does not reflect the new legislation nor actual practice in a number of firms. Unlike the various pieces of British legislation on profit sharing which have been enacted since the late 1970s, *intéressement* covers schemes which may be related to output, productivity, quality and so on. The only real requirement is that the system should link an element of reward to the overall results of an establishment or an enterprise. A significant minority – some 15% – of recent agreements on *intéressement* have, in fact, been value-added or plant efficiency schemes rather than profit sharing.

The other notable feature of the growth of *intéressement* is the relatively large number of deals compared to the still restricted proportion of the national workforce affected. It is clear that many of the agreements cover a small number of employees, especially when one considers that a handful of the 3,000 or so agreements on *intéressement* cover many thousands of people, in companies such as Peugeot, Renault, Aerospatiale, Rhône-Poulenc and Alcatel.

Government and employers alike stress continually that *intéressement* is not intended to substitute for any of the pay packet or pay award. This again is unlike the intention of the legislators in Britain who introduced the latest profit-related pay (PRP) scheme, coincidentally also in 1986, with the express intention of encouraging the substitution of a variable element for part of the 'normal' wage or salary.

But what does seem to have happened in certain cases in France is that employers have been able to limit the size of basic pay increases at some establishments by introducing *intéressement*, arguing that employees were better off in net terms as a result. The Belgian chemical company, Solvay, which introduced *intéressement* at a number of its French establishments a few years ago, has been able to depress some basic pay rises below the inflation rate in this way.

The issue has clearly worried French unions – who are campaigning for stricter controls on such agreements – and employers' bodies such as the UIMM, which continue to advise their members that *intéressement* should not be a substitute for normal pay. For the UIMM '*intéressement* is tending to rediscover its original role. Many firms which have looked to it as an element in their pay policy realise that introducing *intéressement* can produce effects in areas which are a priori far removed from remuneration: quality or communications for example, without forgetting productivity of course, which can be the basis for the scheme.'[5]

Currently the yield under *intéressement* is limited to 20% of gross pay in any one year. This is also the limit for tax relief on PRP in Britain and the similarity is not accidental: the figure is directly attributable to Weitzman, who argues that the macroeconomic benefits to be gained from the widespread adoption of profit-related systems can only be realized if a sufficiently high proportion of basic pay is variable.[6]

However, the French scheme is likely to be revised in the face of a general realization that the vast majority of employees are unhappy at putting such a high proportion of their pay at risk.

A few French firms (notably in the high technology sectors of engineering) have had exceptionally high *intéressement* payments, approaching 20%, but the norm in industry is reported to be well under 10%. A recent survey of management pay in about 100 large firms by the CEGOS consultancy (see below) found that payments in 1988 averaged only 2.6% of the pay bill for managers and 4% of the total pay bill in those companies with agreements – just over 40 firms in all.

Although employers' organizations are formally opposed to a reduction in the limit, the consensus seems to be that tighter controls on pay fluctuations will not have much effect on actual payments and may make the policy more widely acceptable.

2.3 A Rising Tide of Merit Pay

Alongside the growth of *intéressement* the other key development in France has been a marked increase in merit or performance pay ('*individualisation*'). Linking part or all of a pay rise to individual merit is certainly not new in France, but there has been a shift in management awareness about performance pay. As one employer put it: 'many of our companies have been rather like Monsieur Jourdain in the play by Molière who was surprised to learn from his tutor that he had been speaking prose for years.'

It is thus impossible to quantify the extent of the changes taking place. A survey conducted in 1987 by the regional engineering employers' association for the Paris region (the largest in France, with firms employing some 600,000 people) found that around 25% of firms intended to stick to general increases, while at the other extreme some 15% were adopting a totally merit-based approach. There was, however, a spectacular rise in the number of employers intending to combine general increases with merit awards: from 20% of firms in 1985, to 40% in 1986 and 60% in 1987.[7]

These figures reflect the intentions of firms for the 1987-88 pay round, not necessarily the final outcome. And they also do not distinguish between categories of employee, most notably between executives, who now very generally have a merit element in their salary throughout the private sector, and the rest of the workforce, where the situation is far less clear.

Although major French employers have consciously broken from the practice of setting any bench marks for pay – the UIMM even refrains from any predictions of changes in the cost of living – they recognize that inflation still plays a significant role. The best estimate of the normal value of merit awards in the engineering industry is between a quarter and a third of the total increase. Thus, for example, the UIMM estimates that of the average company settlement of around 4% during 1989, perhaps 1% on average was set aside for individual awards. With a range of settlements of around 2% to 6%, some engineering companies are allocating perhaps 2% as a merit budget. This compares fairly closely with the size of such budgets in those British firms which operate merit systems. But the French payments in many cases cover manual workers, while this remains relatively rare in Britain.

The global figures from the UIMM also match up to the merit pay pool in some of the larger French chemical firms. Rhône-Poulenc, for example, has a budget of up to 1.5% of the pay bill for individual awards for those subsidiaries which chose to use it.

Three general points need to be borne in mind here, which apply as much (or more) to the British and Italian experience. The first is that these are average pay bill costs. Individual awards may of course be considerably larger in some cases. Secondly, there is evidence from several French firms that what appear to be individual awards may in fact be measures to reward employees for qualifications or skills. The budget for individual awards at Rhône-Poulenc, which covers all employees, is available for skill-related increases as well as performance pay. Further, some merit awards are in fact more or less disguised measures to overcome recruitment and retention problems. Thirdly, the spread of merit pay among firms in the Paris region, and the much higher merit awards in evidence there, suggest that cost-of-living and external labour market pressures have been at work, along with internal pressures to pay more at head office.

A case in point is the fertilizer company Norsk Hydro Azote, part of the Norwegian transnational Norsk Hydro. Here a very wide range of individual pay rates emerged as a result of some years of individual merit awards. By February 1989 when the company came to review the situation the pay ranges for skilled manual workers in the three main plants varied by between 2.8% and 20.2%. But the range of salaries in most job categories at the Paris headquarters was between 30% and 50%, and in one case nearly 70%.

The company has now negotiated a new national agreement with the unions which provides a 12% merit pay range in each category and harmonizes the structure between the different units, consolidating a number of premiums into basic pay. The previous chaotic situation partly resulted from the takeover of companies, but it also shows what can happen with uncontrolled merit pay policies in multi-plant firms.

2.4 Towards a More Orderly System?

The potential for an arbitrary approach to individualized pay, leading to wage and salary drift and to a potential backlash from executives and other groups subject to merit awards has led to growing concern in larger companies that merit pay policies should be more soundly based.

At the end of 1986, for example, the UIMM told its members that it might well be appropriate to think in terms of no general increase at all or perhaps one-off unconsolidated bonuses. But a little more than 12 months later a note of caution appeared. A working party set up to look at individualization warned that firms should not adopt merit pay to 'conform to a fashion but only if it fitted in with an overall strategy.' The working party also made it clear that the introduction of merit pay demanded great care, very thorough preparation and 'procedures designed to minimise the risks of arbitrary decisions, procedures which must be perfectly plain to all concerned.'[8]

In November 1988 the UIMM published a booklet of guidance to its members[9] and at the same time agreed some ground rules with the managers' union, the CGC, with the emphasis on measures to increase the transparency of merit pay systems as well as the need for rights of appeal and the duty of employers to provide information during annual negotiations on the amount of the pay bill set aside for merit awards.

2.5 Contrasting Approaches

Drawing up a balance sheet of the French experience is far from easy. The situation is still in flux and there are evident divisions among French managers about the way forward. For some there is a contradiction between linking reward to collective performance, as with *intéressement*, and merit pay, which is seen as reinforcing individualism at the expense of the group.

Nor is decentralization of pay always seen as desirable. The two large supermarket groups – Casino and Carrefour – have, for example, both opted for systems which tend to reinforce corporate identity. For Casino '*intéressement* was put in place to reinforce the solidarity among staff throughout our group. There are some supermarkets which are struggling against competitors, others which profit on the basis of location. In this situation there can be no question of decentralizing *intéressement*. We are thinking in terms of national market share.'[10]

Concern about strengthening individualism at the expense of 'team spirit' is central to the opposition to merit pay expressed by Antoine Riboud, President of BSN, in an interview published in January 1988:

> In my view one can only really speak about individual merit when the degree of initiative exercised by the individual reaches a level where it can really have a personal influence on performance. It's totally right for a senior manager who has all the scope to really be meritworthy. But it's totally wrong for a worker, in trades where everything is in upheaval because of technological change.
>
> The process of manufacturing creates a bond between those involved. There is already a pay hierarchy because of the hierarchy of functions. To break up that bond even more, at every level, by merit pay is to go against good management practice and the efficiency of a manufacturing process which requires teamwork.[11]

Riboud's personal politics are different from the mainstream of French businessmen, but some of these concerns find an echo in companies such as BP France and Saft (the batteries subsidiary of the CGE group), both of which have introduced individual performance bonus systems linked to defined objectives.

Such systems have been termed 'new individualization of pay'[12] and hitherto seem almost entirely confined to executive and professional staff. They have the benefit of avoiding much of the subjectivity implied by a traditional merit pay approach because they should involve targets which are defined and measurable.

They should therefore avoid the 'equalization effect' which has become apparent with merit pay in France and which was highlighted by the recent annual survey of management pay conducted by the CEGOS consultancy. The details of the survey are unfortunately confidential to participating companies, but the main conclusions make some important points about merit pay, which are relevant to countries other than France.

The survey[13] found a narrower range of increases for managers in 1988-89 than in 1984-85 and 'overall hardly any change in selectivity since 1976.' The authors comment that the companies covered by the survey tended to expand individual differentials one year only to narrow them in the next and that over a three year period the pay increases of executives in individual firms tended to converge.

These conclusions are very much in line with the experience of managers who have lived with merit pay for some time. As one senior executive from the engineering industry commented on the CEGOS findings: 'There are very few firms that are prepared to follow the IBM example and base salaries solely on performance or merit. And the scope for individual differentiation quickly finds its limits. It has an effect for one or two years and then things even themselves out.'

More significantly for the longer term policy of firms, CEGOS warns that more rapid progression for young managers in France is limiting employers' room for manoeuvre on merit awards and increasing the potential dissatisfaction of senior managers. At the same time the higher relative salaries of young managers threaten to increase long-term salary costs.

The move away from a stratified approach to management pay has some way to go before it is generally accepted. But one major consequence of the cultural changes now taking hold in some French companies is that pay costs and pressures will be much less predictable.

3. Italy: Large Firms Seek to Break the Mould

Recent developments in pay determination in Italian industry to some extent reflect the same pressures as in France, but there are significant differences. The most important developments have been in the engineering industry, where there have been radical departures in collective bargaining since 1987. Several of the largest firms have moved towards payments tied to company performance.

Centralized pay arrangements at industry level and at national level – through indexation – retain much more authority in Italy than they do in France. In the wake of the January 1987 agreement in the engineering industry, the pivotal deal in Italy's current system of three year agreements, nearly 3,500 factory level agreements covering just over 500,000 workers were signed in some 18 months of local bargaining. But in many cases, including key groups such as Fiat and Olivetti, these were the first substantive company deals in 11 years. And even after the most intensive round of negotiations of the 1980s, locally negotiated rates made up less than 5% of the average manual worker's pay packet in general engineering. The proportion of pay decided by central bargaining or as a result of indexation is nearly 80%, little changed from the early 1980s.[14]

But these figures tell only part of the story. First, as the surveys by the employers' association Assolombarda show, there has been a major change during the 1980s in the proportion of white-collar earnings determined by merit awards – up from an average 12% to nearly 20% over the past five years, with a particularly sharp rise between October 1987 and 1988.

As Carlo dell'Aringa comments: 'Unilateral wage determination, which is not negotiated with unions, has been used by firms primarily to correct the egalitarian effects of wage indexation.' He also notes that the incidence of merit awards seems 'to have widened in the last two years to include the more highly skilled blue-collar groups.'[15]

Secondly, although many hundreds of company agreements on pay do not differ significantly from the industry 'norm' (particularly in small businesses), larger firms, especially in the north, can pay up to 30% above the minimum rates as a result of company bargaining over 'production bonuses' (related to past performance) and the 'superminimo' – locally agreed plus rates. It is this last element in pay which has been the subject of the greatest change over the past two years, primarily in the engineering industry.

Describing the bargaining round which followed the January 1987 agreement, the Fiom (normally considered the most militant of three unions in engineering) admitted that it was 'actually impossible to work out an average...because of the wide variety of increases, the different periods involved and because of the forms in which the increases are paid, certain of them extremely complex.'[16]

3.1 New Departures: Fiat, Zanussi and Olivetti

The new departure was the replacement of standard 'superminimo' award with an increase tied to company performance. Although there have only been a few dozen deals of this sort, the most notable examples – at Fiat, Olivetti and Zanussi – cover some 260,000 employees between them, approximately 20% of the total covered by the industry-wide agreement. The impact of these agreements has therefore been very considerable and they set trends for the wage round that started in 1990 – with engineering leading the way.

So far other sectors have been wary of following the trend. The introduction of a profit-related element at the Italian subsidiary of the British chemical company Tioxide in 1987 was considered something of a milestone, for example.

Although the Fiat, Olivetti and Zanussi agreements have been bracketed together there are distinct differences between them. The Fiat agreement of July 1988 was the first and by far the most controversial because of the divided response of the unions involved and the opposition of the Fiom (the union agreed to take part in discussions on the implementation of the deal and eventually signed it a year later when the final details were agreed).

The initial accord simply paved the way for profit-related pay (with a ceiling of 8% of earnings) but the deal finally agreed is complex, being based on four elements – turnover per employee, turnover on net capital invested, net assets on net capital invested, and a quality factor, the cost of guarantees on turnover – which together make up the *'Premio Performance di Gruppo'* (Group performance bonus). The detailed terms of the agreement effectively operate for two years from January 1990 and improve the original proposals, in that 75% (rather than 50%) of the bonus earned each year is consolidated into monthly pay, the remainder being a lump sum which can vary between fixed limits.

The first major deal of what was dubbed the 'post-Fiat' era was at Zanussi (since 1984 part of the Electrolux group). Here management and unions agreed on two indices linking company pay to productivity rather than profit. Again the agreement came into full operation in 1990, and the basic formula provides for two bonuses, one linked to the productivity of individual production units, the other a three-monthly bonus linked to production targets established at plant level. The latter bonus penalizes absentees, a feature of a number of Italian agreements.

The agreement at Olivetti, as at Fiat, gives the company pay element in the form of lump sums. A guaranteed bonus, payable in June each year, is offset against a second payment (in January) linked to an index of company competitiveness, designed to measure Olivetti's performance. The index is derived from the relationship between gross operating profit and turnover at Olivetti relative to the company's 'largest and most significant competitors.' The maximum yield envisaged is 10%, with a guaranteed 6%, and the agreement (defined as an experiment) was initially intended to last until the end of 1991.

The Olivetti deal, concluded in November 1988, was followed by a number of other agreements which have sought to tie the company pay element to variable factors: a quality index in the case of Italtel; the relationship between gross operating profit and net profit at the Ericsson subsidiary, Sielte; or a two-tier efficiency index based on direct and indirect costs at the Agusta aerospace company. The significance of some of these subsequent agreements is that they came in state-controlled firms which had previously been noted for their fixed pay structures.

3.2 After Fiat...?

It is not easy for those outside the Italian industrial scene to assess the importance of these agreements. Within the companies concerned, to quote one top manager at Fiat, they represent 'an undoubted contrast with the tendency constantly to extend guaranteed aspects of income – and therefore limit the uncertainty factors – which was typical of the Italian factory tradition. This represents an important step in "modernizing" industrial relations in Italy.' For other employers, according to Sergio Pininfarina, head of the employers' association Confindustria, the Fiat accord showed 'that we are no longer in the crazy seventies, when unions considered pay to be an independent variable.'[17]

So the agreements certainly reflect a change in mentality, but the flexibility involved seems very small, at least to an outsider. The context has also to be considered. In the case of Fiat and Olivetti, these were the first company pay offers in many years. A survey of 6,000 company agreements concluded between January and August 1988 – i.e. before the impact of Fiat, Zanussi and Olivetti – highlighted the introduction of flexible pay, but confirmed its relative insignificance when compared to total pay. In none of the agreements analyzed did the variable element exceed 2%, and in most cases the mechanism for determining this element had still to be defined.

This survey[18] also highlighted 'a tendency for large company groups to give one-off payments or annual bonuses' contrasting a tendency for smaller firms to grade increases so as to expand differentials. The detail of large company agreements certainly confirms the prevalence of flat-rate lump sums (apart from production bonuses paid according to grade) as a means of paying additional money without building up long-term pay costs. But it is also the case that there are problems about how the 'superminimo' should be distributed in a number of large firms.

Under the weighted percentage distribution defined in the industry-wide agreement, increases are scaled to a set pattern, rising in steps from 100% in category 1 to 200% in category 7. This formula (widely used to determine increases in company pay) has also been adopted by some of the companies which have introduced profit-related pay, for example Olivetti. At Fiat, however, management has insisted on a distribution which results in a flat-rate bonus payment for the first four categories (the bulk of manual workers) with larger rises in the higher supervisory and specialized grades, thus widening differentials.

This variation of the industry weighting is one way in which some firms are adapting the system to reflect technological change and effectively create additional company job categories for workers with enhanced skills. In many cases – although not at Fiat – this is done with the full backing of the unions, for example where there are no workers in the lowest grades.

Though the parameters evolve over time through negotiation, the system is rather less flexible than in France, where firms can if necessary design the pay structure they want and fit it notionally into the industry coefficients. In Italy, the relatively high proportion of fixed pay elements, at least for manual workers, makes this more difficult, or expensive.

The commitment of some major employers to decentralized bargaining can also be questioned. Representatives of the Federmeccanica, the engineering employers' federation, have on several occasions put forward proposals for an agreement which would determine company pay awards at national level, leaving scope locally only for increases related to merit, increased skills or efficiency.

The experience of the 1980s in Italy is that centralization has served employers well since the modification of the *'scala mobile'* indexation rules. But such proposals go against the idea that companies need to determine their own pay policies in concert with their own employees, which is a central theme of the recent pathbreaking company accords.

3.3 Rigidity in Management Pay

The relative rigidities of the Italian system are nowhere more noticeable – nor more irksome to the large firms – than with management pay. The national agreement for *'dirigenti'* lays down tight rules on indexation and seniority increases as well as supplementary bonuses, fringe benefits and certain individual payments. National agreements for managers usually run for a two-year period, with the main increase in the first year. The degree of centralization means the linking of pay to managers' performance remains uncommon in Italy, a factor which inevitably limits the spread of performance pay among other employees.

According to the consultancy BSI, the bonuses that are paid are linked to overall results, such as pre-tax earnings or return on investment, rather than individual performance. Bonus payments for meeting targets and improved performance are more common in transnational firms and may become more widespread with the international transfer of executives.

American companies such as the speciality chemical firm Rohm & Haas and the battery manufacturer, Duracell, have fixed international performance pay systems which apply to Italian managers (and in Duracell at lower levels). But indexation means that 'all-merit' policies operate in theory but not in practice. Firms such as Rhône-Poulenc, which have more recently adopted performance pay as an international, company-wide philosophy, have as yet not been able to introduce this in Italy.

The Italian companies which stand out against this general pattern are, not surprisingly, the well-known transnational firms such as Olivetti and Fiat, along with a few national companies such as Alitalia.

Fiat has in fact been responsible for introducing performance pay for managers at the Iveco Ford joint venture in Britain. Whereas Ford applied a general across-the-board increase to all staff except the very top managers, Iveco introduced all-merit reviews for senior managers and undertook an intensive job evaluation exercise (using the HAY system) shortly after the management structure was changed in 1986. Lower down the management hierarchy the company has so far retained a general award, with a limited merit allocation.

In the context of the widespread belief in the 'cultural hostility' of Italian managers to performance pay this example shows that the introduction of new practices is not all one way.

4. Britain: Fragmentation and Labour Market Problems

The context of changing company pay policies in Britain differs from the rest of Europe in many respects. The structures of pay determination have been decentralized for many years and industry-wide agreements have a quite different role and status from that on the continent. The sharp divide between manual and white-collar structures which still exists in all but a small minority of manufacturing firms means that quite distinctive sets of policies and practices may remain for different groups of employees at the same establishment. A variety of craft and general trade unions, often well entrenched at the workplace, has meant that the focus of change in manufacturing has more and more been at establishment level, rather than the industry or even company level. Some specific – and controversial – pay issues which have been aired in Britain over the past few years can thus seem quite alien to those in other countries.

4.1 Integrated Pay and the Japanese Influx

One fairly new development, for example, is the move towards integrated pay structures covering manual and white-collar workers. These have generally been associated with a radical overhaul of working practices at plant level or new systems of industrial relations on greenfield sites. Japanese companies such as Nissan, Toshiba and Komatsu have been widely quoted as a catalyst for change, but it is established firms, such as Shell and Cummins Engine, which are more important because the changes have been negotiated at existing plants. The Japanese companies have usually benefited from being able to draw up pay and working arrangements, select a union and only then proceed to recruit workers.

It is useful to look at these Japanese firms, however, because they do not usually conform to the 'model' of individualized pay and the strong emphasis on merit which is very much in vogue in Britain and France. On the contrary, many of them have resisted the trend.

An example is Sony, which on the whole chooses to reward experience and contributions to a team performance rather than promoting individualism. Although there is performance appraisal for managers which is linked to pay there are not big financial rewards or penalties. In the same vein the company does not have incentives for manual workers. As one experienced Sony manager commented, 'we need people to raise problems. If performance is judged on an individual basis they are not likely to be honest. The balance is difficult to achieve. Britain has gone too far towards individual assessment. It is important, but not at the expense of the team.' Nissan, in contrast, pays performance-related awards to its employees – but it is noticeable that the company has so far paid large general increases as well.

The flexibility that Nissan, Sony and other Japanese firms are developing is much more related to the functions employees perform than the jobs they do. Thus in contrast to the vast majority of firms in Britain which grade people by job, Sony's workers are graded according to their skills – there are no job descriptions. Nissan has only two grades of manufacturing worker (excluding team leaders) so as to maximize job flexibility.

4.2 The Resilience of Established Payment Systems

Bonus and incentive payment systems have been widespread among manual workers for many years, with periodic bargaining over targets and premiums as systems have become corrupted or outdated because of new technology. There is no particular pattern to such incentive schemes, although obviously piecework is heavily concentrated in the textile, clothing and engineering industries. The regular surveys conducted by the regional engineering employers' association in the West Midlands, for example, indicate that more than half the manual workers in the industry are on piecework. This includes workers employed at large firms in the motor components industry, such as Lucas and GKN, as well as Massey-Ferguson.

Piecework is unusually concentrated in the West Midlands, partly because of the relatively strong presence of the traditional engineering industry. But a survey of 200 firms conducted by the Engineering Employers London Association in October 1989 also shows the continuity of established payment practices. The survey highlighted the fact that some 20% of the firms concerned said they were planning to change their schemes because of changes in organizational structure, the introduction of new business systems or new technology: payments under some schemes were felt to be 'too remote' to motivate workers.[19]

This survey also found that some 25% of firms claimed to link manual workers' pay to merit or performance appraisal. This is a much higher proportion than in large companies, which have faced considerable trade union opposition to merit pay for manual workers.

Some companies such as Cummins Engine and Rhône-Poulenc have sought to introduce assessment, but this has been confined either to skills assessment linked to a pay-related training programme or to appraisal which is not linked to pay.

4.3 Merit Pay and New Working Practices

Recently, however, some firms in process industries such as food and pharmaceuticals have been significantly developing the role of skilled maintenance workers, giving them greater responsibility for controlling the work process. At the same time the wider adoption of forms of group working has led to a changing role for production workers.

As part of these changes two Unilever subsidiaries – Birds Eye Wall's and Elida Gibbs – have introduced appraisal with payments linked to defined sets of criteria such as development of skills, knowledge, initiative etc. These agreements apply to craftsmen at Elida Gibbs, where the payments are consolidated into basic rates, and to all manual workers at Birds Eye, where merit payments are made as annual lump sums. These agreements were both reached with the unions concerned and there is union involvement in both the allocation and the size of the payments. In both cases the payments are separate from the annual pay review.

There is a different philosophy behind the two schemes because while the scheme at Elida Gibbs will require renewal once particular skill standards have been reached, the scheme at Birds Eye is open-ended. Birds Eye management argues that it wants 'to be able to recognise each individual's contribution' within the context of group working and that 'new working arrangements require more initiative from each worker, creating more scope for measuring a particular individual's contribution.' The company has also been making moves towards harmonizing manual and white-collar conditions of employment and saw the introduction of an appraisal scheme as another step in this direction.[20]

The Birds Eye view contrasts strongly with the approach of Sony and with the arguments of BSN President, Antoine Riboud, quoted earlier. It will be interesting to see what happens in the British factories recently acquired by BSN from Nabisco.

There are undoubtedly other large firms which are thinking along the same lines as these Unilever subsidiaries, particularly where technical and organizational change is leading to the elimination of certain indirect and supervisory functions and group working is becoming more efficient.

Harmonization of employee conditions is also a factor in companies such as Pilkington, the glass manufacturer, which has moved to integrated pay structures with a salary range for manual workers. However, so far most firms are at a preparatory stage or, like Pilkington, still pay a standard wage in practice.

4.4 Productivity Bonuses or Merit Pay?

The latter half of the 1980s has seen a renewal and extension of bargaining over productivity and efficiency across a wide range of industry, which echoes an earlier period – the late 1960s – when major employers sought to codify industrial relations and exert shop floor control with new pay systems. This was a period which saw a new style of agreement, particularly in the oil and chemical industries, and the beginning of a management campaign to abolish piecework in the car industry and elsewhere and replace it with pay systems less susceptible to control by workers.

A major problem which resulted was the demotivation of workers and as a consequence the recourse to new output-related bonuses and incentive schemes. As we have seen the constant revision of incentives continues to be an underlying feature of many company pay policies in Britain. So far the recourse of companies to 'input-related' systems such as merit pay is too limited to assess its impact among manual workers. In France some employers and commentators have drawn attention to the demotivating impact of pay policies which are too subjective. In Britain there are few signs of this as yet, but, in the words of one Marconi manager, 'people can tolerate reasonable pay differentials between individuals doing the same job but we run risks if the differences become too noticeable.'

4.5 White-Collar Payment Systems and Market Forces

Service-based incremental systems remain widespread for staff in Britain but employers have in many cases made progress beyond the mid-point of salary scales subject to a performance 'bar' or have introduced assessment or discretionary increases at the top end. Examples include the large defence electronics companies such as Ferranti, GEC, Marconi and Plessey and many of the building societies and insurance groups.

The finance sector has been particularly prominent in the move to progression based entirely on merit, partly as a reaction to a tradition of rigid structures but mainly because of the competitive pressures for staff which followed deregulation. Payments described as merit or performance-related have frequently been disguised responses to skill shortages.

Companies in the South East where competitive pay pressures have been strongest have resorted on a wide scale to supplementary payments or accelerated progression to recruit and retain employees.

Some developments which appear to be 'policy-driven' in Britain are therefore more properly described as market-driven.

Most of these firms have retained the practice of awarding general annual pay increases to their white-collar staff, with incremental payments riding on top. However, 'all-merit' pay policies have become more widespread, especially for engineering and computer staff and scientists, where companies have sought more flexibility to hold and recruit key groups which are in short supply. For senior managers this approach is now the practice in a number of large firms but all-merit reviews covering all staff are less common. The well-known cases include the American computer companies – such as IBM, Unisys, Hewlett-Packard etc. – but there this is also the policy of continental European firms such as Petrofina and Rhône-Poulenc, which completed a transition to all-merit reviews for all white-collar staff in 1987. Such policies, it must be said, frequently result in a similar increase for the great majority of employees, and the companies concerned usually apply a basic general increase to their pay scales.

4.6 Decentralization Nears Its Limit

Britain's long tradition of fragmented pay arrangements and the absence of a legal framework for pay and industrial relations has been enriched by even more decentralization over the past few years. The legal props to industry-wide bargaining were removed, which further reduced the role of national agreements. Companies such as Pilkington and BICC moved away from company-wide bargaining. GEC, the country's largest engineering firm, left the employers' federation and pursued a policy of devolving responsibility for pay to local profit centres which at its most extreme resulted in 13 separate company agreements on one site.

These changes have had mixed results. In the early 1980s companies to some extent succeeded in breaking away from the concept of the 'going rate.' But in circumstances of economic revival and a higher inflation rate than most other European countries pay pressures re-emerged. In 1988-89, after unions and employers in the engineering industry failed to agree first on an increase in minimum rates and subsequently on working time, negotiations moved entirely to the local level.

Certain key manufacturing employers clearly feel that even indicative national agreements of the British type are an anachronism given the diversity of companies covered by them. The desire to relate pay to the needs of the business, the conservatism of smaller firms and in some cases moves to longer-term agreements have all contributed to this mood.

Where employers have abandoned sectoral bargaining altogether, however, they have usually retained company-wide bargaining rather than move to pay determination at regional or site level. The most prominent examples are the banks and the supermarket chains. Company-wide bargaining is, however, rare in manufacturing, with a few prominent exceptions such as Ford, ICI and privatized firms such as British Telecom.

4.7 Profit-Related Pay – A Damp Squib

Profit sharing in Britain has increased steadily since fiscal incentives were introduced in 1978. The number of approved schemes under the (amended) 1978 legislation on deferred share schemes grew to over 600 by 1987, although some of these were schemes which had existed for many years and were simply taking advantage of the tax concessions. Several large British companies with a 'paternalistic' tradition – such as ICI and the retail firm John Lewis – have schemes dating back to the 1920s.

The exact extent of profit sharing and share ownership schemes in Britain is unknown but research into large firms conducted at the end of 1987 revealed 231 organizations employing over a million people which operated one or more schemes. Just under a third were cash based schemes – i.e. not eligible for tax relief.[21]

The new departure in 1986 was Profit-Related Pay which, as noted earlier, was unlike traditional profit sharing in that it was specifically designed to become a flexible portion of basic pay. Since mid-1987 the number of PRP schemes has risen from an initial 145 to just over 1,100, covering some 225,000 employees. This seems impressive, but a significant proportion of the total simply results from the abolition of a tax concession to employee trusts. Several established profit sharing schemes thus 'converted' to PRP during the last three months of 1989, when the number of employees covered by PRP rose by 60%. Most firms with PRP are small; there are just six schemes which together cover about 62,000 employees, nearly 30% of the total. The main employers involved are the tobacco firm Gallaher; the chemical firm Tioxide; Van den Bergh, a subsidiary of Unilever; John Lewis (a 'converted' scheme); and two financial institutions, the Nationwide Anglia Building Society and the Norwich Union insurance company.

Although employers' organizations generally welcomed the concept of variable pay, many large firms have been sceptical. In addition the regulations involved are fairly cumbersome. So far this very explicit attempt to promote flexible pay in Britain appears to have failed.[22]

5. West Germany: Flexibility within a Stable Framework

If Britain represents one extreme, with its apparently endless fragmentation, then Germany seems to represent the other. The shake-up taking place in France and, to a much lesser extent, in Italy needs to be balanced against the continuity of stable central authority in Germany, with powerful employers' associations and trade unions and a strong central bank. One explanation for this continuing stability is that the system of pay determination is less rigid and centralized than it might appear.

Minimum pay for most employees is fixed by collective agreements signed for their specific industry at regional and national level. Once signed, agreements are legally enforceable and can be extended by the authorities to become 'generally binding' for all employees in a particular industry. Only some 500 collective agreements, of a total of around 45,000, are generally binding in this way: but the sectors concerned (including construction, commerce and clothing and textiles) together employ about 4.5 million people, almost a quarter of the total West German workforce, according to the Federal Ministry of Labour survey of January 1988.

Although there are around 8,000 agreements involving 2,000 companies, many of these arrangements are old and marginal. The few large companies which have gone their own way are concentrated in the oil industry – Shell, BP, Texaco and Veba – plus the national champions Volkswagen and Lufthansa. All these agreements have been established for many years, and it is rare for prominent firms to abandon industry arrangements. One recent example involved the large publishing firm, Gruner & Jahr, which left the employers' federation after an agreement in the printing industry which put limits on weekend working. The company's argument was that an existing house agreement with the union (IG Druck) took precedence.

The chief reason for this paucity of company bargaining is the parallel system of works council agreements which, among other matters, can cover 'remuneration arrangements' within an establishment, including both the principles of remuneration and 'the introduction and application of new remuneration methods.' The works councils play a major role in applying industry pay and grading agreements at plant level, with the outcome typically expressed in a works agreement.

The result is a considerable variation in both grading and the make-up of pay. In the engineering industry as a whole, the larger firms typically pay 15 - 20% above the regional rates, according to the employers' federation, Gesamtmetall. But in less competitive companies – the shipyards, for example – pay levels are only 2 or 3% higher than the agreed minimum. In the car industry the rate for the same job in the major factories can vary by up to a third compared to the industry reference wage, depending on local grading arrangements and company pay elements.

Large companies thus have considerable scope to vary industry pay arrangements according to the market, skill requirements etc. Payment-by-results systems – individual or, more commonly, group-based – remain widespread. A 1989 survey of the commercial vehicle industry by the engineering union, IG Metall, found that around 60% of manual workers were on PBR systems. In the view of Gesamtmetall these systems 'are certainly not in decline' and provide employers with the opportunity to link pay to the performance of the individual.

What is certainly much less common is merit pay on the Anglo-Saxon or French model. However, there are some signs of change. One interesting example is the chemical company, Henkel, which introduced an element of individualized pay from 1990. Its new arrangements replaced an output-based bonus which became outdated because of extensive capital investment. Now all employees can receive individual performance-related bonuses. The sum available for distribution is to be set annually by management in the light of any general pay awards and the economic situation of the firm, although it is likely to be around 10% of the pay bill, defined in terms of the agreed industry rates. Actual merit awards to individuals may be higher than this: the allocation and amounts involved will be the responsibility of supervisors.

Henkel is a major employer by any standards, with some 30,000 employees worldwide, and 12,000 at its main site in Düsseldorf, but it is much smaller than the Big Three of the German chemical industry – Bayer, Hoechst and BASF. Unusually for a firm of this size, control is still entirely in the hands of the family owners – publicly issued shares are non-voting. Such factors may help to explain a more innovative approach to pay than is normal, but the catalyst for change was the single-status pay structure agreed in the chemical industry at national level in 1987. Henkel used the opportunity to simplify pay arrangements which had been unchanged since the mid-1950s.

How far such moves will be emulated in other German firms is an open question. It is significant that the introduction of these arrangements, which would have excited considerable comment elsewhere, has passed virtually unnoticed in Germany. There is in general far less concern about the relationship between company pay determination and economic performance than in France or Italy, let alone the obsession that there is in Britain. Profit sharing schemes, or other forms of employee financial participation, are largely governed by industry collective agreements under the Capital Formation legislation passed since 1975. Nearly 95% of eligible employees are entitled to a collectively agreed capital formation payment from their employer. Some firms – such as Henkel – do make annual share offers to employees, which are generally seen as a way of ensuring greater loyalty to the firm or, in some cases, a retirement bonus. There is hardly any interest in profit sharing as a form of variable pay.

As yet there is no sign of large firms promoting any substantial modification of systems which have stood the test of time. Fragmentation is more likely among the *Mittelstand* – the mass of small to medium enterprises which are restless at some of the rigidities of the system. This is especially noticeable with negotiations over working time. The large firms can more easily concede cuts in hours because they have the production volumes, the capital equipment and the labour force necessary to adopt more flexible patterns of work. Smaller firms will find it extremely costly to follow suit.

There remains the large question of the impact of the upheavals in the East. There is bound to be friction over wages in East Germany and the most likely outcome – at least in the interim – is a series of works agreements covering some of the old *Kombinate*. But it is hard to see how a parallel system could persist independently alongside the established industry-wide arrangements. Renewed debate about the merits of a more formalized system of two-tier bargaining is likely to be one consequence of German reunification.

6. Policy Trends within Transnational Firms

Against the background of diversity we have considered so far (without even touching on the contrasting conditions of Spain or the smaller countries of the Community), it is obviously dangerous to generalize too much about the behaviour of transnational firms, which have to operate within national rules – sometimes more strictly than their purely national counterparts. But there are some common features and points of convergence.

The tendency towards the decentralization of decision-making about pay to country level (and to different subsidiaries within a country) is very general. A broad spectrum of companies – such as 3M, Rhône-Poulenc, Solvay and Alcatel – agrees that while decisions about top management pay need to be made group-wide – along with those decisions with long-term cost implications, such as pensions – policy on pay increases and industrial relations must be left to country managers. This may seem obvious – and some companies have always had this approach – but it is not so long since prominent American firms, for example ITT, insisted on a strong supranational input.

The vetting of agreements with trade unions was not purely an American habit. There were French firms, such as Bull, which required monthly reports from expatriate managers. There seem to be few firms with such centralized policies today. The exceptions are generally 'single-product' companies such as Duracell, the US-owned battery manufacturer, which has a common appraisal system and staff grading structure across 14 countries in Europe. Pay reviews have to be agreed with the European headquarters, although the pay levels of industrial staff are of course decided locally. This is quite different from, say, Rhône-Poulenc, where the British company reports on just eight salaries to the French parent. The move towards giving local managers authority is symbolized by the way in which the American transnationals have been changing in the last few years, replacing expatriate national and regional managers with a European management team.

Within this general framework of devolved authority, however, convergence is taking place and certain corporate policies are being promoted. Increasingly this is a process of cross-fertilization – new policies do not always come from the centre.

The British chemical company Tioxide, for example, applies a common job evaluation system across Europe – the HAY system – as do a number of 'Anglo-Saxon' companies, and others such as Fiat (some more flexibly than others, recognizing that the HAY system itself varies from country to country). Rhône-Poulenc has used HAY in Britain, Brazil and the US since 1983 and is now gradually adopting it in France. The company is linking its own system with HAY and encouraging other subsidiaries to adopt it. The idea is that a common approach provides a way of 'translating' different national systems – perhaps helping to overcome the institutional barrier of the hierarchy of *cadres* in France, for example, or making it easier for French management to accept the transfer of a young engineer from abroad on a higher salary than expected.

But well-known systems such as HAY do not necessarily meet with universal approval. In some countries the key firms do not use it, for example Holland. The Belgian firm, Solvay, which has been trying to introduce job evaluation at executive level for the first time, commented that rating senior management by a number of points is inappropriate when the jobs towards the top of a firm are increasingly 'individual.' Different national salary policies are required.

Solvay is an example of a 'traditional' firm. There is a decentralized management style but an emphasis on the integration of the company, family ownership etc. Basic pay at management level is still strongly influenced by seniority. This is quite different from the pattern in most British and American companies, but still much closer to the mentality of several of the largest French companies.

In one large French firm, for example, the grading of senior international management is considered too sensitive to reveal to those concerned at the moment. Although this company is changing its philosophy towards an emphasis on management performance rather than service, its major French subsidiaries have yet to adopt this policy wholeheartedly. The identification of 'high-flyers' among the company's younger managers has also caused controversy.

But other leading French firms are much more obviously part of the wider trend towards a stress on performance. Michelin has long been known for its emphasis on the individual and has carried this approach into its foreign subsidiaries. The company continues to insist on strong French ties – including a layer of expatriate managers and work experience placements for French undergraduates abroad. There is a strong technical input from the centre and the French system of job ranking is used as a focal point for international comparisons. The individualistic approach is reflected in the company's rejection of executive status symbols such as company cars, which is based on a belief that employees 'should have the freedom to dispose of their income as they choose.'

This contrasts with the changing approach of a firm such as Rhône-Poulenc. The company has set up two 'action programmes.' One of these emphasizes decentralization through the development of 'home group projects' – centres of group-wide projects located outside the home country. The other is the concept of an 'overall remuneration' package: general increases linked to the market; individual rises depending on increased skills, qualifications and job ranking; and profit sharing in one form or another.

The dynamic for change in Rhône-Poulenc is chiefly the company's dramatic expansion internationally (above all in the US) over the past three or four years. Its major international subsidiaries in Britain, Brazil and now the USA have enjoyed considerable autonomy in the past and have developed a performance-oriented culture faster than their parent. So the impetus for change – such as performance-related pay for senior management – has in some cases come from outside France (in this case from Britain) and has subsequently been adopted by the parent company.

There are still considerable differences in national emphasis. The French companies start their bonus system at a lower salary grade than the British for example. But the performance element in the French salary is fairly small, whereas in Britain the company now pays all its non-manual staff on an 'all-merit' basis. However, the French companies, unlike the British, have up to 1.5% available for distribution in merit or skill awards on the shop floor. The French companies do more skills training and reward employees accordingly.

Rhône-Poulenc is one of many companies which is at a transitional stage in developing the coordination of its personnel policies across Europe. The aim, in the words of the British computer company ICL, is to 'develop the compatibility of systems' rather than implement a single system across Europe, which would blur the emphasis on national independence and performance and be very time-consuming to achieve. It is the encouragement of compatibility which above all characterizes those firms which are seeking to transfer larger numbers of professional and managerial staff between countries.

The need for such internationalization is strongest in companies which are seeking to become truly transnational. An increasingly familiar aim is the development of centres of excellence outside the 'home' country – promoting decentralization, but in a way which enables the company to deploy the necessary international resources to compete.[23] Rhône-Poulenc speaks of the need to mobilize the diversified international expertise within the firm, for example

British pharmaceutical research which is strong and very cost-effective or the superior technical engineering skills of the French. A wider range of people need to be available as an international resource.

It is in this context that the promotion of performance culture needs to be seen. Much of the theorizing of performance pay, profit-related pay and 'flexibility' in general emphasizes the macroeconomic consequences or the advantages for firms in achieving more control of costs. In fact these developments have much more to do with the dynamics of international competition between firms. The pressures of this competition are tending to drive up pay: the question facing companies, in the words of one British manager, is how 'to ensure that every £1 spent on payroll gives good value in terms of attracting, retaining and motivating employees – particularly the good performers.'[24] The currencies may be different but the arguments in different European countries are much the same.

This aim lies behind the strong initial input of a performance-related approach to management pay by such firms as Fiat, in the case of the Iveco Ford joint venture in Britain, or by Tioxide in the case of takeovers in France and Germany. The general view is that takeovers provide a unique opportunity for the introduction of performance-related pay for managers, which may then trickle down to other parts of the company.

7. Towards a European Model?

Large transnational manufacturing firms are leading the way in modifying the impact of national systems which do not fit their business needs. In doing so many of their policies are tending to converge, even while they emphasize the decentralized nature of decision-making about most matters to do with employee relations. Can one therefore perceive the outlines of a future 'European model' for the firm?

There are four factors which suggest we may be moving broadly in this direction.

1. Transnational companies have a tendency to pay at the upper quartile of the national market – sometimes as a conscious policy, sometimes because they have to be seen to be good employers. This is particularly noticeable outside the 'home' country. A company may aim to pay around the average of the majors at

home, but abroad it often has to be more 'aggressive' because it is unable to offer staff the same career paths. This applies most obviously to managers and professionals, but it tends to influence pay throughout a company.

2. As we have seen, large transnational firms are increasingly promoting performance-related policies – individualized, profit-related, linked to the performance of a business unit, or a combination of these. Within the distinctive national markets and systems where they operate, these companies now seem to be gravitating towards similar policies.

3. The increased number of short-term transfers within Europe at executive level (and in some cases lower down the organization) means there is a need for compatible structures, common approaches to job evaluation, common understanding of relativities. The high cost of traditional 'expatriate' pay packages is also making companies look at ways of making their national systems fit together. If you can move away from a 'home' policy, transfers become less expensive.

   Internal company policies will therefore tend to converge, but this may not simply mean conformity to a home country 'norm.' As firms strive to develop centres of international excellence in their different national companies, it becomes less appropriate to have policies strongly identified with a single national approach. Personnel managers within these firms are increasingly meeting on a regular basis – twice a year in Rhône-Poulenc, once every two months in Iveco – to ensure the common approach is understood and that the experience of one country is spread to others.

4. The need for a high quality, high value added, approach to products and to manufacturing, in the face of lower cost production from newly industrializing countries in Asia and Latin America, suggests that an emphasis on training, the personal development of employees, and good and stable relations with trade unions will become more important for competitiveness. A more 'corporatist' approach at the level of the firm may emerge.

But there are also a number of factors to set against these tendencies.

1. There are very different conditions and traditions within Europe, which tend to die hard – especially when it comes to management pay.

2. A 'foreign' firm cannot ride rough shod over the rules and in fact is often more constrained than purely local firms.
3. There are different structures of ownership within firms which mean, for example, that the generalized introduction of profit sharing in national companies is impossible, or not to the liking of the parent.
4. Strongly entrenched trade union organizations among manual workers in countries such as Germany, Britain, Holland and, to some extent, Italy are likely to persuade companies to trim their sails or adapt some of their policies significantly.
5. There are countervailing tendencies such as:
   • the limitations of the changes taking place in Italy, even in firms such as Fiat and Olivetti;
   • the dangers from the uncontrolled development of individualization which we may be seeing in France;
   • the impact of labour market pressures on company policies which is evident in Britain.
6. Some highly successful – and influential – firms, most notably German and Japanese, are reluctant to go down the road of decentralization and performance pay.
7. Finally, there is the serious obstacle to change inherent in the different national pensions and social security regimes. Companies will try to link their policies, but until there is legislative change pension differences will remain a block in the minds of many managers.

At the moment we are in a period of transition. If one were to hazard an opinion it is that we are somewhere near the start of a process of convergence in the policies and practices of major parts of European manufacturing industry. The impact of this in the long term may be profound but the process will be long, faltering and uneven.

Notes

1. '1992: Personnel Management and the Single European Market,' Income Data Services/Institute of Personnel Management, October 1988.
2. See the paper by Daniel Vaughan-Whitehead for the Groupe Lacroix:'Négociations salariales en Europe – continuité et changements.'
3. Negociation Collective, Bilan du CNPF – 1987 et 1988 (Liaisons Sociales: Legislation Sociale 6235, 9 May 1989).
4. Annual Report of the Union des industries Métallurgiques et Minières for 1987/88.
5. 'L'intéressement', Union des industries Métallurgiques et Minières, 1987.
6. *The Share Economy,*. Harvard University Press, 1984.
7. Annual report of the UIMM for 1987/88.

8. Union des industries Métallurgiques et Minières, Annual Reports.
9. 'Une individualisation des salaires?' UIMM, November 1988.
10. Armand Mella, Human Resources Director, Casino quoted in Liaisons Sociales Mensuel No. 25, January 1988.
11. Ibid.
12. For example in a seminar on bonus pay at the 1989 conference on human resources organiZed by Liaisons Sociales.
13. Reported in *Les Echos*, 18 October 1989.
14. Data from the Fiom-Cgil union's review of the bargaining round ('Meta,' November-December 1988) and the Associazione Industriale Lombarda employers' association pay survey, October 1988.
15. 'Wages in Italy,' Paper prepared for the EC working group on 'Wages in Europe,' September 1989.
16. 'Meta,' op. cit.
17. *Wall Street Journal*, 23.January.1988. Mr Pininfarina's own company negotiated a rather more modest two-tier company agreement with a small variable 'managerial efficiency premium' in October 1988.
18. Survey by the CER research organization, quoted in IDS European Report 327, March 1989.
19. 'Enquiry into Incentive Schemes for Manual Workers.' Engineering Employers London Association, October 1989.
20. These agreements are discussed in full in a recent IDS Study: 'Appraising Manual Workers' Performance,' September 1989.
21. 'Developments in Profit Sharing and Employee Share Ownership,' Centre for Research into Industrial Democracy and Participation, University of Glasgow, June 1987.
22. The more usual forms of cash profit sharing, however, continue to pay out substantial sums. In 34 such schemes, covering well over 800,000 employees (heavily concentrated in the finance sector and retailing), the 1989 payments were mainly between 5% and 10%, usually pro rata to salary. The highest payments – over 20% – were at John Lewis (figures from IDS Report 551, August 1989).
23. The process is well described in a recent book by Christopher Bartlett and Sumantra Ghoshal: *Managing across Borders: The Transnational Solution*, Harvard Business School Press, 1989.
24. Richard Coles, formerly Personnel Policies Manager, Ferranti International, now Head of Human Resources, Christian Salvesen, in 'A New Look at Pay Structures.' Paper presented to the 1988 conference of the Institute of Personnel Management.

6. Industrial Relations and the Role of the State in the EEC Countries

Carlo Dell'Aringa

1. Introduction

There is widespread agreement that both industrial relations systems and the role of the state in wage regulation have been under great pressure in recent times, although the reaction to that pressure has varied quite considerably from one country to another.

There have also been different sets of economic pressures. The first were macroeconomic – the oil shocks of the 1970s and early 1980s. By macroeconomic one usually refers primarily to those forces that determine domestic wage and price changes, hence linking these changes to the level of economic activity i.e. unemployment, and sometimes to growth rates as well. Each country has reacted differently to a common external pressure such as the oil shocks, and this can be explained by the differing characteristics of their industrial relations systems and the roles played by the state in regulating the functioning of the labour market. These varying reactions are at the same time linked to different results in macroeconomic performance. The deterioration of economic activity has varied greatly from country to country. The worst performances occurred in the EEC countries, whilst the Scandinavian countries, Austria, Switzerland, Japan, the US and Canada fared relatively better in terms of unemployment and inflation (Table 1).

Table 1. Growth, unemployment and inflation 1974-87:
An international comparison. (GNP, prices: % change from previous year; unemployment: average over period)

	Real GNP	Standardized unemployment rates	Consumer prices
Japan	3.78	2.27	5.94
Switzerland	1.06	0.49	3.71
Austria	2.19	2.86	5.13
Norway	3.94	2.16	8.88
Sweden	1.79	2.35	8.99
Germany	1.86	4.83	3.79
Denmark	1.90	7.42	8.87
Finland	2.90	4.86	9.90
Netherlands	2.05	7.81	5.00
Belgium	1.84	9.15	6.82
Australia	2.77	6.57	10.16
United Kingdom	1.71	8.15	11.14
Italy	2.85	8.30	14.10
France	2.16	7.01	9.41
United States	2.49	7.22	6.98
Canada	3.47	8.61	7.96

Source: OECD, Economic Outlook, No. 44.

The relationship between industrial relations and economic performance has been explained in different ways. Some interpret differences in economic performance according to the degree of corporatism found in the various countries (Tarantelli 1986, Crouch 1985, Bruno and Sachs, to name a few), whilst others associate economic success with flexibility and market forces (as in the case of some OECD studies). Other scholars take into consideration both corporatism and market forces when explaining empirical evidence (Calmfors and Driffil 1988, Freeman 1988c and Olson 1988 recently); wage moderation can be achieved in both kinds of industrial relations systems.

In neocorporatist countries, characterized by large interest groups representing substantial sections of society, we find institutional structures that facilitate tripartite consultation and permit incomes policies based on consensus to be effectively applied. Conflict is generally low, and negotiation occurs primarily at a centralized level. This system is typical of the Scandinavian countries and of Austria. Some of the most important factors that enable these systems to operate are the size of coalitions, the proportion of the cost of each intervention sustained by each coalition (Olson 1982), and the extent to which industrial relations are centralized.

The second system which allows real wage moderation is the complete opposite of that described above, and is composed of competitive markets, weak interest groups, fragmented wage negotiations and industrial relations that take place primarily at individual firm level. In these countries, wage moderation is imposed by market mechanisms. In the 1970s and 1980s, the economic situation of the United States and Canada featured wage moderation and relatively good inflation and employment growth performance although their employment record is somewhat less positive than that of the corporatist countries.

Those countries with an industrial relations system that falls between these two opposite poles, such as Italy, France and the UK, are in the worst situation: interest organizations are strong enough to impose their conditions during the negotiating process, but are not encompassing enough to sustain the social costs of their actions.

2. The Empirical Analysis

Analyzing the relationship between industrial relations and macroeconomic performance has interested and occupied many economists, political scientists and students of industrial relations. The most common methodology used for empirical analysis is to correlate rankings of the various countries according to indicators of economic performance, the level of corporatism and the centralization of the industrial relations systems.

The most commonly used performance indicators are unemployment and inflation rates, or a mix of these two, such as the Okun index which is the sum of these rates. The indicators used to determine a country's degree of corporatism are often similar, even though the importance given to each may differ from author to author. Some underline the degree to which collective bargaining is centralized, whilst others, especially political scientists, underline the importance of consensus, social cohesion and integration between the labour market, firms and government.

Table 2. Rank orderings of countries according to their degree of centralization.

Tarantelli	Schmitter	Cameron Sachs	Bruno & Driffil	Calmfors	Blyth	Dell'Aringa
Austria	Austria	Sweden	Austria	Austria	Austria	Austria
Japan	Norway	Norway	Germany	Norway	Norway	Norway
Germany	Sweden	Austria	Netherlands	Sweden	Sweden	Sweden
Denmark	Denmark	Belgium	Norway	Denmark	Denmark	Denmark
Finland	Finland	Finland	Sweden	Finland	Finland	Finland
Norway	Netherlands	Denmark	Switzerland	Germany	New Zealand	Germany
Sweden	Belgium	Netherlands	Denmark	Netherlands	Australia	Netherlands
Netherlands	Germany	Germany	Finland	Belgium	Germany	Belgium
Belgium	Switzerland	UK	Belgium	New Zealand	Belgium	Switzerland
France	USA	Australia	Japan	Australia	Netherlands	Australia
Australia	Canada	Switzerland	New Zealand	France	Japan	Japan
Italy	France	Italy	UK	UK	France	France
UK	UK	Canada	France	Italy	UK	UK
Canada	Italy	USA	Italy	Japan	Italy	Italy
USA		France	Australia	Switzerland	USA	Canada
		Japan	Canada	USA	Canada	USA
			USA	Canada		

Continued...

Table 2. (cont.) Rank orderings of countries according to their degree of corporatism.

Tarantelli	Schmitter	Cameron	Bruno & Sachs	Lehner	Dell'Aringa
Austria	Austria	Sweden	Austria	Japan	Japan
Germany	Norway	Norway	Germany	Switzerland	Switzerland
Japan	Sweden	Austria	Netherlands	Austria	Austria
Sweden	Finland	Belgium	Norway	Sweden	Norway
Norway	Denmark	Finland	Sweden	Norway	Sweden
Denmark	Netherlands	Denmark	Switzerland	Netherlands	Denmark
Australia	Belgium	Netherlands	Denmark	Belgium	Germany
Netherlands	Germany	Germany	Finland	Germany	Finland
Finland	Canada	UK	Belgium	Denmark	Netherlands
Belgium	France	Switzerland	Japan	Finland	Belgium
Canada	UK	Australia	New Zealand	Australia	Australia
USA	Switzerland	Italy	UK	UK	UK
France	Italy	Canada	France	Italy	France
UK		USA	Italy	USA	Italy
Switzerland		France	Australia	Canada	UK
Italy		Japan	Canada	France	Canada
			USA		

Table 3. Corporatism and economic performance. (Differences in average percentage changes).

	Okun Index				Growth rates			Inflation rates		
	74-82/ 60-73	83-87/ 74-82	74-87/ 60-73	74-87/ 60-73*	74-82/ 60-73	83-87/ 74-82	74-87/ 60-73	74-82/ 60-73	83-87/ 74-82	74-87/ 60-73
Concordance	1.65	-4.12	0.17	-3.33	-4.89	1.15	-4.48	1.08	-4.70	-0.60
High corporatism	4.16	-1.99	3.45	0.65	-1.67	0.18	-1.61	0.93	-2.70	-0.03
Medium corporatism	8.50	-1.83	7.85	3.82	-3.06	0.52	-2.88	4.38	-4.83	2.66
Weak corporatism	12.08	-3.69	10.76	4.21	-2.44	0.38	-2.30	9.28	-7.91	6.45
Pluralism	8.80	-4.02	7.36	3.50	-1.99	1.79	-1.35	5.94	-5.51	3.97
Japan	3.01	-6.58	0.66	-4.51	-5.82	0.31	-5.70	2.17	-7.24	-0.41
Switzerland	0.29	-1.67	-0.31	-2.15	-3.97	2.00	-3.26	-0.02	-2.16	-0.79
Austria	2.26	-1.04	1.89	-1.14	-2.96	-0.61	-3.17	1.89	-3.25	0.73
Norway	4.60	-1.86	3.94	2.26	0.08	0.19	0.15	4.39	-2.55	3.48
Sweden	5.63	-3.07	4.54	0.85	-2.14	0.94	-1.81	5.43	-3.77	4.09
Germany	4.19	-0.08	4.16	1.11	-3.38	0.58	-3.17	1.36	-3.43	0.14

Continued...

Table 3. (cont.) Corporatism and economic performance. (Differences in average percentage changes).

	74-82/60-73	83-87/74-82	74-87/60-73	74-87/60-73*	74-82/60-73	83-87/74-82	74-87/60-73	74-82/60-73	83-87/74-82	74-87/60-73
Denmark	9.95	-3.38	8.74	3.97	-2.52	1.21	-2.08	4.72	-5.87	2.62
Finland	9.03	-6.09	6.86	1.26	-3.21	0.44	-3.05	6.56	-6.60	4.20
Netherl.	6.67	-0.73	6.41	1.94	-2.85	0.05	-2.83	1.67	-5.38	-0.25
Belgium	9.88	-0.02	9.87	5.65	-3.19	-0.56	-3.39	4.34	-3.83	2.97
Austral.	11.28	-0.68	11.04	8.97	-3.24	1.38	-2.75	7.64	-3.86	6.26
U.K.	12.66	-5.09	10.84	4.27	-2.62	2.60	-1.69	9.19	-10.08	5.59
Italy	13.76	-4.64	12.10	4.57	-1.88	-0.63	-2.11	12.02	-7.90	9.20
France	9.81	-1.35	9.33	3.78	-2.81	-0.84	-3.11	6.62	-5.75	4.56
U.S.A.	8.23	-5.41	6.30	2.35	-1.57	2.36	-0.73	5.51	-5.69	3.48
Canada	9.36	-2.63	8.42	4.66	-2.40	1.23	-1.96	6.37	-5.33	4.46

Note: * (average unemployment rate 1974-87 + average inflation rate 1985-87) less (average unemployment rate 1960-73 + average inflation rate 1960-73).

An example of the latter factors are Japan and Switzerland, whose industrial relations systems are relatively decentralized, but have, as Lehner (1988) says, a high level of 'concordance,' or social agreement. Social cohesion and stability are features of the political system as a whole, rather than of the narrower system of industrial relations, but they nevertheless could prove the most important indicators in explaining economic performance. The concept of corporatism generally referred to has a wider scope than the concept of centralization of industrial relations systems; we might say that corporatism includes centralization amongst the other aspects of social life and political organization. Government involvement in wage negotiation, for example, is a necessary ingredient of corporatism. For some authors (but not all), corporatism also implies that political and ideological similarities exist between unions and governments (e.g. Paloheimo 1988).

Each country goes through phases in which the levels of corporatism and/or centralization of industrial relations increase or decrease considerably, so when their ranking is defined, the period of reference is important. An example is Australia, where the changes which started in 1983 would cause this country to be ranked amongst those with a high level of corporatism.

Table 2 shows how different authors have ranked the levels of corporatism and centralization for the major industrialized countries. The order differs according to whether the indicator used is that of centralization or corporatism, and we find the greatest differences amongst the relative positions of Japan, Switzerland, Germany and the Netherlands, which rank high in the area of consensus systems (corporatism) but are in an intermediate position from the point of view of centralization. The ranking of these countries in the corporatism classification varies according to the weight each author attributes to consensus and centralization factors.

For the empirical analysis that follows, two rank orderings have been constructed. The first (CORP) embodies Lehner and Tarantelli's corporatist rankings, where Japan and Switzerland are at the top, whereas the more truly neocorporatist countries – Austria, Norway and Sweden – make up the next group. In an intermediate position are Germany, Denmark, Finland, Australia, Netherlands and Belgium. In some of these countries unionization is high, although the unions themselves are generally divided for linguistic or religious reasons (Belgium, the Netherlands) or for ideological reasons (Finland) and negotiations are held primarily at sectoral level.

The countries with a low level of corporatism are Italy, France and the United Kingdom; their industrial relations systems are fragmented and unstable, unionization is relatively high (with the exception of France) and many of the most powerful unions are divided along ideological and political lines, making it difficult to coordinate and implement effective incomes policies. Bargaining occurs at various levels in these countries, but no coordination exists between them.

Finally there are the North American countries (US and Canada), with pluralistic systems of low unionization, extremely decentralized bargaining at firm level, and a lack of cooperation and involvement mechanism between government and unions. The ranking of centralization levels (CENTR) differs from the previous one in so much as Japan and Switzerland are now in intermediate positions; the simple correlation coefficient between the two rankings is 0.75.

Table 3 shows several performance indicators for these groups of countries in the two periods following the oil crisis of 1973: the stagflation period (1974-82) and that of economic recovery (1983-87). These indicators are variations between the annual averages for each period and those of the preceding period. It is interesting to note the relationship between the degree of corporatism and/or centralization, and the variations of economic performance in the critical periods as compared to the previous one.

In fact, we can observe a general worsening of economic performance for the entire period 1974-87, and for the crucial period 1974-82 when compared to the base period, but this decline varies from country to country. In the 'concordance' countries economic performance declined only slightly, whereas it deteriorated increasingly in countries with strong, average and weak corporatism. Pluralistic countries performed similarly to those with a medium degree of corporatism, and we thus find something of a 'U' relationship between the two.

Table 4. Changes in performance and corporatism-centralization ranking: correlation coefficients.

		Corporatism	Centralization
GNP	74-82/60-73	0.28	-0.18
	83-87/74-82	0.22	0.41
	74-87/60-73	0.35	-0.03
Standardized	74-82/60-73	0.46	0.24
unemployment	83-87/74-82	0.47	0.24
rate	74-87/60-73	0.50	0.23
Inflation	74-82/60-73	0.74	0.48
rate	83-87/74-82	-0.49	-0.55
	74-87/60-73	0.72*	0.40
Okun index	74-82/60-73	0.82	0.49
	83-87/74-82	-0.12	-0.35
	74-87/60-73	0.82*	0.43
Adjusted	74-87/60-73	0.73*	0.28

Notes:
Okun index**
* Significant at the 0.001 level.
** Okun 74-87=average unemployment rate 1974-87 + average inflation rate 1985-87.

Table 4 gives some descriptive statistics that draw the same conclusions by using the Pearson correlation coefficients between corporatist and centralization rankings and those of economic performance indicators. The resulting positive coefficient for the inflation, unemployment and Okun indicators shows that the higher the level of corporatism or centralization, the better the performance.

The correlation coefficients are positive and the coefficients are high for both the entire 1974-87 period, and that of 1974-82; coefficients for the corporatist ranking are higher than those for centralization. The concordance countries exert a major influence on the results for corporatism, as their performance in terms of unemployment and inflation is very good, and they stand at the top of the corporatist ranking.

The results for the 1983-87 period are totally different, particularly when performance is compared to that of the previous period. Here the correlation is almost inverted, that is, performance improves as the level of corporatism declines. The same conclusions can be reached by looking at the results of several linear regressions presented in Table 5.

Table 5. Corporatism, centralization, conflict and performance: regression analysis (1974/87)-(1960/73).
Dependent variable: change in the Okun Index.

	A	B	C	D	E
CONSTANT	1.79	3.41	-1.74	-1.84	2.67
	(1.67)	(1.72)	(-1.08)	(-1.07)	(1.79)
CORP	0.64				
	(5.25)				
CENTR		0.35		0.03	
		(1.76)		(0.23)	
L(GPS)			1.77	1.72	
			(4.99)	(4.56)	
CORPU					0.51
					(3.02)
R^2	0.63	0.12	0.66	0.64	0.35
F	27.60	3.11	30.29	14.10	9.10

Notes:
Variables: CORP, CENTR = corporatism and centralization rankings (see Table 3).
L(GPS) = logarithm of the average days lost through strikes in the 1965-86 period.
CORPU = corporatism ranking U shaped: Japan, Switzerland, United States, Canada, Austria, Norway, Sweden, Italy, France, United Kingdom, Germany, Denmark, Finland, the Netherlands, Belgium, Australia.
For the group of regressions relative to the latest period, CORPU is constructed placing at the top of the ranking the pluralist countries: United States, Canada, Japan, Switzerland, United Kingdom, Italy, France, Austria, Norway, Sweden, Germany, Denmark, Finland, Australia, Belgium, the Netherlands.
Dependent variable: Change in Okun index between period averages. Cross-countries OLS, 16 countries (t-statistics in parentheses).

Table 5a. (1974/82)-(1960/73).

	A	B	C	D	E
CONSTANT	2.64 (2.45)	3.87 (1.98)	-1.70 (-1.29)	-1.77 (-1.26)	4.10 (2.49)
CORP	0.66 (5.36)				
CENTR		0.41 (2.09)		0.28 (0.22)	
L(GPS)			1.94 (7.37)	1.90 (5.89)	
CORPU					0.45 (2.43)
R^2	0.64	0.18	0.79	0.78	0.25
F	28.70	4.37	54.35	25.20	5.92

Notes: See Table 5.

Table 5b. (1983/87)-(1974/82).

	A	B	C	D	E
CONSTANT	-2.38 (2.25)	-1.28 (-1.08)	-0.52 (-0.34)	-0.20 (-.13)	-4.74 (-4.61)
CORP	-0.05 (-0.43)				
CENTR		-0.17 (-1.4)		-0.10 (-0.75)	
L(GPS)			-0.48 (-1.58)	-0.35 (-1.01)	
CORPU					0.23 (2.18)
R^2	-0.06	0.06	0.09	0.06	0.20
F	0.19	1.96	2.50	1.49	4.77

Notes: See Table 5.

The estimates, which are based on cross-country data, consider the impact of corporatism and centralization on variations in the Okun index.

In an effort to detect the 'U' relationship between industrial relations systems and economic performance, other corporatist rankings besides that of Table 2 (which ranks the countries in descending order) were tried. The 'U' rankings (CORPU) place batches of countries in an alternating sequence, thus ranking both concordance and pluralistic countries in the top positions, strong and weak corporatist countries second, and those with an intermediate level of corporatism in last place.

The degree of corporatism in its monotonic specification is the explanatory variable that statistically shows the best results in producing changes in the Okun index, for both the 1974-87 period when compared to before the oil crisis, and the 1974-82 period. The level of centralization, in contrast, appears to be of less significance. The consensus systems appear to produce the best performances in terms of variations of the Okun index, a point revealed by the inclusion of an indicator for the level of conflict in each country among the explanatory variables. In accordance with McCallum (1986), this indicator is measured by the logarithm of the number of days lost for strikes.

3. The Role of the State

The reason why most corporatist countries were able to keep unemployment levels low during the years of stagflation must, to a certain extent, be attributed to the policies followed by the governments of that time. Full employment was maintained primarily through employment growth in the public sector, activist labour policies (especially in Sweden) and expansive fiscal and monetary policies in Austria and Norway (see Table 6).

Many structural aspects of labour markets changed during the 1980s; an increasing need for flexibility was the result of new economic pressures on both the system of industrial relations and the regulatory role of the State. The world was increasingly dominated by the financial preoccupations of firms, and this threatened stable industrial relations, as investment in human resources and in improving the employer-union relationship no longer appealed to firms more intent on short-term profits.

Table 6. Employment in the private and in the public sector: percentage change (1973-82).

	Private sector	Public sector
Australia	5	31
Austria	-3	30
Belgium	-9	29
Canada	21	22
Finland	1	25
France	-1	13
Germany	-8	19
Italy	5	23
Japan	7	16
Netherlands	4	22
Norway	15	46
Sweden	-3	45
Switzerland	-7	16
United Kingdom	-8	9
United States	17	13

Source: Schmidt, 1988, p.16.

Technological change was another important economic pressure, undermining the old mass assembly line system, and introducing a more 'customized' system of production. The market found itself under pressure to augment its 'flexible specialization' capacities and to find different market niches: emphasis was laid on change, rather than stability in industrial relations. Once more, collective bargaining relationships dependent on continuity tended to be undermined by such developments.

The systems which suffered most from these economic pressures were the most highly centralized: the growing complexity of productive organization and the shift towards flexibility cannot be regulated by a monopolistic and centralized system. Bargaining began to be more decentralized, and this inevitably brought with it an increasing differentiation in industrial relations patterns. In this context 'deregulation' becomes the dominant theme, and is used against not only the rigidities of industrial relations, but also the rigidities found in all regulatory approaches, and consequently social life as well. The need for 'control' seemed to fade, starting with incomes policies, once the concern of concerted action in the past.

The most highly centralized and corporatist system seemed to show an intrinsic instability and social democratic governments were substituted by conservative regimes for a certain number of years. There was less room for manoeuvre in the market as a result of slowing growth rates and increasing public deficit levels, and those factors which eroded the consensus system during the 1980s are tied to this situation. In addition, different categories of workers (white collar and public employees) took on a new and greater importance, hence reducing the capacity of central labour organizations to put together unified demand packages, and increasing the number of disputes, especially in the public sector. The traditional wage round, where the industrial sector was still the wage leader, at this point collapsed, and this role seems to have been assumed by the public sector, protected and not exposed to international competition. The result has been lower wage flexibility and higher wage dispersion.

The data on performance indicators used here show a certain decline in the economic performance of the highly corporatist countries as compared with other countries. This observation is valid for the years of deflation (1983-87) when we consider the variations of most variables for this period on the previous period (Table 5); Japan and Switzerland registered relatively positive performances, whilst the Scandinavian countries and Austria showed rather poor results in comparison to the nations with a more fragmented system.

Whether assessing variations in the Okun index or changes in the GDP growth rate between 1983-87 and that of the preceding period (1974-82), one notes a ranking that is almost the inverse of that for the stagflation years. In fact, with the exception of the concordance countries, improved performances (which show negative variations in the Okun index) increase as the level of corporatism decreases.

Nevertheless, it should be remembered that the period 1983-87 under examination is in fact very short, and the different results obtained are not sufficient to modify the overall picture emerging from an analysis of the last 15 to 20 years, during which, on average, the most highly corporatist countries showed the best macroeconomic performances. Nonetheless, these four years cannot be ignored, and should perhaps be considered as a turning point, or at least the signal of a possible turnaround in trends.

4. Conclusions

Among the advanced industrial countries, those of the EEC experienced the greatest upsurge of unemployment in the years following the oil crises. They are also the countries with the most conflictual and difficult industrial relations systems, composed of unions powerful enough to impose their interests in the bargaining process, but at the same time too numerous and not encompassing enough to internalize the results. In those countries with systems closest to the neocorporatist model (Denmark and Germany), the prevailing tendency in the 1980s was towards more decentralized and conflictual industrial relations, where works councils play a more important role in the bargaining process.

European economic integration will surely have a strong impact on the industrial relations systems of its member countries, if only because of its repercussions on the economic performance of various sectors, and the pressure it will bring to bear on the regulation of labour-management relations and labour costs.

The questions raised at this point are the following: what type of modifications to the industrial relations system may be necessary (and feasible) to improve employment performance in the EEC countries? What effects will European integration have on these systems?

Although it is impossible to answer these questions at this stage, several interesting elements have emerged from the analysis we report here. The first is that European countries will have to live with the problems that fragmented unions and lack of consensus and social cohesion create. The second is that bargaining at firm level looks certain to increase, but sectoral bargaining will generally maintain its present level of importance. This, at least, is what we may predict for the foreseeable future.

Some authors in fact forecast that it is precisely at sectoral and local levels that the bargaining process will develop most in the future. The 'r' level of bargaining, they say, offers a real alternative to neocorporatism and neoliberalism – at this level we already have examples of cooperation between social and political partners, such as the Italian geographical 'districts.' Cooperation between firms and unions at this level could be utilized to increase investment in activities such as vocational training and research and development, which have become so strategic in sustaining growth and productivity. These activities can be regarded as the 'public goods' of firms and single employees.

It is for this reason that higher level bodies, such as sectoral level unions, can solve the problems of positive externalities that individual firms cannot internalize. Whilst this is certainly true, we should bear in mind that in many countries bargaining at sectoral level has been the main feature of that kind of fragmented industrial relations responsible for the worst effects in terms of economic performance. Cooperation within each sector is possible and bargaining can become a positive-sum game, but competition between the large sectoral coalitions in the wider arena of the entire economy can impede achievement of full employment and price stability. These latter two elements are in themselves public goods that sectoral unions are often incapable of producing.

A more competitive international market reduces national unions' chances of monopolizing power; even if sectorally fragmented they would face a worse trade-off between employment and wages and higher elasticity of labour demand. Wage moderation could be a possible result – by increasing competition in the product market, the process of integration can lead to a positive effect such as this.

If coordination is to develop amongst national unions, it should be between central and broad-based unions, not those at a sectoral level. If these latter unions are to join together at European level, the national fragmentation found in present-day industrial relations would only be reproduced at a transnational level. The consequences might well be harmful, even more so if the internal market is highly protected in order to keep out the external, non-Community nations. Therefore, if coordination is to evolve, it must be based on unions with national coverage, as only these organizations will be able to put their actions into effect at a trans-European level. Social dialogue should consider this as one of the most urgent goals to be achieved.

7. Conclusion: Pay Policies for the Single European Market

Raymond Hara, David Marsden and Jackie Morin

1. Introduction: The Search for Flexible Solutions to Common Problems

How to make a success of economic and monetary union will be the biggest economic problem facing the Community over the next few years. Failure in an area so central to the construction of a new European Community would be tantamount to failure of the Community itself. Although the progressive implementation of economic and monetary union demands similar sacrifices of autonomy in economic policy from all member countries equally, the positions from which each of the Twelve enters this process differ greatly. Examples of the great differences in levels of average wages and in long term inflationary performance were given in the first chapter.

The task of this chapter is to identify some of the policies in the area of wages and wage policy that might help make a success of economic and monetary union. Although there is much scope for cooperation and consultation over national economic and wage policy formation, it is clear that no one policy will be good for all countries. Their starting positions are too diverse. What may be good for Germany or the Netherlands could be a disaster for Spain or the UK (v. chapter by de Molina and Perea). Equally, policies necessary in some countries may be wholly unnecessary in others. The goal of wage policy, in relation to EMU, should be one of selecting those policies for individual member economies that enable each to succeed within the new economic framework. Inevitably, greatest concern is for those countries which will experience the greatest difficulties, and the policies suggested will reflect this. This may give the appearance of proposing common policies, but it is rather a common menu that is being proposed, with some policies being of greater appeal to some of the Twelve than to others.

Three critical problems need to be addressed by any discussion of wage policies for the Community: the divergence in inflation performance; productivity; and social cohesion and social justice. The level of pay settlements, whether negotiated jointly between worker and employer representatives, or decided unilaterally by employers will come to have a critical effect upon the competitiveness of different regions within the Community. The types of reward systems established also have a critical role, through their potential ability to reconcile the needs of firms for greater flexibility and productivity, and to foster different kinds of motivation among employees, and changing employee aspirations. Finally, the success of European economic integration depends upon a continuing political will, which in turn depends ultimately upon acceptance by citizens of each of the member countries. As a matter of practical politics, their views of social justice, of the acceptable degree of inequality, and the desireable levels of solidarity, will determine the long-run survival of the Community itself.

Thus, pay policies for the Single Market have to resolve the familiar tensions between equity and economic efficiency that occur within nation states, but the degree of economic diversity is greater, and unlike in Europe's nation states, the contours of social solidarity are as yet inchoate. This new unit is more diverse than any one of its member countries as concerns economic institutions, and their approaches to pay determination; and whereas many of the bonds of national solidarity have been formed over hundreds of years, there is no equivalent historical accumulation of a capital of European solidarity.

In Britain and Italy, during the 1970s, incomes policies were based on the idea that those paid poorly needed greater protection from the ravages of inflation than their more highly skilled and highly paid fellow workers. In both countries, there was eventually a revolt by the skilled and managerial workers, thus showing the limits of social solidarity even within long established nations.

The tasks then of pay policy within the Community cannot rest on centralization and harmonization at the Community level as this would require a breadth and depth of consensus which do not yet exist. Equally, if we consider that most national institutions of pay determination rest on a hard-won compromise, there is a danger that their effectiveness could be jeopardized by arbitrary attempts to create uniform structures and rules. Instead, policies are needed that will enable individual countries and their economies to work effectively within the framework of the Single Market: that is, policies which take account of the diversity of national labour markets and pay determination institutions, and of the great spread of economic positions from which different countries enter into the process of integration.

This task would be impossible were it not for the existence of a number of common tendencies to be found in the labour markets and pay institutions of member countries, some of which may have been stimulated by integration to date.

1.1 Common Tendencies amid National Diversity

Inflation performance among Community countries varied greatly during the 1980s. If we consider the extremes, labour costs in the highest inflation countries rose at more than 10 times the rate of the lowest ones. However, the overall Community position is helped in part by the fact that the dispersion of inflation rates among the majority of Community countries is considerably smaller than that between the extremes. It is also helped by the convergence, at least in terms of absolute rates, owing to the slowing of inflation. This reduces the rate at which individual countries would see their competitiveness eroded, thus giving them more time to take corrective action.

Labour costs also vary greatly among member countries and regions for comparable jobs and levels of skill. As was shown in the first chapter, the gap in hourly labour costs between Portugal and the Netherlands ranged from 75% below the Community average to over 25% above it. These differences have given rise to fears of 'social dumping.' Among the high wage countries, it is feared that low wage countries will seek to depress labour costs in order to sustain their comparative advantage for longer than necessary. Among low wage countries, it is feared that high wage ones will seek to cut their own labour standards in order to compete more effectively on price.

Although the gap between the extremes is considerable, in fact, the majority of Community countries cluster within a narrower range of labour costs (eight lie within plus or minus 25% of the Community average). Diversity is further reduced when account is taken of productivity. This means that those countries with low labour costs contain considerable potential for increases of productivity which remain untapped. The above average growth of countries such as

Spain and Portugal is also likely to help narrow the productivity gap further.

Low wages, in themselves, do not guarantee attractiveness for productivity enhancing investment, as they may discourage the search for productivity increases (and the substitution of capital for labour), and they may not be sufficient to offset the disadvantages arising from the lack of a good infrastructure and a good training system (v. chapter by de Molina and Perea).

Nevertheless, the general process of creating the Single Market should ease those cases where a shortage of local capital prevents the use of more effective production methods. It should attract the many firms locating facilities abroad that believe they can improve on local productivity levels by exporting their own methods of human resource management and their technical know how.

1.2 Centralization of Pay Determination Systems

Among economies in which trade unions and employer organizations are relatively strong, centralized and more coordinated,[1] pay bargaining systems appear to be better able to achieve lower rates of inflation for a given level of unemployment than decentralized ones (v. chapter by Dell'Aringa). This is particularly relevant in the European context because, although union membership varies greatly among member countries, the share of workers whose pay is covered by collective agreements is uniformly high, as compared with many other parts of the industrial world, notably the United States. The social partners play a central role in wage determination, and the way in which they are organized conditions the outcomes obtained.

Their ability to conduct either centralized or decentralized negotiations, but in a coordinated way, depends very much upon the structure of their organizations and the degree of support they are able to command. Although there have been some movements in individual countries' position in the rank order of centralization, on the whole, the relationships are fairly long term. Among the countries with more centralized bargaining structures are Denmark, Germany, and the Netherlands, and among the more decentralized are the UK and Italy.

In many countries, the state also holds a key position, sometimes as an actor in tripartite discussions on pay, and sometimes in the role of umpire and provider of the basic rules. In Italy, the government has frequently been party to tripartite negotiations, as in those of 1983-

84, whereas in France and Germany, the state has sought more often to provide a framework for bipartite discussions or negotiations. In France and the UK, it has also acted in an authoritarian fashion imposing wage and price freezes or statutory limits on their rate of increase. In several countries, public sector pay has from time to time been used as an implicit pay norm for the private sector.

As with pay changes, there appears to have been some convergence among European countries from an initial position of great diversity. In a number of countries more noted for their higher inflation rates there have been recent discussions on how to adapt some of the basic pay rules to the new environment in either a centralized or a coordinated way. For example, in Britain, there has been considerable debate among the unions and the Labour Party over the need for a central forum for discussing pay questions, and in Italy, over the central negotiations on the reform of wage determination which began in June 1991. In Spain, a major new national agreement on pay, inflation and the economy is under discussion.

1.3 Growth of Plant and Company Level Bargaining

Growth of bargaining at the plant and company level is important for two reasons. Firstly, it creates a forum in which work organization and productivity can be discussed, these being issues that typically cannot be dealt with except in very general terms at the industry level. Secondly, it can represent a deepening of the bargaining relationship between employers and their workforces, extending the practices of consultation and joint regulation to a wider range of issues, and often to issues which are less divisive than pay. It thus creates greater scope for a more cooperative approach to employee relations.

Again, the starting point of different European countries is very diverse. In some countries, such as Germany, Italy and the UK, there is a well established system of enterprise level industrial relations. In the former country it is based on legal rights of representation, and in the latter two, upon collective bargaining. In other countries, such as France, enterprise level bargaining, despite recent growth, remains considerably less developed than in the preceding three countries, and is hampered by the small number of trade union members.

In many Community countries, although there has been a movement towards decentralization of wage bargaining over the last few years, it has not always been at the expense of industry level bargaining. It has often been accompanied by an enrichment and broadening of the content of bargaining at the industry level covering a number of non-wage issues, notably, the reorganization and reduction of working time, training, the redefinition of the scope of skills, and various measures to increase flexibility.

The degree of diversity remains considerable both as concerns the structure and effectiveness of the industry level and enterprise level institutions. The growth of enterprise level relations in many countries may facilitate the search for greater productivity, especially where new technologies and new products require a more cooperative style of working than older, more 'Taylorist' systems.

1.4 Remuneration Methods

The spread of certain kinds remuneration systems may also help to slow the transmission of inflationary pressures, and to boost productivity. Practices in this area too are very diverse, as can be seen, for example, in the large variation among countries in the degree of indexation, the size of occupational pay differentials, the importance attached to length of service in rewards (e.g. CERC 1988), and in the extent of profit sharing schemes.

Nevertheless, a number of similar changes have been under way in member countries: the abandonment or dilution of the indexation of wages on the cost of living, the growth of non-wage elements of pay, the use of of performance related pay, and the spread of various forms of collective financial involvement of employees (*intéressement*, employee share ownership etc.).[2]

One of the problems of the 1970s and early 1980s was the speed with which inflationary pressures were transmitted through some national economies, a process in which various forms of indexation were instrumental. Examples of recent reduction of indexation can be found in many countries. In Italy, the degree of protection of employee pay from cost of living rises has been reduced by the dilution of the *Scala Mobile* in the early 1980s. In France, public sector pay was also de-indexed from 1983, and in Britain, employers have been successful in breaking the presumption among pay bargainers that wage increases should automatically compensate for changes in prices.

Non-wage labour costs have increased across the Community. The importance of wages paid for time worked has declined, and there has been a shift towards deferred pay, notably in the form of pensions, of social insurance, and of paid sick leave and holidays. The fact that countries have on the whole been moving in the same direction and towards greater non-wage elements in recent years softens the impact of national diversity in wage structures.[3]

Further changes in payment systems have produced some convergence as employers, unions and governments (in particular through their role as employers in the public sector) seek to tackle the common problems of workforce change, and economic change. Greater recognition of the first problem can be seen in the signs of a movement towards employees being offered greater choice in the way they are paid through *à la carte* systems of remuneration (basic pay plus bonuses, pensions, profit sharing etc). A degree of choice is offered as concerns the share of bonuses to basic pay, which sales staff might prefer to have in greater proportion, as compared with older workers who might prefer pensions to represent a greater share of their remuneration.

More important than these moves have been the steps taken by employers and governments to foster a greater interest among employees in the progress of the firms for which they work, and to make pay more responsive to the quality of effort put in. This can be seen in the spread of 'merit pay' and of profit sharing schemes.

Performance pay, or the linking of the pay of individual employees to management's evaluation of their performance, has grown considerably in a number of countries, notably, Italy, France, and the UK. In the latter two countries, its growth has been particularly strong in the public sector, reflecting a desire by management to break away from the automaticity of age and service related pay increments towards practices that are more widespread in the private sector, and more appropriate to modern management methods. It also represents an increased role for the enterprise, and factors affecting it, in pay determination.

Profit sharing, employee share ownership, and other schemes designed to link part of employees' income to the fortunes of their employers have several objectives, including making labour costs more variable, and fostering greater employee commitment to, or interest in, their employer's firm. Employer interest in such methods, in part stimulated by government offers of tax incentives, has increased in a number of countries, notably France, Italy and the UK. In all three countries, this coincides with an enhanced role for the enterprise in pay determination.

Performance pay and profit sharing represent, therefore, a form of wage policy able to contribute to macroeconomic wage flexibility (and potentially, to a smaller role for the state in pay determination).

200

Moreover, the new forms of remuneration policy may enable firms to acquire greater room for manoeuvre (notably by means of productivity gains) in the new competitive environment.

2. The Tasks of Contemporary Pay Policies

Three main tasks for pay policies have been identified in the preceding chapters:

1. The need to contain inflationary pressures and minimize their impact on competitiveness, which involves:
  • greater coordination of pay settlements;
  • pay systems with more flexible rules.
2. Compensating for excessive wage growth, and adaptation of newly 'exposed' sectors to greater competition involves:
  • the promotion of productivity growth within firms;
  • encouragement of greater flexibility in enterprise internal labour markets.
3. Assisting adjustment across markets, which involves:
  • facilitating economic restructuring;
  • improving the coordination of firms' labour forces across national borders and developing the possibilities for labour mobility between countries.

This section examines these tasks and how different kinds of pay policies are able to tackle them. It also considers some of their limitations.

2.1 Containing Inflationary Pressures

Although there are many sources of inflation, such as excessive credit growth, labour markets can be influential both as a source of inflationary pressures, for example, from settlements which exceed the pace of productivity growth, and by transmitting inflationary pressures. The constraints of the exchange rate mechanism, plus the decline of national governments' ability to control the money supply as financial markets have become more sophisticated, give the reform of pay bargaining and remuneration systems an increasingly important part to play in containing inflation.

Pay may grow faster than productivity as a result of the sheer scale of pay expectations among workers, but more often, it is the result of bargaining structure. Structure is important for two reasons. First, a highly decentralized and fragmented structure may put groups wishing to pursue 'moderate' demands in a very difficult position, particularly if they are in competition for membership or for influence. The group that pursues a modest pay claim in the interest of lower inflation may find itself left behind by other groups bargaining more aggressively, especially if they subsequently achieve higher pay settlements. This situation is sometimes referred to as the 'prisoner's dilemma.' Greater communication between the parties concerned may provide a solution so that they can be reassured that a desire to act in the common interest will not be exploited by others. The solution usually recommended is to foster cooperation by reducing competition, and promoting greater communication and coordination between the groups involved.

Structure may also be important because large groups have to live with the consequences of their actions and so are more likely to take a broader view than small ones. In the case of pay bargaining, a large bargaining group representing, or 'encompassing,' a high percentage of the workforce knows that a settlement well above the rate of productivity growth for its members is likely to contribute directly to increased inflation (Olson 1982). Small groups, on the other hand, know that their individual increase is unlikely to have much direct effect on inflation, so they may be tempted to take the risk of pressing a high wage demand. In fact, according to some recent work, coordination rather than centralization of bargaining holds the key to lower inflation. This seems plausible because centralized bodies, especially workers' organizations, have a long history of splits, such that their internal cohesion cannot be taken for granted. Coordination, unlike centralization, stresses the need to maintain a consensus over objectives – most union and employer confederations have only moral powers over their constituent organizations.

The idea that both centralized and highly coordinated bargaining systems and their opposites are associated with below average inflation rates found considerable support in the evidence reviewed in Dell'Aringa's chapter. In contrast, partially decentralized and uncoordinated bargaining systems were found to generate higher inflation for a given level of unemployment.

The transmission of pay increases from one group to another may also be speeded up by certain kinds of bargaining systems and the rules they establish. First, demands based on comparisons with the pay, or the increases, of other groups may help to spread an inflationary impulse from one group across the labour market. Secondly, transmission may be hastened by certain kinds of pay rule: for example, that a uniform rate of pay should apply across the whole of a country or region irrespective of variations in local conditions. The latter kind of rule, in particular, may help generalize a rate of pay increase initiated in a particularly tight regional labour market.

This suggests two avenues for policy on wage inflation: the reform of pay bargaining to enable greater coordination of bargaining outcomes, and the adoption of pay rules that enable a greater degree of adaptation to local labour market conditions, and which reduce the force of comparability, and other forms of indexation.

One important qualification, however, is that centralization and coordination cannot be decreed. They depend upon a high degree of mutual confidence as they entail that some groups should be prepared to forego their immediate short-term bargaining advantage in favour of a broader common goal. Although it is common to think of unions in this context, it applies also to employers. The latter group have been known to disregard the fight against inflation in order to deal with local recruitment difficulties, or with other internal organizational objectives. Mutual confidence, and the associated institutional structures, in the countries using coordinated bargaining have usually been built up over many years, and, mostly were not set up in order to deal with particular crises, only to be disbanded once the immediate threat had passed.

The need for coordination rather than centralization is, in fact, positive news for the more decentralized, higher inflation, countries because coordination and consensus building may be possible within a variety of union and employer organization structures. Given their past history, it is unlikely that centralization could be achieved by most European labour and employer organizations, and even if it were, it might prove fragile.[4] Although coordination and consensus might require much more persuasion, they do not require a uniform type of institutional structure.

Nevertheless, although bargaining systems potentially have a major contribution to make in assisting convergence in the rate of growth of wages, they do not provide a panacea, and one must therefore look to other policies as well.

2.2 The Search for Productivity Increases in General and in Newly Exposed Sectors

The second major task of pay policy is to assist the development of productivity levels both in order to enable general increases in pay across a whole economy, especially when these may exceed those elsewhere in the Community, and to accommodate those sectors most exposed by the removal of protective barriers. The nature of many of the 'newly exposed' sectors was reviewed in the chapter by Vaughan-Whitehead. In the present context, new pay systems have also an important part to play in facilitating the introduction of modern management methods more suited to new production techniques and new consumer demands.

In view of the limited opportunity left by national wage structures for sectors to alter their relative wage levels, much of the competitive pressure on the newly exposed sectors will take the form of demands to raise productivity to reduce unit labour costs. Thus, the tasks of wage policy in connection with productivity are very similar whether they concern raising the general level of productivity in an economy or reversing the fortunes of newly exposed sectors. In either case, the task of raising productivity falls onto enterprise level policies.

The tasks facing enterprise level policies to boost productivity consist of a number of components: to obtain more support for management policies for change; to influence employee motivation; and to make enterprise internal labour markets more flexible.

In many firms, organizational changes hold the key to higher productivity, and productivity bargaining is one of the methods available. According to this, employers make increased pay conditional upon the acceptance of organizational changes designed to raise productivity, and to assist the introduction of new working methods. In recent years, two main kinds of agreement can be identified: those in which increased pay is linked to specific changes in working practices; and those in which an increase is made conditional upon the achievement of a specified increase in productivity. The former has been common in Britain during the 1980s, under the name of 'flexibility agreements' (Marsden and Thompson 1990), while the latter kind has become more widespread in France (Eyraud et al. 1990).

Although the theory of such productivity-linked increases is simple, there is some debate as to whether they are desirable. Productivity bargaining is not common to all countries (Delamotte, 1971). In particular, it is virtually unknown in Germany. Even though employers consult extensively with works councils on work organization issues, such questions are not directly linked to pay bargaining. The German example shows that high productivity can be achieved without productivity bargaining, and it is possible that bargaining over such issues actually increases the cost of change.

That example also illustrates another issue: that productivity bargaining may be a solution to introducing productivity enhancing changes in particular kinds of bargaining systems. Delamotte argued that the two countries in which pay increases were linked to particular changes in work methods were Britain and the United States, where enterprise and plant level pay bargaining are dominant. In addition, in both countries, 'job control'[5] bargaining has been common.

At the industry level, collective agreements could not possibly define working practices in sufficient detail for employers to be sure that they could obtain an adequate increase in productivity to compensate for extra wage concessions. Thus, this kind of productivity bargaining would seem to be relevant mainly to those countries in which pay bargaining at the plant and enterprise level is fairly autonomous of the industry level. Indeed, this local flexibility would seem to be one of the compensating features of the less coordinated bargaining systems.[6]

Two main types of incentive system have recently attracted much attention: individualization, or merit pay on the one hand, and profit sharing and employee share ownership plans on the other (v. the chapters by Shonfield and FitzRoy). Merit pay has been mostly geared towards individual performance, although there has been some discussion of group performance, whereas profit sharing has been geared towards collective performance of the enterprise, or some large section of it.

Merit pay, as discussed in the first chapter and in that by Shonfield, has four main uses for management: to motivate staff; to adapt pay systems to new methods of personnel management; to restore pay differentials and incentives for skilled and managerial staff; and to introduce a greater degree of flexibility to established systems of pay scales and job classifications. Each of these has a potential contribution to make to increasing productivity, although the managerial difficulties of making them effective should not be underestimated.

Merit pay systems that employees experience as badly designed and arbitrary in their application could well prove demotivating, and increase staff hostility towards management, with the possible consequence of reduced productivity. An essential accompaniment to any successful merit pay scheme is a system of performance appraisal that employees trust and believe to be fair. Such schemes are expensive, but the information management derives is useful in a wider sense by providing clues as to where training, work design and other personnel policies might be failing.

The second type of productivity incentive, profit sharing and employee share ownership schemes, has attracted much controversy in recent years. It is essentially a group incentive, and as such may not always be compatible with extensive use of individual incentives such as individual merit pay. A major survey of recent evidence by Blinder et al. (1990) indicates that such incentive schemes can indeed lead to higher productivity. Although sceptics often suggest that a share in future profits is too distant from an individual employee's effort to be an effective motivator, and the danger of 'free-riding' is too great, proponents of profit sharing argue that in a long-term employment relationship, and where group effort is particularly important, profit sharing can be a powerful motivator, and peer group pressures will limit free-riding (v. chapter by FitzRoy).

This difference of assessment suggests that the conditions under which profit sharing is used are very important to its success.[7] Moreover, the weaknesses of profit sharing have to be set in the context of the weaknesses of all other known payment systems. As new technology, and the search for greater quality in production place a greater premium on cooperative work relations than did Taylorist work systems, it can be argued that collective incentives are better adapted than individual incentives to many modern work situations. In addition, innovation requires much sharing of information in the work place (Nonaka 1991), and this would suggest collective rather than individual incentives would be more appropriate in many circumstances.[8]

The choice between individual performance incentives (such as merit pay), and collective performance incentives (such as profit sharing) may depend upon circumstances, but their increased use by employers across the Community indicates dissatisfaction with older, more bureaucratic, systems. This in turn suggests that such incentive payment systems have an important part to play in improving the ability of firms, and other organizations, to respond to a more competitive environment, and more generally, provide an opportunity for those economies with more decentralized bargaining systems to find some way of offsetting their greater inflationary potential.

The third task in this category concerns the role of pay in promoting greater adaptability within enterprise internal labour markets. The majority of employees, once they have completed their initial period of entry into work life, will remain in the same job for 10 or more years (OECD 1984). Thus employee motivation, and the ability of employers to gain the cooperation of their employees in staff redeployment, have a critical contribution to make to productivity.

Until now, in many organizations, the rules of wage and salary systems have placed a premium on age and length of service, leaving employers with dismissal and promotion as the two main sanctions. Widespread use of dismissal would no doubt demotivate many of the remaining employees, and there are limits to the use of promotion. Hence, there remains the problem of motivating the majority of employees who know they probably have no further promotions ahead of them, and for whom length of service increments are exhausted. Merit pay has its part to play in motivating these employees, and has been attractive to many employers for just this reason.

There is, however, another reason for looking at internal labour markets: the expectation employees have of their future earnings growth and job development. The expectation of career development is a major source of inertia in many organizations, and makes their adaptation to changing conditions very dependent upon past recruitment and remuneration decisions. One potential contribution of profit sharing (or similar schemes) to firms' adaptability arises when it represents a substantial proportion of the wage bill, as it reduces the impact of expectations of wage and salary growth on firms' labour costs, and also reduces the amount of the individual employee's investment in the firm which is dependent on a particular career profile. This may both help protect the firm's profit margins against rising age related employment costs, and generate greater flexibility of career paths within it.

2.3 Pay and Restructuring Workforces

The restructuring of European industries, especially those which experience the greatest increases in competition, may be facilitated by a greater degree of labour mobility both within and between regions. There is evidence that interregional wage differences cause some labour mobility (Pissarides and McMaster 1984), thus, if wage structures were more flexible, they might make a greater contribution to the employment adjustments associated with industrial restructuring.

The evidence that wage structures are generally unresponsive to short-run changes in labour market conditions should not obscure the possibility that pay stability may represent economically desirable processes, such as the efficient management of internal labour markets. But it may not always be so. For example, the high pay levels of certain industries resulting from workers and employers sharing rents derived from a dominant position on their product markets are less defensible (v. chapter by FitzRoy).

Apart from the attractiveness of low wage countries to new capital investment, the amount of capital restructuring and merger activity in the Community at present raises one important question: integration of firms will demand greater merging of the teams of managers and technical specialists needed to run them. Nationally based remuneration policies of subisidiaries could prove a serious obstacle to such integration. Current rules for expatriate staff are very expensive, and could discourage greater integration among European firms.

Organizational integration across the Community will almost certainly routinize movements of staff between production locations on both a short and a long term basis. Current career remuneration policies in many organizations probably leave too little scope for compensation of those staff required to be mobile, as one has to consider what should be their pay in relation to that of those of a similar grade remaining in their home country, and what should be the pay of those returning after a period of absence in another Community country. Thus remuneration policies may have an important part to play in facilitating the integration of the international management and technical teams that should follow the progressive integration of European companies.

2.4 Trade Offs between the Different Axes of Pay Adaptation

Although the three main tasks are to a large extent complementary, there are a number of difficult choices, as the policies appropriate to one may undermine those appropriate to one of the others. Tensions may arise between:

- productivity related pay increases and coordinated bargaining;
- the autonomy needed to experiment with new solutions, and coordinated or centralized bargaining;

• internal labour markets with their scope for productivity enhancing work reorganization, and occupational markets with their scope for deployment of labour between firms and industries.

The first of these concerns the problem that can arise when productivity is increasing faster in some sectors or firms than in others. Linking pay generally to increases in productivity could then lead to increasing inequality among firms and sectors, and this is likely to generate considerable pressures on any system of coordinated bargaining, especially from those groups in sectors where there is no ready source of productivity growth.

Secondly, tensions may arise between those firms and sectors that need to raise productivity, and those that do not. The first group may wish to devolve bargaining autonomy to the lowest level possible, so that managers can negotiate specific changes in working practices. They may also desire to experiment with new kinds of deals, perhaps adapted to new conditions experienced in individual firms. This would potentially undermine attempts to coordinate bargaining. Hence, there may be occasions when the demands of coordinated bargaining conflict with the search for greater productivity. Indeed, during much of the time incomes policies were in force during the 1970s in the UK, productivity deals were outlawed.

Thirdly, some kinds of labour market are much more sensitive to local labour market pressures than others, and this can cause problems for both coordinated bargaining and enterprise policies. Enterprise internal labour markets tend to be relatively insulated from them, except at the main entry points. In contrast, occupational labour markets tend to be much more competitive, both for recruitment and retention of skilled labour.

Because workers engaged in internal labour markets are relatively protected from local labour market pressures, their bargaining power declines less than that of other groups as unemployment rises. They may therefore be less responsive to calls for wage moderation in periods of rising unemployment. In contrast, the bargaining power of workers on occupational markets varies more with unemployment, because their skills are often highly sought after by many employers. Thus the sacrifices demanded by coordination vary among groups at different points of the business cycle.

Equally, firms using labour from both types of labour markets (usually in different occupations) may find that fluctuations in the difficulty of recruitment and retention of workers on occupational markets may disrupt their internal pay policies. For example, a firm may be tempted to use merit pay in order to retain workers with scarce skills recruited from an occupational market whatever the quality of their performance. This could be the thin end of a wedge that gradually destroys the integrity of this kind of payment system.

Both types of labour market structure provide different, but somewhat incompatible, types of flexibility to firms. Internal labour markets potentially give greater internal functional flexibility, and provide employers with more scope to organize work in the way they need, but the supply of skilled labour, being developed internally, is harder to expand quickly. Equally, workers on internal labour markets have much to lose if they are laid off, and so both workers and employers place a premium on employment stability. The extra freedom employers gain in pay determination arising from the employment stability of internal labour markets has its price in a relatively inelastic labour supply. In contrast, occupational markets give employers a more elastic short-run labour supply, but at the expense of being more bound by local labour market pressures.

In practice, well-designed policies may attenuate some of the tensions between these different policy options, and it is to these that we now turn.

3. Wages and Remuneration Policies in the European Community

If we take progressive economic and monetary integration as the goal, then the task of wage policy becomes that of ensuring its success. Macroeconomic policy coordination among Community countries should be concerned with achieving compatible outcomes, such as convergence towards lower rates of inflation, and towards higher rates of labour productivity and real incomes. The role of wage policy should be to help member countries achieve a greater degree of convergence, to ease the strains of EMU, and to avoid the build up of pressures that could lead to its break down. At the same time, the experience of the 1970s shows that wage policy is likely to fail unless other demand and monetary policies are running in the same direction.

'Convergence from within diversity' might serve as a description of the task facing European pay policies. The large differences among the labour markets of member countries, notably in pay, mean that the problems facing individual countries vary greatly. For some, the task of permanently breaking high underlying inflationary tendencies is the key to successful integration into the Single European Market (e.g. Italy and the UK). For others, the most difficult task is that of attracting productivity enhancing investment so that low current levels of real wages can be brought closer to the Community average (e.g. Portugal and Spain). For yet other countries, a mixture of these two problems has to be faced. Thus, making a success of EMU entails different policies for different countries.

Against this background of diversity, policy coordination is needed to ensure that countries refrain from macro- and microeconomic policies likely to undermine those of their Community partners. Equally, individual countries, or the Community as a whole, should not insist on policies which place too great a strain on the social and political consensus in other member countries. For example, if citizens of one country experience EMU as a massive rise in unemployment, or a severe drop in living standards, it is unlikely that their support for membership of the Community will continue for long.

The pressures to be tackled by pay policy derive from three main sources:
- the problem of divergence in inflationary tendencies originating within labour markets;
- the need to help poorer and lower productivity countries to draw closer to the Community average;
- and the need to maintain a consensus among the citizens of member countries in favour of European integration.

To deal with these, our recommendations cover three broad themes: greater coordination in macroeconomic policy in general, and in pay determination in particular; the promotion of pay policies that can enhance the growth of productivity; and the need to sustain a wider social consensus in favour of European integration.

3.1 Greater Coordination in Pay Determination Policies

Coordination of macroeconomic policies among Community countries has been developing over recent years. The establishment of the Single European Market increases the need to extend this, and should encourage member countries to discuss more intensely their policies on pay determination and labour markets which up until now have been the 'forgotten link'[9] in international policy coordination. Much of the work on pay policies has to be done at the national level as this is the level at which the social partners are currently organised, but there are a number of linkages that can be established between Community-level economic policy discussions, and national level pay determination policies. They are summarised in Figure 1.

Figure 1. Pay policies for the Single European Market.

1. Adaptation to the SEM.

This requires:
- convergence of rates of wage inflation;
- greater coordination of national macroeconomic policies;
- greater coordination in pay determination policies;
- faster reactions to increases in inflation.

Instruments:
- increase awareness of the social partners of current and expected rates of wage rise in other member countries;
- provide guidelines on sustainable pay increases for each country, taking account of productivity;
- set out a range of forecast pay increases for each country;
- better short-term labour market indicators.

2. Tasks for the social partners.
- coordinate pay bargaining nationally;
- integrate macroeconomic considerations into pay bargaining;
- establish lasting procedures for pay determination;
- assume responsibility for bargaining outcomes.

3. Firm level pay policies.
- greater use of incentive pay, and link pay increase to:
  - individual performance;
  - company performance;
  - the general growth of national prosperity.
  avoid full indexation;
- permit regional variation in rates of pay across the EC, but also between regions within countries.

4. Role of governments.
- support the attempts of the social partners to set up coordinated bargaining;
- maintain social cohesion, and prevent labour market inequalities from becoming too great;
- act on low pay;
- watch the relationship between fiscal policies and non-wage benefits;
- coordinate social security systems across the Community.

The most important of these linkages concerns information to industry and company level negotiations in the member countries on how their settlements stand, in relation to those in other member countries. We propose the development of general guidelines for pay negotiations in member countries, a radical improvement in information on pay developments across the Community, and the development of a long-term framework for building consensus on desirable pay trends in individual member countries, and for coordinating pay bargaining within countries. Although wage moderation by employers and unions may enable European economies to be run at lower rates of unemployment, it remains essential that policies on pay and other aspects of the economy, notably demand and monetary policies, should be consistent.

3.1.1 Guidelines for Feasible Rates of Pay Increase within the Single Market

Pay determination is primarily undertaken within member countries, and for the great majority of the Community's workforces is likely to remain so for the foreseeable future. Yet the degree of interdependence between settlements across the Community is greatly increased by economic and monetary union, in particular, because of the likely impact on competitiveness. Therefore pay bargainers working at the industry, company, and plant levels in one country will need to know how pay is changing elsewhere in the Community, especially in the same sectors in other member countries. Two main alternative approaches can be identified: use of a Community-wide anticipated rate of wage increase; and the establishment of a range of current and expected increases for member countries and for sectors within these across the Community.

A Community-wide anticipated rate of wage increase would comprise two elements: one is a forecast, and the other an attempt to bring down inflationary expectations. It is therefore partly positive, and partly normative. Such an anticipated rate would be designed to inform member pay bargainers as to what would be both a sustainable rate of increase at the Community level, and a target towards which negotiations in their own country should seek to converge over a number of months or years. A policy of this kind, at the national level, was used successfully in France in the years after 1983 to bring inflation down towards the German level, and was included as part of the 1986 national agreement in Spain, although the unions have been sceptical of the government's forecasts.

Publication of such an anticipated rate of inflation has the considerable advantage of simplicity and clarity for pay bargainers. However, in some Community countries, its very simplicity could be counter-productive as pay bargainers interpret the anticipated rate as the minimum likely rate of inflation. There is a good deal of evidence from the incomes policies in Britain that government fixed norms for the maximum increase allowed were seen by workers, and their union representatives as the minimum or the average rate to be achieved. If one got less than the norm, then a loss of real pay was seen as the likely consequence (v. Lipsey and Parkin 1970, and Henry and Ormorod 1978). Any self-respecting negotiator should get at least the norm for his or her members.

This suggests that a richer signal should be given to bargainers, and this might be publication of up to date information on current levels of pay settlements and likely future trends in the same sectors in other member countries. In this way, pay bargainers would be informed of how their own settlement targets were likely to stand in relation to those of their 'competitors.' On the union side, they would thus have the responsibility for getting the best deal for their members without putting their jobs at risk, and on the employers' side, they would know better what were the likely cost increases their competitors in other member countries would be facing.

Although the emphasis of the first is on central direction whereas that of the second is on informing the social partners, and leaving them to take responsibility for their own decisions, the two options are not mutually exclusive. The first could be supplemented by the second, and the second could take the first, in a weaker form, as additional information. The balance between the two could vary among countries depending on their past experience with counter-inflation policies.

3.1.2 The Need for Better Short-term Information on Pay Developments

Currently, there is no uniform short-term (monthly or quarterly) indicator of pay developments across the member countries, and even data available on an annual basis are usually only published a year or more afterwards. Many member countries have their own short-term indicators (monthly or quarterly) although the precise concepts measured are not comparable between countries. In addition, some countries use fixed weight indices and others do not, so that some indices are like price indices for labour, whereas others are more akin to an index of firms' expenditure on labour.

There is therefore an urgent need for good short-term indicators of pay movements across the Community. Otherwise, pay bargainers are left in the dark as to the likely impact of their agreements upon competitiveness and jobs.

There is another reason for developing a good short-term indicator. Having given up a number of familiar instruments of macroeconomic control, governments have a more limited arsenal with which to tackle a surge of inflation in their own country. Hence, it will be more important for them to have early warning of any relative speeding up of wage inflation so that it can be dealt with before it builds up momentum. With the present state of pay statistics it is difficult to gain more than a very impressionistic view of current trends in pay in some of even the most important economies in the Community so that the all important view of relative inflation is not available.

3.1.3 The Need to Build Consensus on Sustainable Pay Increases, as a Basis for Coordinated Bargaining

Government imposed pay restrictions do not have a good record of success over a long period, which indicates that voluntary action by the social partners should lie at the centre of any long-term strategy on pay determination. A stable forum of union and employer representatives is needed in order to establish a consensus on sustainable rates of pay increase over the short and longer run, and in order to respond to any sudden acceleration of pay increases. Such a forum should act as a focus for coordinating pay bargaining within member countries.

Building a consensus among the social partners over their wider economic objectives is necessary because collective bargaining can only resolve distributional disputes if those represented believe that those bargaining on their behalf are getting the best deal available. Both unions and employers' organizations rely on their members' support. This can be withdrawn, as sometimes happens especially with unions when the membership refuse to accept the terms of the agreement that has been reached. Similar pressures exist in employers' organizations, although they are usually less widely reported. Unless the unions and employers' associations are seen to be involved in discussing the constraints on pay bargaining outcomes, it is difficult for them to convince their members that the best is being done on their behalf, albeit in the longer rather than the short run.

The framework for building consensus should be a lasting one, even though the need to react to a burst of inflation may arise only periodically.[10] The reason is that the determination of macroeconomically sustainable rates of pay increase involve a significant element of judgement as to what kinds of settlement workers will accept, and employers can afford. As information on both of these will affect the outcome of negotiations, it is highly sensitive and can only be exchanged in an environment of mutual confidence. Building trust is a slow process, and depends upon repeated acts by either partner that are consistent with cooperative behaviour. It therefore cannot be summoned up to deal with individual short-term crises, nor can it be decreed by central governments.

Consensual arrangements for coordination work best if those concerned feel they are responsible for their smooth working, and for the outcomes. Hence, excessive government intervention could prove damaging as it introduces the temptation to let politicians take responsibility for unpopular decisions. Faced with the very uneven strength and representativeness of union and employer organizations among countries, and the considerable variations in the degree of centralization and coordination, governments may be reluctant to let a major part of their counter-inflation strategy depend upon action by the social partners.

Although the coverage of collective bargaining is generally high, levels of union membership density vary greatly from between 70% and 80% in Belgium and Denmark to possibly below 20% in France, Portugal and Spain (v. Table 1). Unions cannot be assumed to have the same degree of representativeness across the Community. Bargaining structure also varies greatly, as shown in Dell'Aringa's chapter, from the more centralized and coordinated systems in Denmark, Germany and the Netherlands to the greater decentralization in Britain and Italy. Whereas the first three have a long, if sometimes interrupted, tradition of consensual discussion of economic constraints on pay growth, the others do not.

In those countries in which the social partners do not have an established pattern of coordination, governments can use persuasion, and they can encourage the growth of a procedural framework for collective bargaining in order to promote greater stability. Again, the French experience, where successive governments of both right and left have sought to promote more stable collective bargaining, provides some examples. There, on a number of issues such as monthly payment of wages, training, and working time, governments have amended legislation in order to leave room for the social partners to fix detailed norms by negotiation, the intention being that regular contact over substantive issues should feed the growth of a web of procedural rules encouraging regular contact and discussion.

Finally, the state has two important sanctions with which to prod the social partners into greater discussion of pay problems, notably, the threat of imposing limits on pay increases, and competition policy. Although imposing limits on pay increases may free the social partners of their responsibilities, the costs to them are high because of the rigidity of state imposed norms. Firms cannot adjust wage structures to suit their own managerial needs, and rigid norms prevent the resolution of cases of injustice between different groups of workers.

The second sanction, stiffening competition, is already part of the agenda of the Single Market. This should make it more difficult for leading national employers, who often have a key role in bargaining within the national context, to pass on excessive pay increases to the consumer. The reduction of market dominance of some national firms will be beneficial to the general process of controlling inflationary pressures arising from pay bargaining, and notably those connected with wage leadership.

Overall, causing rates of pay increase to converge to lower levels across the Community should rely on building a consensus over targets and procedures among the social partners, guided by improved information on wage trends in other member countries. Only in the last resort should governments intervene to impose pay targets or limits. The price of doing so is to slow down the process of consensus building among the social partners.

3.2 Productivity and Enterprise Level Pay Policies

Many of the key decisions relating to productivity are made at the enterprise level, and it is here that much of the adjustment to the increased competition of the Single Market will have to be made. Thus, firms should be left as much autonomy to determine their remuneration policies as is consistent with the flexible framework of coordination proposed.

The quid pro quo for employee acceptance of this is that the best guarantee of their jobs lies in the competitiveness of their enterprises, and raising productivity is the only way to expand purchasing power without causing inflation in the long run. However, their acceptance may be rewarded by some kind of 'contract' linking their pay to changes in the economic situation of their firm and its environment.

A small number of common principles may be identified for company remuneration policies that would help them to work within the new framework by providing a greater degree of flexibility and yet remain within the general pay guidelines agreed nationally. First, increases in real wages should remain within the limit of increases in productivity. Nevertheless, it should be recognised that national productivity growth, which is the ultimate limit so long as national currencies remain in force, has three main sources. The first two are those obtained directly within the enterprise, either by the workers directly involved working more efficiently, or by investment and organizational decisions at that level. The third arises from general productivity improvements throughout the economy, for example, as a result of an improved infrastructure or improved services.

These suggest three different types of incentive:

• the first is linked to the work done by individual workers or the work groups to which they belong, which requires clear and open performance appraisal criteria;
• the second is linked to the performance of the enterprise: it requires schemes such as profit sharing which should be created and encouraged among the member countries;
• the third is linked to the growth of national prosperity. As all firms benefit from general productivity gains, this suggests a priori the need for general wage increases.

Performance related pay, although not a panacea for all incentive problems, may help motivate employees at a time of stagnating employment, and slower career advancement. It may also be an important instrument for firms as they try to move to newer and less bureaucratic styles of management. The psychological evidence discussed earlier (Chapter 1) suggests it also has much to offer, provided certain steps are taken by management, notably: employee performance appraisal; clarity in the definition of employees' objectives; and clarity in its application.

Performance pay also requires additional attention by management to training where staff have deficiencies, and some form of appeals procedure in order to enhance employee confidence in its fairness. This may seem a high price for management to pay in the short-run, but introducing these additional elements, apart from being necessary to obtain any return from the investment in additional payments, could also improve management generally. Even with these safeguards, performance pay schemes are difficult to operate fairly and accurately, so it seems unwise to make too great a part of an employee's pay dependent upon it.

The additional policies required to accompany performance pay indicate that it should only be used in more sophisticated types of work. Traditional output incentives may still be appropriate where output is easily measured, as in routine assembly work. But these are declining as a share of employment, and, in many parts of the services and manufacturing industries, where quality and innovation have come to be at a premium, more sophisticated methods of management and remuneration are necessary.

Profit sharing and employee share ownership schemes are ways of sharing the results of the firm's performance with its employees. They may be based upon overall financial performance of the whole firm, or that of the group, the enterprise, the establishment, or even the workshop.[11]

Profit sharing allows a degree of flexibility which helps protect firms from external shocks while preserving the level of employment. Indeed, the variable component of pay may depend upon the results of the firm, and its reduction, or even its temporary disappearance may enable the firm to survive a difficult period. However, this reversibility will only remain operative as long as the variable component is limited in size, especially for those on low or average earnings.

More generally, although desirable to promote pay systems that favour productivity and flexibility, it should be stressed that such schemes are not a panacea for all types of adjustment problems. Financial difficulties are not usually the result of the size of a firm's wage bill only, and even though it is common to cut this in the first instance, the cause of the difficulties is also to be found in its commercial strategy.

Finally, two other principles concern rather what might be avoided: full indexation, and a lack of regional variation in basic rates of pay. The more complete the degree of indexation of pay on prices or on average earnings the more it accelerates the transmission of inflationary pressures. Certain exceptions may be envisaged, such as for groups of workers with a very weak bargaining position or those not allowed to bargain. But other pay formulae could also be considered, such as special committees of enquiry to ensure fair treatment.

The second concerns regional variation in pay. National pay agreements are only one source of national uniformity in basic rates of pay.[12] Many companies and other large organizations also have their own internal rates which apply nationally. National uniformity of pay removes one (albeit minor) incentive for interregional labour mobility, and makes poorer regions less attractive for new investment, especially in labour intensive activities. Greater wage differentiation among regions might help absorb some unemployment, while at the same time being more equitable once account is taken of differences in the cost of living.

However, such differences should remain limited for reasons of social cohesion and overall economic effectiveness. As far as possible, competitive bidding between regions as a means of reducing interregional inequalities should also be avoided.

3.3 The Maintenance of Social Cohesion and the Role of the State

Apart from its role in encouraging coordinated pay bargaining, and in promoting the use of certain kinds of payment systems, the state may also help maintain social cohesion by preventing labour market inequalities from growing too large. It should also keep an eye on the wider implications for labour markets of policies agreed between the social partners. This may also be done jointly with them, taking advantage of their greater closeness to labour market problems. Three issues stand out for particular attention: low wages; the effects of fiscal policies on certain elements of remuneration, in particular on non-wage benefits; and the coordination of the social security provisions.

For social and economic reasons, minimum wage provisions exist in the majority of member countries. Without going back over the underlying arguments, two issues deserve special attention: notably, improving the pay and conditions of workers in low paid employment, and improving access to jobs by allowing greater regional and sectoral variation in minimum wages, and by reducing other employment costs for low paid workers.

Although the most effective long-run way to improve the condition of low paid workers is to improve their skills, this is not always feasible. For example, in sectors where work is organized along Taylorist lines, or in certain regions, such options are not always available. Action on pay then becomes necessary. Its potentially adverse effect on employment can be mitigated in a number of ways.

Firstly, national level minimum wage protection could be partially devolved to the social partners at the sectoral and regional levels. A national minimum set at a somewhat lower overall level could be supplemented according to sectoral production requirements, and regional variations in living costs. Secondly, by making employers' social contributions more progressive in their incidence, the degree to which they penalize the employment of low paid workers could be reduced.[13] It should be added that these are essentially short- to medium-term policies, linked to the current period of high unemployment, rather than major long-term policies, which would be incompatible with the systematic quest for high value added activities.

A considerable proportion of non-wage labour costs are determined by governments' fiscal policies, for example, employers' social security contributions. Thus, government fiscal policy can be a major determinant of differences in the cost of employment among member countries. In 1984, the share of employers' social security contributions in total labour costs varied from 7% in Denmark to 45% in the Netherlands. As many of these schemes involve contributions that are not fully proportional to basic pay, they are effectively a regressive tax on employment, damaging the opportunities of the lowest paid.

Tax concessions also have a profound influence on the structure of labour costs, not just in terms of fringe benefits such as company cars, but also in the allocation of deferred income, notably, in pensions or employee saving schemes. Although less influential on employment policy than employer social security contributions, the incidence of other benefit schemes may also affect the structure of employment by making certain categories of workers more or less attractive.

Finally, governments have a major contribution to make by greater coordination of regimes of social security. One of the principal institutional barriers to labour mobility among Community countries, over and above problems of language and adaptation to different cultures, is the lack of coordination among regimes of sickness insurance and retirement pensions. The question is made more complex by the number of different systems in place, sometimes even within the same country.

Apart from being an obstacle to greater labour mobility between countries, it probably works to the disadvantage of the least skilled groups who have in the past been among the most likely to seek work in other member countries. The big migrations of the 1950s and 1960s were among unskilled workers from Spain and Portugal to France, and from Italy to northern European countries. Lack of coordination among social security regimes makes it all the more likely that the low pay of such workers will be accompanied by inadequate social security protection.

These proposals are not intended as the basis for a common standard. Rather they are put forward as an array of policies that could help promote greater convergence in the social domain but yet be consistent with the severe economic pressures on countries as they adapt to life in the Single Market. Just as the economic pressures of the Single Market are pushing countries towards greater convergence on inflation for example, so one might envisage, in the social domain, the social equivalent of convergence from the broad to the narrow bands for the European currencies. However, as with the economic convergence, the important thing is the practical outcome in terms of living and working conditions, and not the precise route by which each country gets there.

Notes

1. Centralization of pay bargaining usually involves national level negotiations between peak level representatives of workers and employers for a whole industry, or a situation in which there is a tight control over regional bargains from the national level. Coordinated bargaining refers to a looser arrangement whereby bargaining takes place in many different units with an effort being made to take account of similar constraints, and to arrive at compatible outcomes.
2. Capital integration, whether at the level of large or small enterprises, could contribute to greater convergence of remuneration systems practiced in the different member countries. A high degree of interregional mobility currently takes place within large firms: the homogeneity of payments systems facilitates such movement.
3. It also suggests some convergence to what has been described as a European model of social insurance, at least as compared with the United States and Japan.
4. The experience of Britain, Italy, and France suggests that centralization may not be easily achieved. Both Britain and Italy have had successful but short periods of centrally coordinated pay restraint in the mid-1970s. However, in Britain they were subsequently undermined by bargaining at the local and plant levels, and in Italy, the system of indexation then set up had economically damaging side-effects. In France, attempts at coordinated action by the communist and socialist oriented unions on wages have proved dependent upon the quality of relations between the Communist and Socialist parties.
5. Job control bargaining refers to extremely decentralized bargaining in which part of the agreement, explicitly or implicitly, is taken to cover the set of tasks constituting workers' jobs.
6. This was undermined in Britain by attempts to run incomes policies as productivity deals which quickly degenerated into a device for gaining increases above the norm specified by the incomes policy.
7. Some recent work on the impact of employee share ownership schemes in Britain on employee attitudes and on company performance in the UK has produced more sceptical conclusions as to its efficacy (Dewe, Dunn, and Richardson 1991).
8. The importance of group incentives to encourage team working has been stressed by an extensive review of recent work by Levine and Tyson (1990).
9. Edwards, R. and Garonna, P. (1991).
10. This point is stressed in Dore's analysis of consensus building behind the system of synchronized pay bargaining in the Japanese 'Spring Offensive,' (Dore 1990).

11. The period of reference should be related to the basis chosen: annual in the case of the overall financial results (even though the money may be withheld for a number of years so that employees can take advantage of tax breaks).
12. In a recent study, Elliott, R. F. and Hemmings, P. J. (1991) showed that, in Britain, lack of regional variation in pay could not be attributed wholly to the presence of national pay agreements.
13. It is not a question here of reducing the overall volume of social security contributions, which are needed in order to have a high level of social protection which is a feature of the European model, but to modify their structure so as to avoid penalizing those groups most affected by unemployment.

References

Acs, Z.J. and Audretsch, D.B. (1989a) 'Editors' Introduction,' *Small Business Economics*, Vol.1, No.1, pp. 1-6.

Acs, Z.J. and Audretsch, D.B. (1989b) 'Job Creation and Firm Size in the US and West Germany,' *International Small Business Journal,* Vol.1, No.2.

Acs, Z.J. and Audretsch, D.B. (1988) 'Innovation in Large and Small Firms,' *American Economic Review* 78, pp. 678-90.

Acs, Z.J. and FitzRoy, F.R. (1989) 'Inside the Firm and Organizational Capital: A Review Article,' *International Journal of Industrial Organization*, Vol.7, No.2.

Akerlof, G. and Yellen, J. (eds.) (1986) *Efficiency Wage Models of the Labor Market.*, Cambridge University Press, Cambridge.

Akerlof, G.A. and Yellen, J. (1988) 'Fairness and Unemployment,' *American Economic Review*, No. 78, pp. 44-49.

Aoki, M. (1988) *Information, Incentives and Bargaining in the Japanese Economy*, Cambridge University Press, Cambridge.

Aschawer, D.A. (1989) 'Is Public Expenditure Productive?,' *Journal of Monetary Economics* 23, pp. 177-200.

Atkinson, J. and Meager, N. (1986) *Changing Working Patterns: How Companies Achieve Fexibility to Meet Their Needs.* National Economic Development Office, London.

Baker, G.P., Jensen, M.C. and Murphy, K.J. (1988) 'Compensation and Incentives: Practice vs Theory,' *The Journal of Finance* 43, pp. 593-616.

Belman, D. (1988) 'Concentration, Unionism and Labor Earnings: A Sample Selection Approach,' *Review of Economics and Statistics* 70, pp. 391-97.

Best, M.H. (1988) *The New Competition*, Polity Press, London.

Best, S. (1984) *And Now for Something Completely Different: a Report on Personnel Management in Sumitomo Metal Industries,Japan*, British Steel Corporation, London.

Bishop, J. (1987) 'The Recognition and Reward of Employee Performance', *Journal of Labor Economics*, Vol. 5, No. 4, pt. 2, pp. 536-56.

References

Blanchard, O.J. and Summers, L.H. (1988) 'Beyond the Natural Rate Hypothesis,' *American Economic Review* 78, pp. 182-87.

Blanchflower, D., Oswald, A. and Garret, M. (1990) 'Insider Power in Wage Determination,' Centre for Labour Economics, London School of Economics, Disc. Paper 319, August 1988; *Economica.*

Blinder, A.S. (1988) 'The Challenge of High Unemployment,' *American Economic Review* 78, pp. 1-15.

Blinder, A.S. (ed.) (1990) *Paying for Productivity,* Brookings Inst., Washington, DC.

Blyth, C.S. (1979) 'The Interaction between Collective Bargaining and Government Policies in Selected Member Countries,' *Collective Bargaining and Government Policies,* Washington Conference, OECD, Paris.

Brock, W.A. and Evans, D.S. (1989) 'Small Business Economics,' *Small Business Economics,* No. 1, pp. 7-20.

Brown ,W. A. (1973) *Piecework Bargaining,* Heinemann, London.

Brown, W.A. (1976) 'Incomes Policy and Pay Differentials', *Oxford Bulletin of Economics and Statistics,* Vol. 38, pp. 27-49.

Brunowsky, R.D. (1988) *Das Ende der Arbeitslosigkeit,* Piper Verlag, Munich.

Burda, M.C. (1988) 'Reflections on Wait Unemployment in Europe, II,' INSEAD Working Paper No. 88/48.

Burda, M.C. and Sachs, J. (1988) 'Institutional Factors in High Unemployment in the Federal Republic of Germany,' NBER Working Paper 224.

Butera, F. (1974) Mutamento dell'organizzazione del lavoro ed egemonia' *Economia e Lavoro.*

Cahill, J. and Ingram, P. (1988) *Changes in Working Practices in the British Manufacturing Industry in the 1980s: A Sudy of Employee Concessions Made during Wage Negotiations,* Confederation of British Industry, London.

Calmfors, L. and Driffil, J. (1988) 'Bargaining Structure, Corporatism and Macroeconomic Performance,' *Economic Policy, A European Forum,* No. 6, pp. 13-47.

Cameron, D.R. (1984) 'Social Democracy, Corporatism, Labour Quiescence and the Representation of Economic Interest in Advanced Capitalist Society,' in Goldthorpe, J.H., *Order and Conflict in Contemporary Capitalism,* Clarendon Press, Oxford.

Cecchini, P. (1988) *The European Challenge, 1992: The Benefits of a Single Market.,* Wildwood House, Aldershot.

Centre d'Etude des Revenus et de Coûts (CERC) (1988),*Les structures de salaires dans la Communauté Economique Européenne,* Documents du CERC, No. 91, La Documentation Française, Paris.

Chabanne and Lollivier (1988) 'Les salariés de 1967, quinze ans après' *Economie et Statistique,* No. 210, May, pp. 21-32.

Clegg, H. (1971) *How to Run an Incomes Policy.* Heinemann, London.

Creedy, J. and Whitfield, K. (1988) 'Earnings and Job Mobility over the Life Cycle: Internal and External Processes' *International Journal of Management,* Vol. 9, No. 2, pp. 8-16.

Crouch, C. (1985) 'Conditions for Trade Union Wage Restraint,' in Lindberg, L.N. and Maier, C.S., *The Politics of Inflation and Economic Stagnation,* The Brookings Institution, Washington, DC.

Delamotte, Y. (1971) 'British Productivity Agreements, German Rationalisation Agreements, and French Employment Security Agreements' *Bulletin of the International Institute for Labour Studies,* ILO, pp. 30-44.

Dell'Aringa, C. (1988) *Raporto sui salari 1988,* ASAP Unità Studi, Franco Angeli, Milan.

Dell'Aringa, C. and Lodovici, M. S. (1989) 'Industrial Relations and Economic Performance' Paper for the International Industrial Relations Association conference, *Labour Relations in a Changing Social, Economic and Technological Environment,* Brussels.

Della Rocca, G. (1989) 'Produttività e salari nelle relazioni industriali: l'esperienza Italiana', Paper for the conference *Salari e produttività: esperienze internazionali e Italiane,* organized by the Fondazione Regionale Pietro Seveso and Nomisma with the support of the CNEL, held in Rome, April 1989.

Dewe, P., Dunn, S. and Richardson, R. (1988) 'Employee Share Ownership Schemes: Why Are Workers Attracted to Them?', *British Journal of Industrial Relations,* Vol. 26, No. 1, March, pp.1-20.

Dickens, W.T. and Katz, L.F. (1986) 'Inter-Industry Wage Differences and Industry Characteristics,' in Lang, K. and Leonard, J. (eds.), *Unemployment and the Structure of Labor Markets,* B. Blackwell, London.

Doeringer, P.B and Piore, M. J. (1971) *Internal Labour Markets and Manpower Analysis.,* Lexington, Heath.

Domowitz, I., Hubbard, R.G. and Peterson, B.C. (1988) 'Market Structure and Cyclical Fluctuations in US Manufacturing,' *Review of Economics and Statistics* 70, pp. 55-66.

Dore, R. P. (1990) 'Building an Incomes Policy to Last' *Taking Japan Seriously: A Confucian Perspective on Leading Economic Issues,* Athlone Press, London.

Economic Commission for Europe (ECE) (1982) *Economic Survey of Europe in 1981,* United Nations, New York.

References

Edwards, R. and Garonna, P. (1991) *The Forgotten Link: Labor's Stake in International Economic Cooperation,* Rowman and Littlefield, Savage, Maryland.

Elliott, R. F. and Hemmings, P. J. (1991) 'Are National Agreements a Source of Nominal Wage Rigidity in the Depressed Regions of Britain?' *Regional Studies,* Vol. 25, No. 1, pp. 63-69.

European Commission (1988) 'Differing Wage Cost Levels in the Community' Working Paper of the Commission services for the Social Dialogue on the Community level, *Group 'Macro-economics',* 'Directorate-General for Financial and Economic Affairs, November, Brussels.

Eyraud, F., Jobert , A., Rozenblatt, P. and Tallard, M. (1989) *Les classifications dans l'entreprise: production des hiérarchies professionnelles et salariales,* Ministère du Travail, de l'Emploi et de la Formation Professionnelle, Paris.

Eyraud, F., Marsden, D. W. and Silvester, J. J. (1990) 'Occupational and Internal Labour Markets in Britain and France', *International Labour Review,* Vol. 129, No. 4, November, pp. 501-18.

Finegold, D. and Soskice, D. (1988) 'The Failure of Training in Britain: Analysis and Prescription', *Oxford Review of Economic Policy,* Vol. 4, No. 3, pp. 21-53.

Finseth, E. (1988) 'The Employment Behaviour of Profit Sharing Firms: An Empirical Test of the Weitzman Theory,' Honours Thesis, Harvard University.

FitzRoy, F.R. (1981) 'Work Sharing and Insurance Policy: A Cure for Stagflation,' *Kyklos* 34, pp. 432-47.

FitzRoy, F.R. (1988) 'The Modern Corporation: Efficiency, Control and Comparative Organization,' *Kyklos,* pp. 41- 2.

FitzRoy, F.R. (1989) 'Firm Size, Efficiency and Employment: A Review Article,' *Small Business Economics,* Vol.1, No.1.

FitzRoy, F.R. (1990) 'Profit Sharing Agreements: Their Macro- and Microeconomic Effects,' Paper presented to ASAP Conference, Rome.

FitzRoy, F.R. and Acs, Z.J. (1989) 'The New Institutional Economics of the Firm and Lessons from Japan,' mimeo, WZB, January .

FitzRoy, F.R. and Funke, M. (1988a) 'Relative Wages and Employment in West German Manufacturing Industries,' mimeo, WZB.

FitzRoy, F.R. and Funke, M. (1988b) 'Imperfect Competition, Wages and Employment: A Disaggregate VAR Study,' mimeo, WZB.

FitzRoy, F.R. and Funke, M. (1988c) 'Monopolistic Competition and Labor Demand in U.S. Manufacturing,' mimeo, WZB.

FitzRoy, F.R. and Hart, R.A. (1990) 'Wage Component Behavior in Japanese Manufacturing Industries,' in König, H. (ed.), *Recent Developments in Wage Determination,* Springer Verlag, Heidelberg-New York.

FitzRoy, F.R. and Kraft, K. (1985) 'Participation and Division of Labor,' *Industrial Relations Journal* 16, Winter, pp. 68-74.

FitzRoy, F.R. and Kraft, K. (1986) 'Profitability and Profit Sharing,' *Journal of Industrial Economics,* December, pp. 113-30.

FitzRoy, F.R. and Kraft, K. (1987) 'Cooperation, Productivity and Profit Sharing,' *Quarterly Journal of Economics,* February.

FitzRoy, F.R. and Mueller, D.C. (1984) 'Conflict and Cooperation in Contractual Organization,' *Quarterly Review of Economics and Business* 24, Winter, pp. 24-49.

FitzRoy, F.R. and Schwalbach, J. (1990) 'Managerial Compensation and Performance in West German Corporations,' Paper presented to EARIE Conference, Lisbon.

FitzRoy, F.R. and Vaughan-Whitehead, D. (1989) 'Efficiency Wages, Employment and Profit Sharing in French Firms,' mimeo, WZB, January.

Frank, R.H. (1984) *Choosing the Right Pond,* Oxford University Press, Oxford.

Freeman, R. (1971) *The Market for College-Trained Manpower.* Harvard University Press, Cambridge, Mass.

Freeman, R. (1988a), 'Union Density and Economic Performance,' *European Economic Review,* Vol. 32, August, pp. 707-16.

Freeman, R. (1988b) 'Evaluating the European View that the United States Has No Unemployment Problem,' *American Economic Review,* May, pp. 294-99.

Geroski, P.A. and Jacquemin, A. (1985) 'Industrial Change, Barriers to Mobility and European Industrial Policy,' *Economic Policy,* November, pp. 172-217.

Guest, D. E. (1987) 'Human Resource Management and Industrial Relations', *Journal of Management Studies,* Vol. 24, No. 5, September, pp. 503-21.

Guest, D. E. (1991) 'Personnel Management: The End of Orthodoxy?' *British Journal of Industrial Relations,* Vol. 29, No. 2, June, pp. 149-76.

Hall, R. E. (1982) 'The Importance of Lifetime Jobs in the US Economy', *American Economic Review,* Vol. 72, No. 4, September, pp.716-24.

Hall, R.H. (1988) 'The Relation between Price and Marginal Cost in US Industry,' *Journal of Political Economy* 96, pp. 921-47.

Hart, R.A. (1987) *Working Time and Employment,* Allen and Unwin, London.

References

Hart, R.A. (ed.) (1988) *Employment, Unemployment and Labor Utilization,* Unwin Hyman.

Hart, R. A. (1989) *Non-wage Labour Costs,* Report for the European Commission.

Henry, S. G. B. and Ormorod, P. A. (1978) 'Incomes Policy and Wage Inflation: Empirical Evidence for the UK 1961-1977, *National Institute Economic Review,* August, pp. 31-39.

Ioannou-Gianakis, C. (1990) *Collective Bargaining, Incomes Policy and Relative Wage Flexibility in Greek Manufacturing 1966-88,* PhD Thesis, London School of Economics, University of London.

Jackman, R. (1989) 'Unemployment and Public Expenditure: Some International Comparisons,' Centre for Labour Economics, LSE, Wp. 1152.

Jones, A. (1973) *The New Inflation,* Penguin, Harmondsworth.

Kahnehan, D., Knetsch, J. and Thaler, R. (1986) 'Fairness as a Constraint on Profit-seeking:Entitlements in the Market', *American Economic Review,* Vol. 76, No. 4, September, pp. 728-41.

Karier, T. (1988) 'New Evidence on the Effect of Unions and Imports on Monopoly Power,' *Journal of Post Keynesian Economics* 10, Spring, pp. 414-27.

Kay, N.M. (1989) 'Competition, Technological Change and 1992,' mimeo, Heriot-Watt University.

Kochan, T.A., Katz, H.C. and McKersie, R.B. (1986) *The Transformation of American Industrial Relations,* Basic Books, New York, NY.

Krueger, A.B. and Summers, L.H. (1988) 'Efficiency Wages and the Inter-Industry Wage Structure,' *Econometrics* 56, March, pp. 259-94.

Kruse, D.L. (1988) 'Profit-Sharing and Employment Variability,' mimeo, Rutgers University.

Lawler, E. (1971) Pay and organisational effectiveness

Layard, P.R.G. (1982) 'Youth Unemployment in Britain and United States Compared', Freeman, R.B. and Wise, D.A. (eds.) *The Youth Labour Market Problem: Its Nature, Causes and Consequences,* National Bureau of Economic Research, University of Chicago Press.

Layard, R. (1989) 'European Unemployment: Cause and Cure,' Centre for Labour Economics, L.S.E. Disc. Paper 368.

Layard, R. and Bean, C. (1988) 'Why Does Unemployment Persist?', Centre for Labour Economics, L.S.E. Disc. Paper 321.

Lehner, R. (1988) 'The Political Economy of Distributive Conflict', Castles, F., Lehner, F. and Schmidt, M., *Managing Mixed Economies*, Walter de Gruyter, Berlin and New York.

Levine, D. I. and Tyson, L. (1990) 'Participation, Productivity, and the Firm's Environment', Blinder (ed.) *Paying for Productivity,* Brookings Inst., Washington, DC.

Lipsey, R. G. and Parkin, F. (1970) 'Incomes Policy: A Reappraisal', *Economica* May, pp. 115-38.

Lyon-Caen, G., and Pélissier, J. (1989) *Droit du travail,* Editions Dalloz, Paris.

Marc, G. (1987) 'Les etrangers en France', *Données Sociales 1987*, INSEE, Paris.

Marsden, D. W. (1981) 'Internal Labour Markets', *Manpower Studies,* Spring.

Marsden, D. W. (1988) 'Short Run Wage Flexibility and Labour Market Adaption in Western Europe,' *Labour*, Spring, pp. 31-54.

Marsden, D. W. (1990a) 'Institutions and Labour Mobility: Occupational and Internal Labour Markets in Britain, France, Italy, and West Germany', Brunetta, R. and Dell'Aringa, C. (eds.) *Labour Relations and Economic Performance,* Macmillan, London.

Marsden ,D. W. (1990b) *The Fexibility of Relative Wages and Changing Economic Conditions,* Paper prepared for the International Labour Office, Geneva.

Marsden, D. W., Morris, T., Willman, P. and Wood, S. (1985) *The Car Industry: Labour Relations and Industrial Adjustment,* Tavistock, London.

Marsden, D.W. and Ryan, P. (1989) 'The Transferability of Skills and the Mobility of Skilled Workers in the European Community', Background paper prepared for the Pertica Report, *The Forgotten lLnk: Labour's Sake in International Economic Cooperation* by Edwards, R. and Garonna, P., Peritaca, Rome.

Marsden, D.W. and Ryan, P. (1990) 'Institutional Aspects of Youth Employment and Training Policy in Britain', *British Journal of Industrial Relations*, Vol. 28, No. 3, November, pp. 351-70.

Marsden, D. W. and Thompson, M. (1990) 'Flexibility Agreements and their Significance in the Increase in Productivity in British Manufacturing since 1980', *Work, Employment and Society*, Vol. 4, No. 1, March, pp. 83-104.

Maurice, M., Eyraud, F., d'Iribarne, A. and Rychener, F. (1988) *Des entreprises en mutation dans la crise: apprentissage des technologies flexibles et émergence de nouveaux acteurs,* Laboratoire d'Economie et de Sociologie du Travail (CNRS), Aix-en-Provence.

Maurice, M., Sellier, F. and Silvestre, J. J. (1982) *Politique d'éducation et organisation industrielle*, Presses Universitaires de France, Paris.

McCallum, J. (1983) 'Inflation and Social Consensus in the Seventies,' in *The Economic Journal,* Vol. 93, No. 372, December, pp. 784-805.

References

Ministère du Travail, de l'Emploi et de la Formation Professionnelle (1989) *Bilan 1988 Annuel de la Négociation Collective*, Document Travail Emploi, La Documentation Française, Paris.

Nerb, G. (1986) 'Employment Problems: Views of Businessmen and the Work Force,' *European Economy*, Commission of the European Communities, No. 27, March.

Nonaka (1991) 'Product Innovation.', Imai Kenichi (ed.) (forthcoming).

OECD, 'Employment Outlook,' Paris, 1984, 1985, 1987 and 1989.

Oi, W. (1962) 'Labor as a Quasi-Fixed Factor', *Journal of Political Economy*, Vol. 70, No. 6, December. pp. 538-55.

Olson, M. (1982) *The Rise and Decline of Nations: Economic Growth, Stagflation, and Social Rigidities*, Yale University Press, New Haven.

Olson, M. (1988) *The Rise and Decline of Nations*, Yale University Press, New Haven.

Padoa-Schioppa, T. (1987) *Efficacité, stabilité et équité: une stratégie pour l'évolution du système économique de la Communauté Européenne*, Rapport du groupe d'étude nommé par la Commission des Communautés Européennes et présidé par T. Padoa-Schioppa.

Paloheimo, H. (1990) 'Between Liberalism and Corporatism: The Effect of Trade Unions and Governments on Economic Performance in Eighteen OECD Countries', in *Labour Relations and Economic Performance*, Macmillan, London.

Piore, M.J. and Sabel, C.F. (1984) *The Second Industrial Divide: Possibilities for Prosperity*, Basic Books, New York, NY.

Pissarides, C. and McMaster, I. (1984) 'Regional Migration, Wages and Unemployment: Empirical Evidence and Implications for Policy', *Centre for Labour Economics Discussion Paper N. 204*, London School of Economics.

Porritt, J. (1990)*Where On Earth Are We Going?*, BBC Books, London.

Prais, S. (1981) *Productivity and Industrial Structure,* Cambridge University Press, Cambridge.

Rebitzer, J.B. (1988) 'Unemployment, Labor Relations and Unit Labour Costs,' *American Economic Review* 78, pp. 389-94.

Reynaud, B. (1989a) Institutions, controle de l'intensité du travail, modes d'organisation du travail et formes de salaire', mimeo, CEPREMAP.

Reynaud, B. (1989b) 'Les systèmes de rémunération ouvriers dans la crise: quels choix stratégique', *Economie et Prévision*, No. 90, November.

Richardson and Nejad (1986) 'Employee Share Ownership Schemes in the UK: An Evaluation', *British Journal of Industrial Relations*, Vol. 24, No. 2, July, pp.233-50.

Richardson, R. (1990) *The Costs of Premature Monetary Union in Europe*, Italia Oggi.

Saunders, C. T. (1978) *Engineering in Britain, West Germany and France: Some Statistical Comparisons*, Sussex European Papers, No.3, University of Sussex, Brighton.

Saunders, C. T, and Marsden, D. W. (1981) *Pay Inequalities in the European Community*, Butterworths, Sevenoaks.

Scardillo, P. (1977) *I sindacati e la contrattazione colletitiva*, Etas Libri, Milano.

Schleifer, A. and Vishny, R.W. (1988) 'Value Maximization and the Acquisition Process,' *Journal of Economic Perspectives* 2, pp. 7-20.

Schmidt, M. (1987) 'The Politics of Labour Market Policy: Structural and Political Determinants of Rates of Unemployment in Industrial Nations,' in Castles, F., Lehner, F. and Schmidt, M., *Managing Mixed Economies*.

Schmitter, P. (1981) 'Interest Intermediation and Regime Governability in Contemporary Western Europe and North America,' in Berger, S.D., *Organizing Interests in Western Europe*, Cambridge University Press, Cambridge.

Sellin, B. (1989) *The Recognition and/or Comparability of Non-university Vocational Training Qualifications in the Member States of the European Communities*, Interim Report, CEDEFOP, Berlin.

Sengenberger, W. (1987) *Struktur und Funktionsweise von Arbeitsmärkten: die Bundesrepublik Deutschland im internationalen Vergleich*, Campus Verlag, Frankfurt.

Silvestre, J. J., Dell'Aringa, C., Marsden, D.W. and Meurs, D. (1991) *La régulation des salaires dans le secteur public: France, Grande-Bretagne et Italie*, Report for the International Labour Office, Geneva.

Smith, S.C. (1988) 'On the Incidence of Profit and Equity Sharing,' *Journal of Behavior and Economic Organization* 9, 1988, pp. 45-58.

Solow, R. (1990) *The Labor Market as a Social Institution*, Blackwell, 1990.

Steedman, H. and Wagner, K. (1987) 'A Second Look at Productivity, Machinery and Skills in Britain and Germany', *National Institute Economic Review*, No. 122, November, pp. 84-95.

Stewart, M. (1990) 'Union Wage Differentials, Product Market Influences, and the Division of Rents', *Economic Journal*, Vol. 100, No. 403, December, pp. 1122-1137.

References

Stiglitz, J.E. (1985) 'Credit Markets and the Control of Capital,' *Journal of Money, Credit and Banking* 17, pp.133-52.

Stiglitz, J.E. (1987) 'Technological Change, Sunk Costs and Competition,' *Brookings Papers on Economic Activity* 3, pp. 883-937.

Streeck, W. (1981) 'Qualitative Demands and the Neo-corporatist Manageability of Industrial Relations', *British Journal of Industrial Relations*, Vol. 19, No. 2, July, pp.149-69.

Tarantelli, E. (1986) *Economia Politica del Lavoro*, Utet, Torino.

Uvalic, M. (1990) 'The PEPPER Report,' European University Institute.

Vaughan-Whitehead, D. (1989) 'Marché interne et stratégies de délocalisation', mimeo, Cellule de Prospective, European Commission.

Vaughan-Whitehead, D. (1990) 'L'mpact economique de la participation financière en France,' European University Institute, Florence.

Venturini,A. (1988) 'An Interpretation of Mediterranean Migration', *Labour*, No. 2, Autumn.

Visser, J. (1988) 'Trade Unionism in Western Europe: Present Situation and Prospects', *Labour and Society*, Vol.13, No. 2, April, pp. 125-82.

Weitzman, M. (1984) *The Share Economy,* Harvard University Press, Cambridge.

Weitzman, M. and Kruse, D. (1990) 'Productivity and Profit Sharing,' in Blinder, A. (ed.) *Paying for Productivity*, Brookings Inst., Washington, DC.

Willard, J.C (1983) 'Conditions d'emploi et salaires de la main d'oeuvre étrangère', *Economie et Statistique*, No. 162, January, pp.15-27.

Williamson, O.E. (1985) *The Economic Institutions of Capitalism: Firms, Markets, Relational Contracting*, Free Press, New York.

Zabalza, A., Turnbull, P. and Williams, G. (1979) *The Economics of Teacher Supply,* Cambridge University Press, Cambridge.

Zighera, J. (1989) *Coûts de la main d'oeuvre dans six pays de la CE*, mimeo, Laédix, Université de Paris X Nanterre.

Index

Index